Bloom's Modern Critical Interpretations

Bloom's Modern Critical Interpretations

Elie Wiesel's
Night
New Edition

Edited and with an introduction by
Harold Bloom
Sterling Professor of the Humanities
Yale University

BLOOM'S
LITERARY CRITICISM
An imprint of Infobase Publishing

Bloom's Modern Critical Interpretations: Night—New Edition

Copyright © 2010 by Infobase Publishing
Introduction © 2010 by Harold Bloom

Bloom's Literary Criticism
An imprint of Infobase Publishing
132 West 31st Street
New York NY 10001

Library of Congress Cataloging-in-Publication Data

Elie Wiesel's *Night* / edited and with an introduction by Harold Bloom. — [New ed.]
    p. cm. — (Bloom's Modern Critical Interpretations)
    Includes bibliographical references and index.
    ISBN 978-1-60413-867-2 ((hardcover : alk paper) : alk. paper) 1. Wiesel, Elie, 1928– Nuit. 2. Authors, French—Biography—History and criticism. 3. Holocaust, Jewish (1939–1945), in literature. 4. Judaism and literature—France. I. Bloom, Harold.
PQ2683.I32N8534 2010
940.53'18092—dc22   2010003481

Cover design by Alicia Post
Composition by Bruccoli Clark Layman
Cover printed by IBT Global, Troy NY
Book printed and bound by IBT Global, Troy NY
Date printed: May 2010
Printed in the United States of America

10 9 8 7 6 5 4 3 2 1

This book is printed on acid-free paper.

Contents

Editor's Note

My Introduction addresses Holocaust literature in general, rather than focusing spcifically on Wiesel's memoir novel, which originally was published in France as *Un di velt hot geshvign* in 1956 and was followed by a shorter version, *La Nuit*, two years later and an English translation, *Night*, in 1960.

HAROLD BLOOM

Introduction

Elie Wiesel's *Night*

Rather than comment directly upon Elie Wiesel's *Night*, which is the subject of all the essays in this volume, I will address myself to the larger question of Holocaust literature. My starting point will be Geoffrey Hartman's poignant and brilliant *The Longest Shadow: In the Aftermath of the Holocaust* (1996). Trauma, primary and secondary, respectively that of survivor or of audience, is at the center of Hartman's insights.

I am hardly the first to worry about the increasing prevalence of psychic numbing accompanied by fascination which is usually the consequence of *primary* trauma. It would be ironic and sad if all that education could achieve were to transmit a trauma to later generations in secondary form. In this fifth decade after the collapse of the National Socialist regime, the disaster still has not run its course. No closure is in sight: the contradictory imperatives of remembering and forgetting are no less strong than before.

But that leads to the question of artistic representation: can you, should you try to transmute the Holocaust into literature? Hartman defends the possibility of this transmutation against the Frankfurt Jewish philosopher, Theodor Adorno:

After the Holocaust there is a spiritual hunt to de-aestheticize everything—politics and culture as well as art. As Adorno phrased in his harshest and most famous statement, it is a sign of the barbaric (that is, of lack of culture) to write poetry after Auschwitz. He refused the arts a role even in mourning the destruction, because they might stylize it too much, or "make unthinkable fate appear to have some meaning." Yet art creates an

1

unreality effect in a way that is not alienating or desensitizing. At best, it also provides something of a safe-house for emotion and empathy. The tears we shed, like those of Aeneas when he sees the destruction of Troy depicted on the walls of Carthage, are an acknowledgment and not an exploitation of the past.

To acknowledge without exploiting is a difficult burden: are any of us strong enough for that? Hartman crucially goes on to consider a great poet, Paul Celan, Romanian Jewish by birth, who wrote in a purified German. Celan's parents were murdered in the Holocaust; the poet himself survived a labor camp, but killed himself in Paris, at the age of fifty. His art was one of reticence, stripping words of their images. Hartman again is precise and eloquent upon the effect:

> Trauma is given a form and disappears into the stammer we call poetry, into a fissure between speech on the page, seemingly so absolute, and an invisible writing that may not be retrievable. This is, in truth, a disaster notation.

Paul Celan was a great (and very difficult) literary artist. Elie Wiesel is an eminent Witness, but hardly a canonical writer of narrative. Yet only a moral idiot would react to Wiesel's *Night* by refusing the burden of secondary trauma. A purely aesthetic reaction to *Night* is impossible and not to be urged upon anyone. There remains what I find most problematical for Wiesel's reader: how to find the strength to acknowledge *Night* without exploiting it?

TED L. ESTESS

Elie Wiesel and the Drama of Interrogation

I pray to the God within me that He will give me the strength to ask
Him the right questions.[1]

Elie Wiesel is typically identified as a Holocaust writer. As such, he joins
such figures as Josef Bor, Zdena Berger, Primo Levi, Eugene Heimler, and
André Schwarz-Bart, all of whom have attempted in varying ways to find a
voice with which to articulate the experience of the "final solution." Against
a reality so grotesque and unsettling, we might well expect the imagination
to go dumb. Indeed, with this group of writers, *what* and *how* they speak
may not be so remarkable as *that* they speak at all.

While the critical response to Wiesel's artistry has appropriately emphasized his identity as a Holocaust writer, we need also to appreciate the
manner in which his writing participates in broader currents of contemporary
sensibility. It is important to interpret Wiesel as more than a representative
of Job in the twentieth century and to see his literature as more than a con-
venient example of the death of God. An approach which places Wiesel in a
wider context need not neglect the specifically Jewish and the narrowly religious elements of his literature, nor need it soften his witness to the unique-
ness of the Holocaust. What it might do is to enrich our awareness of how
Wiesel's creative verve transmutes his special life experience into art which is
pertinent to the self-understanding of any person.

The Journal of Religion, Volume 56, Number 1 (January 1976): pp. 18–35. Copyright © 1976
University of Chicago Press.

An initial step toward such an approach to Wiesel involves emphasizing that his characteristic stance toward the human mysteries is one of interrogation. In its subject matter and, more importantly, in its fundamental vision, his art portrays that "the essence of man is to be a question, and the essence of the question is to be without answer" (*TBW* 186). While his questions certainly involve the Holocaust experience, the genesis of his interrogative vision resides in pre-Holocaust religious intensity.[2] Indeed, the opening scene of his first narrative initiates the process of questioning as Moché the teacher speaks to Eliezer: "Man raises himself toward God by the questions he asks Him. . . . That is the true dialogue. Man questions God and God answers. But we don't understand His answers. We can't understand them. Because they come from the depths of the soul, and they stay there until death" (*N* 16). The night of the Holocaust, in stripping away the answers of 3,000 years of Jewish religious and cultural history, was not the origination but the intensification of the very questions which sustained that history.

The questions which permeate Wiesel's literature are largely religious in character. They are religious in the ordinary, or what Tillich called the "narrow," sense of the word insofar as God, evil, and suffering are involved. With regard to this sense of the religious, it should be emphasized that through questioning Wiesel avoids a preemptory rejection of ancient patterns of religious meaning. Indeed, the stance of questioning is precisely that interpretative posture which maintains creative tension between the individual and the tradition. Moreover, as a specifically Jewish writer, his task is not to reject but to retrieve, not to invent but to repeat. His creative powers turn to renovate— with hermeneutical violence, to be sure—the tradition in which he stands.[3]

Wiesel's questioning, however, is religious in a broader sense as well, if by "religious" we intend "asking passionately the question of the meaning of our existence and being willing to receive answers. . . ."[4] In his literature this willingness to question takes the distinctively modern shape of inquiry into the nature of the self. Following Nathan Scott's observation about contemporary sensibility, we might locate the expansive meaning of Wiesel's religious interrogation: "In a time of the eclipse of God, the most characteristic form of the religious question becomes the question of authenticity, of how we are to keep faith with and safeguard the 'single one' or the 'true self'—in a bullying world."[5]

Yet questions remain authentic only in the dialectic of question and answer, in the interaction of yes and no. While the presiding principle of creative integrity is that of the question, Wiesel's literature is also assertive. Other writers, such as Kafka and Beckett, with whom he shares affinities, are interrogative; yet their literatures linger more in the state of suspended interrogation than does his. Wiesel's work, parabolic and elliptical as it is, adds ethical intensity and human fullness through its attempt to provide an ideationally significant response to painful religious, social, and psychological dilemmas.

The questioning spirit in itself of course gives no special distinction to Wiesel. Man is questioner, as almost every significant philosophical anthropology from Plato and Aristotle to Heidegger and Lonergan has emphasized. What finally distinguishes Wiesel is the shape his questioning takes and the significance that questioning has for meaningful dwelling in the world. The shape of his questioning is an ancient one—that of storytelling. And it is the stories that we ourselves must interrogate and be interrogated by in order to disclose the import and, possibly, the redemptive vision hidden in and evoked by Wiesel's questioning. In our interrogation, we will do well to remember with Wiesel that "these riddles are hard to solve, for the key is not found in our brains but in our hearts" (*BJ* 116).

INTERROGATION AND SELF-IDENTITY

"When he opened his eyes, Adam did not ask God: 'Who are you?' He asked: 'Who am I?'" (*O* 11). The question of the first man is also the question of Wiesel: "Reduced to a mere number, the man in the concentration camp at the same time lost his identity and his individual destiny"; hence the survivor was compelled to enter onto a path of creation and discovery of self (*LT* 211).[6] Wiesel embarked on this path by writing in quick succession three novellas, which, taken together, constitute a triptych of self-definition. Eliezer in *Night,* Elisha in *Dawn,* and the nameless "I" of *The Accident* are characters without a future; they have only a past cruelly presided over by the smoke of the Holocaust and a present nostalgically punctuated by childhood memories of what was lost in the flames. The "I" has curled into a question mark.

After the manner of Job, Eliezer seeks to understand himself by questioning God. This questioning must be understood in light of Moché's teaching: "You will find the true answers, Eliezer, only within yourself" (*N* 16). External answers failing, Wiesel follows the path which characterizes almost the entirety of modern literature when he turns to "the within, all that inner space one never sees."[7] For the early Wiesel, the community and the family are in flames and the self is left "terribly alone in a world without God and without man" (*N* 74). The only place to go is within. This story of initiation into the drama of interrogation leaves the self not in the place where initiation rites should end—in a new community beyond the trials of the initiatory ordeal—but alone in the nadir of death. Yet, for all its power of muted outrage and endless suffering, *Night* is not a final answer to the question of the self; hence Wiesel's second book questions *Night*.[8]

Dawn questions precisely the notion that the answers will be found within by the solitary individual. Elisha again presents an image of the self as questioner: "So many questions obsessed me. Where is God to be found? In suffering or in rebellion? When is a man most truly a man? When he submits or when he refuses? Where does suffering lead him? To purification or to bestiality?" (*D* 24). As Eliezer's life of study was interrupted in Sighet by the overpowering force from the outside, so is Elisha surprised by Gad, who strides into his life like one out of the grand tradition of Jewish rebels and mysterious messengers. Gad refuses to allow Elisha to remain in his solitude, and in disturbing that solitude, he suggests that the context for authentic questioning is that of the self not in isolation but in relationship.

Strangely enough, the relationship into which Elisha enters is that of executioner to victim. By way of Elisha's killing a British hostage as part of the struggle to create the state of Israel, the narrative suggests that all persons are related, even when they violate that relatedness with so profane an act as murder. In making his protagonist an executioner, Wiesel is not relativizing the unique guilt of the Nazis, nor is he merely suggesting that all persons are capable of murder. He is disclosing, rather, that all persons stand (or fall) together in finitude and moral ambiguity. As a later character remarks, "The man who tries to be an angel only succeeds in making faces" (*TBW* 188). Hence, the "dawn" to which the title refers is a dawning of the possibility for human community, not in moral perfection or self-righteousness, not in a division of the good from the evil, but in the acknowledgment that all persons share a common destiny: all are exiled from the garden of innocence.

The Accident marks the end of the first period of Wiesel's literary development and raises the issue of the invention of a new self to central thematic prominence. The protagonist again poses the question of self-identity: "You want to know who I am, truly? I don't know myself" (*A* 77). It seems from this admission that Wiesel's character is back at the point from which Eliezer begins in *Night*. What is happening, however, is a characteristic movement in Wiesel: he returns to the beginning with every book, as if seeking in the origin of things some secret to assist the process of creativity within a new situation.[9] His protagonists begin again and repeat the same process, either in the present time of the novel or in memory. With each repetition, the protagonist's stepping back to the beginning allows him, by the end of the narrative, to move further forward toward significant identity. This pattern embodies the recognition that the journey of the self is not one-dimensional but is a process in which one recoils repeatedly to the origins in order better to engage the fluid succession of present time.

In an important turn for Wiesel, the protagonist of *The Accident* unexpectedly decides to invent another self. If the "reality" of the self is insufficient or unbearable or nonexistent, then one option is to fictionalize another self by taking a mask.[10] As the protagonist says, "It's absurd: lies can give birth to true happiness. Happiness will, as long as it lasts, seem real" (*A* 126).

Self-invention as an answer to the problem of identity is, however, called into question by an artist named Gyula. Gyula's portrait of the protagonist functions to question the mask through which the protagonist has been seeing himself. Surely the mask of suffering and isolation behind which the protagonist has been hiding is authentically in touch with his life experience. But the interpretation of the self solely in negative terms is a dishonest masquerade which shields the person from the rich diversity of life. Viewing the portrait, the protagonist decides cynically to take another mask, this one of happiness. Sensing what has been decided, Gyula, in a violent and parabolic act of friendship, burns the portrait. With this, he emphasizes that the mask of solitary suffering must be rejected—it belongs more to the dead than to the living; it does not tell the whole story of the self. More importantly, Gyula's act suggests—and here Wiesel differs sharply from an artist such as Beckett—that an interpretation of the self as a series of inauthentic masks is an inadequate model of personhood. As Wiesel writes in another place, "A Jew has no right to wear disguises" (*OGA* 100).

While Wiesel rejects the inauthentic assumption of masks as an adequate model of the person, there is still a recognition that the self is unfinished. He writes that "reflected in all my characters and their mirror games, it is always the Jew in me trying to find himself" (*OGA* 213). The mirror for his protagonists is a friend. By looking into that mirror, the Jew—who on one level is every person for Wiesel—begins to question his habituated modes of self-interpretation and moves to imagine alternative ways of seeing himself. Ortega y Gasset sets the matter for Wiesel's characters: "It is too often forgotten that man is impossible without imagination, without the capacity to invent for himself a conception of life, to 'ideate' the character he is going to be. Whether he be original or a plagiarist, man is the novelist of himself...."[11] What Wiesel's protagonists have difficulty realizing is that one is not necessarily lying or pretending in acts of love and friendship. For, as later characters see, such acts are creative human possibilities which belong authentically to a person.

Wiesel's narrative strategy itself reflects the search for self which we have seen in the early stories. That strategy, reminiscent of the exploration of consciousness which occurs in Bergson, Proust, and Beckett, displays that the life of the self is not a straight-line march into the future but involves considerable dissociation and disunity. Evident in his early narratives and more prominent in the later ones, the rearrangement of the moments of clock time shows the self carrying into the future an ineradicable weight from the past. Through the familiar technique of montage in which the narrator associates, for reasons not always clear, one incident with another, the narrative pattern itself becomes a metaphor of the attempt of the self to find unity in the heterogeneity of experience.

The process of interrogation keeps the self open to new possibilities in the early novels of Wiesel; it, in the words of Amos Wilder, keeps "open the incursions of grace."[12] Just as evil and horror intrude with great surprise into the life of Wiesel's characters, so does grace unexpectedly enter in the form of love and friendship. As one character says, "The mystery of good is no less disturbing than the mystery of evil" (*BJ* 254). The interrogative stance, if it is to exercise fidelity to its own executive principle, must question the significance of those moments of goodness.

INTERROGATION AND AUTHENTIC INTERSUBJECTIVITY

Moving through the night of self-enclosed solitude and through a struggle with angelism, Wiesel carried his interrogation toward the day of dialogic intimacy in *The Town Beyond the Wall* and *The Gates of the Forest*. There are hints in this direction in the earlier novels, indicating that even in the darkest moments of his long night he has remained open to the full gamut of his life experience. But the voyage to recognizing the secrets in one's own experiences of authentic intersubjectivity is a lengthy one. As Yeats said, "It is so many years before one can believe enough in what one feels even to know what the feeling is."[13]

The process of interrogation is the central structural component of *The Town Beyond the Wall*. The entire narrative is related while Michael is being interrogated by Hungarian police about his illegal entry into the country. Ironically, this interrogation is called "prayer," since the prisoner, like a praying Jew, must stand until he confesses or goes mad. Since the Holocaust, Wiesel's prayers have largely been questions, but the "prayers" in this book are no longer inquiries directed to God but are questions posed to Michael: Can he suffer the agony of this "prayer" to save a friend? It is Michael the interrogator who is being interrogated: his fidelity in friendship is on trial.

The journey of the self as portrayed in Michael recapitulates much of what we have observed in the earlier protagonists. Following the war, Michael retreats into isolation to "create a new skin . . . a new life," firmly convinced that "love is for those who can forget, for those who seek to forget" (*TBW* 67, 87). Yet Michael's solitude is invaded by Pedro, who calls forth from Michael the capacity for friendship, a capacity which is exercised when Michael refuses to betray Pedro to the police during the interrogation. More importantly, Michael remains faithful to Pedro when he turns to "resume the creation of the world from the void" by retrieving a fellow prisoner from an almost catatonic silence. He repeats with another person what Pedro has done for him. The place to begin creating a town beyond the wall of death and despair is in the immediate situation, which, in Michael's case, is with the one fellow prisoner.

Michael, in a tendency increasingly important in the vision of Wiesel, translates the man/man relationship into an enactment of the God/man relationship. The Hasidic notion of God's hiding in the least likely stranger, ready to surprise the unsuspecting, informs the movement to attribute revelatory intensity to friendship. Michael—the name means "Who is like God?"—discovers transcendent presence in those persons close at hand. Again, Pedro is the repository of wisdom: "He who thinks about God, forgetting man, runs the risk of mistaking his goal: God may be your next-door neighbor" (*TBW* 123).

The drama of interrogation leads to a re-cognition of the significance of relatedness in the lives of Wiesel's characters, while at the same time it discloses that relatedness is prior to and foundational for any interrogation whatsoever. Michael suggests as much when he remarks: "But to say, 'What is God? What is the world? What is my friend?' is to say that I have someone to talk to, someone to ask a direction of" (*TBW* 187). Even the possibility of asking a question is founded on the recognition that we are not, as Eliezer assumes in *Night,* finally "alone in the world." Furthermore, realizing authentic intersubjectivity is less a matter of building relationships than it is of interrogating the meaning of those relationships in which and by virtue of which one already dwells in the world.

But the element of questioning carries a still further significance in *The Town Beyond the Wall,* since a simple question—Why does Michael wish to return to his hometown?—provides the chief element of narrative suspense. This question is resolved when Michael confronts the spectator, a man who stood passively at a window while the Jews were being deported from the city. How can a human being remain an indifferent spectator?—that is the question which compels Michael to return to his home.

In one of the most dramatic moments in all Wiesel's literature, Michael indicts the spectator with the sin—no, the punishment—of indifference.[14] That indictment brings further into question the model of the self that we observed in *The Accident,* the model in which a person plays an invented role, in which there is a split between the self and its role, between being and acting. To play at living, Michael suggests, is insufficient; merely to pretend at happiness, friendship, and love leads only to an indifference in which the real action and death of men are viewed as morally neutral. In Michael's perspective, the Holocaust is a final repudiation of an ethical nihilism which he sees implicit within the metaphor of life as a game: "If living in peace means evolving in nothingness, you accept the nothingness. The Jews in the courtyard of the synagogue? Nothing. The shrieks of women gone mad in cattle cars? Nothing. The silence of thirsty children? Nothing. All that's a game, you tell yourself. A movie! Fiction: seen and forgotten. I tell you, you're a machine for the fabrication of nothingness" (*TBW* 172).

Against the view that life is a game and the self is a player, Michael affirms what Pedro calls "simplicity," in which there are no disguises and no pretending. "'I believe in simplicity,' Pedro said. 'When one loves, one must say: I love you. When one wants to weep, one must say: I want to weep. When one becomes aware that existence is too heavy a burden, one must say: I want to die. . . . In driving Adam out of Paradise . . . God merely deprived him of the power of simplicity'" (*TBW* 124–125). For Michael a return to simplicity means things as ordinary as working, loving, being a friend, and having a family (*TBW* 173). In redeeming his own lifetime, Michael moves to recover that "condition of complete simplicity," the simplicity "costing not less than everything."[15]

But we misunderstand the complexity of Wiesel's interrogation of the self if we think that his world divides neatly into such categories as victims, executioners, and spectators; that in the world there are persons who are simply playing at living while others embody the life of simplicity. As the various representatives of these life possibilities dialectically confront one another, Wiesel's literature suggests that the self is multidimensional. Michael seizes the insight: "Down deep, I thought, man is not only an executioner, not only a victim, not only a spectator: he is all three at once" (*TBW* 174). It is not, furthermore, a question of either being a person who invents himself or being a person who simply is what he is. It is a matter of dwelling in the dialectical tension of being both persons at the same time; it is a matter of being both authentic and inauthentic together. Not only is the self a quester, without identity and home and firm mooring; the self, speaking out of ancient wisdom, is also teacher and guide, possessing with Gyula and Pedro quiet confidence and deep simplicity.

The movement to simplicity, however, does not bring the stasis of the completed self, for there are other questions to explore. Also, the primary questions of God and evil and suffering remain unanswered because they are unanswerable. Michael's self-progression, however, does bring the equilibrium which accompanies the capacity to commit oneself in compassion to another. In caring one gains and expresses rootedness; in caring one comes home to the only place one can be—where one is—and there, even in a prison cell, one can act to alleviate suffering.[16] Michael's prayer, "God of my childhood, show me the way that leads to myself," finds a response: the way "leads to another human being" (*TBW* 135, 127). In moving toward another, the self finds a place in which the secrets of reality and the questions of man are conjoined in revelatory dialogue. There a person must risk "to ask the great questions and ask them again, to look up at another, a friend, and to look up again: if two questions stand face to face, that's at least something. It's at least a victory" (*TBW* 187). As Gyula says, "Maybe God is dead, but man is alive. The proof: he is capable of friendship" (*A* 123).

The "town" to which Michael returns is in all respects unlike the town from which he was torn by the Holocaust. Yet, to our surprise, it is very much like that town, for it is a place—no, a way—in which persons with integrity of words and actions dialogically share their lives. The lines of Eliot again trace the voyage of Wiesel's characters:

> We shall not cease from exploration
> And the end of all our exploring
> Will be to arrive where we started
> And know the place for the first time.[17]

INTERROGATION AND ACTION

Wiesel's early protagonists are incapable of initiating independently chosen actions. They are characterized more by what happens to them than by what they are able to make happen. Returning from the Holocaust denuded of self and stripped of a community in which to act, these cripples have little interest in doing anything whatsoever.

This inability to interact significantly with the external world reinforces the impression that the primary concern of Wiesel's literature is with character, not with plot or action. Indeed, he at times accentuates the interest in character by telling the reader the outcome of the action at the beginning of the narrative. His plotting in the longer stories is extraordinarily loose, providing only an external frame for the exploration of the interiority of his characters. Unlike what we find in a tightly structured, sequential narrative, the actions of his characters in the external world tend to follow *after* not *from* one another.

Despite the retreat of his characters from action and despite a narrative strategy which de-emphasizes interconnection of events in time, the drama of interrogation in Wiesel is a preparation for action. This occurs in several stages: first, the protagonist secludes himself for a period of introspection; then there occurs an intrusion by a compelling individual who attempts to engage the protagonist with the living; narrative interest increases in the contrast between the protagonist's inaction and his friend's willingness to love and act; finally, the protagonist, after enduring the loss of the friend and after further suffering, evolves to the moment of choice and action. In *The Town Beyond the Wall, The Gates of the Forest,* and *A Beggar in Jerusalem,* this pattern occurs in each of its major components. Gregor, toward the end of *The Gates of the Forest,* exemplifies the culmination of this process when he decides to return to his wife and attempt to rebuild the marriage. Forcefully, he asserts: "I am what I choose to be; I am in my choice, in my will to choose. There is no divorce between self and its image, between being and acting. I am the act, the image, one and indivisible" (*GF* 219).

Wiesel's protagonists move toward action because they wish to gain a story for their own lives. They realize that without action there is no story to life; without action, there is only atmosphere. David suggests as much when he remarks in *A Beggar in Jerusalem*, "I'm also looking for a story" (*BJ* 157). His plan to fight and die in the Arab-Israeli war is his effort to find some definitive action, even if only to die, which will give shape to an amorphous, storyless existence. The plan involves an agreement with an Israeli soldier named Katriel that if one of them should die in the war, the survivor will tell the other one's story. But it is Katriel who is "missing in action"; hence David faces the dilemma of whether he, in addition to telling Katriel's story, should live out that story. Through marrying Katriel's widow, David comes to possess a story for his own existence, as do all of Wiesel's later protagonists.

In sharp contrast to the protagonists' inability to act is the capacity of their close companions to commit themselves. The secret of Katriel's power over David and of the power of Gyula, Gad, and Pedro is that, though they have suffered in the Holocaust and have teetered at the brink of madness, they are still able to engage the living through a self-initiated agency. Katriel is "missing in action"; and it is toward a destiny of being willing to lose one-self in action that Wiesel's protagonists move. Only in that path will they, in addition to being the tellers of the stories of the dead, be able to achieve that little taste of immortality that is given to mankind: that immortality which is gained by having a story of one's own which can be told by another after one is gone.

The resolve to act, while it might appear in this brief synopsis as a dramatic appendage to the development of the characters, is not a shallow voluntarism or a Sartrean turn to Wiesel's sensibility. It is rather the culmination—and by that I do not mean "termination"—of an ongoing process of self-interrogation, self-creation, and self-discovery. We are somewhat surprised when Michael and Gregor and David come decisively to the moment of action; but they apparently realize, in the words of Graham Greene, that "sooner or later . . . one has to take sides—if one is to remain human."[18]

The Hasidic rebbe, who ascends to such a powerful influence in the final pages of *The Gates of the Forest*, brings Gregor to see the unavoidability of choosing. To Gregor's question of how belief in God is possible after the Holocaust, the rebbe replies, "How can you *not* believe in God after what has happened?" (*GF* 192). But, as the rebbe in great wisdom sees, belief or nonbelief is not a final answer. He painfully admits that God "has become the ally of evil, of death, of murder, but the problem is still not solved. I ask you a question and dare you answer: 'What is there left for us to do?'" (*GF* 197). With a despair beyond the antinomy of hope and despair and a faith beyond the opposition of belief and unbelief, the rebbe continues to probe the question of doing. There are no adequate answers, theological or philosophical or psychoanalytical; yet the individual remains to face life and to do what one can to alleviate suffering, to respond to the need of persons to be loved, to act in behalf of friendship. David sets the dilemma: "Do you understand now that love, no matter how personal or universal, is not a solution? And that outside of love there is no solution?" (*BJ* 172). Having only proximate answers to unanswerable questions, Wiesel's protagonists take courage and act.

The movement to the possibility of action indicates something about the drama of interrogation itself. It suggests that the questioning of Wiesel is not a sophistry which engages argumentation for its own sake, nor is it a cynical detachment which relativizes away all differences among human responses, nor is it a thinking severed from the concrete situation of life with others. His interrogation is a process in which the person recovers a reserve of self-integrity, of wholeness, of health. The self comes to what Ortega y Gasset calls *ensimismarse*, "with in-oneself-ness," which is taking a stand within the self so as to empower the person to act freely in the relationships in which he stands.[19] Interrogation, while it involves exploration of what is within, does not finally abstract Wiesel's protagonists from the exigencies of the historical situation in which they dwell but instantiates them in that situation more fully. The end of the process is not self-enclosed thinking or solitary contemplation: it is action in behalf of that which is disclosed in the process of interrogation. As Gregor comes to see in *The Gates of the Forest*, "Nothing is easier than to live in a cloistered universe where I am alone with God, alone against God. . . . The man that chooses solitude and its riches is on the side of those who are against man . . ." (*GF* 219). What confronts us—indeed, what interrogates us—in Wiesel is an ongoing process of enacting those insights which are disclosed through questioning while at the same time questioning those insights which inform action.

In seeing the importance for Wiesel of enacting insight, we do well to remember that the lives of most of his protagonists carry the imprint of two distinct dispensations, one from the mother and the other from the father. It is the mother who carries the son to the Hasidic rebbe for a blessing; it is she who condones, even encourages, an interest in the esoteric wisdom of the cabbalists and the paradoxes of the Hasidim. In dialectical tension with the mother, the father is the active advocate for the concrete needs of persons in the community. The father reminds the son that "God, perhaps, has need of saints; as for men, they can do without them" (*LT* 17). These two dimensions do battle in Wiesel, and surely both are integral to the full image of the self that he portrays. In his literature, the turn toward mystical solitude is checked by an awareness of the desperate needs of persons in history; similarly, the loss of the self in frenetic activism is inhibited by an attentive listening to dark mysteries.[20]

Action comes to occupy a large place in Wiesel's sensibility because he experienced so deeply in the Holocaust the consequences of the failure to act. It was an indifference to life on the part of executioners, spectators, and even the victims themselves which, in Wiesel's view, allowed the destruction of the 6 million. Indifference is the enemy of action; apathy is choosing death in life. And storytelling is Wiesel's action against indifference and for friendship. "We tell the tale of the Holocaust," he says, "to save the world from indifference."[21]

INTERROGATION AND STORYTELLING

Every story, to some extent, is about storytelling. This is true of all Wiesel's tales; yet storytelling fully emerges as the central action in his latest novel, *The Oath*. This action is performed by an old man named Azriel, who is the sole survivor of a pogrom against the Jews of a small European village earlier in this century. Azriel—since that awful irruption of hate and suspicion destroyed the entire village, Gentile and Jew alike—has kept the "oath" of silence, the pledge of every Jew not to narrate the story of the pogrom if he by chance should survive. If speaking of man's atrocities and God's failures were insufficient to accomplish deliverance from such pogroms, then perhaps silence would stir the conscience of mankind and disturb even the indifference of God in a way that speaking did not. Azriel has survived for fifty years, carrying in silence the terrible burden of memory. One night in an attempt to dissuade a young man from committing suicide, he tells the story of death in order to serve life, thinking that in hearing the story the young man will be placed in such a relationship with the dead that he will not forsake the living. Perhaps the young man will choose life, if for no other reason than to interrogate the meaning of Azriel's story.

In placing storytelling at the center of *The Oath*, Wiesel focuses the dynamic which has sustained his writing from the beginning. With the Holocaust, he entered into a night of silence. It seemed that any description of the dignity, faith, and complicity of the victims, that any tale about the hate and indifference of the executioners and spectators—that any act of speaking whatever would betray the victims, immortalize the executioners, and corrupt the living. On what basis could one break the silence and attempt to speak the unspeakable? The protagonist of *The Accident* answers, "I am a storyteller. My legends can only be told at dusk. Whoever listens questions his life" (*A* 77). Or, as David remarks, "Men's tales put me in jeopardy" (*BJ* 159).

Storytelling, at least in Wiesel's view, is an act which initiates the listener into the drama of interrogation. And the moments of that drama, as we have already seen, include inquiring into self, attending to significant relationships, envisaging and effecting chosen actions. In short, the drama of interrogation is a process by which one can come to have a story of one's own. That is precisely what Azriel sees when he dissuades the young man from suicide in *The Oath*. Suicide, Azriel suggests, is a foreclosure on the possibility of having one's own story, for suicide is an answer whose finality cannot be revoked.[22] One gains a story through interrogating experience, and experience belongs only to the living. "Some writings," Wiesel comments, "could sometimes, in moments of grace, attain the quality of deeds" (*LT* viii). Storytelling attains the "quality" of action in Wiesel when it catalyzes a process of questioning that effects change in the life of the hearer and the reader.

If the reader in his own confrontation with the tale is initiated into the drama of interrogation, the action of storytelling must be, as I have proposed throughout this essay, an interrogatory venture for the teller himself. Wiesel comments, "I write in order to understand as much as to be understood" (*OGA* 213). There is, however, in Wiesel a tension between coming to understand through storytelling and coming to understand through rational inquiry. A significant moment for several of his protagonists, and perhaps for Wiesel himself, is their turning to and quickly from philosophy. Also important are the comments scattered throughout his literature which place strictures on the efficacy of a rigidly logical address to the questions which possess the characters.[23] Occurring here is another dimension of the battle between the way of the mother and that of the father: the way of the mother is that of storytelling after the manner of the great Hasidic masters; that of the father is of philosophy. The longer narratives combine both, for in the frame of a story there is considerable talk which has the appearance of philosophizing. But ultimately, narrative succeeds philosophical discourse as the mode of interrogation in Wiesel. Questioning is not the *subject matter* of his narratives; rather, the narratives are his way of questioning any subject matter. Narrative, Henry James observed, "bristles with questions."[24] It does so, Wiesel might say, precisely because narrative is questioning.

This discussion indicates that, for Wiesel, the end of telling a story is not to make an object of beauty which will be the focus of passive contemplation, though his stories are at times beautiful in their aesthetic shape; nor is storytelling playing with words to pass the time, after the manner of someone like Samuel Beckett. Rather, storytelling is Wiesel's mode of inquiring into the nature of things. In this action, he is doing something analogous to what the philosopher attempts to do: to interrogate all experience and attempt to disclose the way in which things cohere in significant patterns of meaning. This is why, I think, we see the gradual expansion of the canvas and of the subject matter in Wiesel's career as a writer. From the brief story which dealt with the Holocaust experience, he has turned to increasingly longer narratives which probe deeper and deeper into Jewish history. Hence, he recently composed

Souls on Fire, a book on the Hasidic masters of the eighteenth and nineteenth centuries, and is presently writing on the patriarchs. His interrogative adventure enlarges as he seeks to incorporate the stories of all men into his own story; it expands as one question leads to another, as he finds in storytelling "answers to all questions and questions for all answers" (*A* 119).

It is precisely this understanding of the nature and function of storytelling and of the literary text that several students of the art of interpretation have with persuasive arguments been attempting for a number of years to lead us to see.[25] Storytelling, indeed all speaking whatever, is, we are told, a coming-into-understanding of that which discloses itself to an attentive inquirer. Moreover, the relationship which, according to these thinkers, characterizes the address of the reader to the story is one of mutual interrogation. The reader brings to the text a history of habituated modes of response and a certain value orientation which, if the confrontation with the literary text is to do what it ought, are placed in question by the horizon of understanding speaking through the text. A challenge comes to the interpreter from the text, a challenge to allow his own perspectives to be interrogated and his horizon of understanding to be altered and expanded. Accordingly, the hermeneutical event involves not merely dissection or explication of the text itself, but a dialogue by which the text and reader act on each other in such a way that neither the reader nor the text will any longer be the same.

The narrator of *The Accident* appears to have this type of dialogic intensity in view when he remarks: "To listen to a story under such circumstances is to play a part in it, to take sides, to say yes or no, to move one way or the other. From then on there is a before and an after. And even to forget becomes a cowardly acceptance" (*A* 95). And, again, after relating the story of a child who served the perverse pleasure of German officers, the narrator comments, "Whoever listens to Sarah and doesn't change, whoever enters Sarah's world and doesn't invent new gods and new religions, deserves death and destruction" (*A* 96). Engaging and being engaged by the story at this deep level is not altogether a consciously intellectual or verbal matter. It involves listening to the silence which resonates through the story. Clara (clarity) has this in view when she speaks to Gregor: "You stop at words. . . . You must learn to see through them, to hear that which is unspoken" (*GF* 176). It is this painfully creative process, with all the risk and courage and sensitive openness which it demands, that situates itself into the life of the hearer of Wiesel's tales. "Do you know that it is given to each of us to enrich a legend simply by listening to it?" (*BJ* 131).

It might appear with this understanding of the act of storytelling, along with the previous discussion of friendship and action, that in the vision of Wiesel the ethical subsumes the aesthetic. It might even appear that there is a submerged moralism in Wiesel, that the interrogative drama opens itself up finally to the soliloquy of the imperative. To be sure, his interrogation, so as not to be an act of bad faith, a dramatic pose, or a mere game, includes an attempt to answer the questions. His interrogation involves an effort to distinguish options and to pursue with appropriate clarity and passion the matters at hand. Patiently, with honest and disturbing self-revelation, Wiesel has negotiated the treacherous movement between forgetfulness and madness. In this movement he has dared, imperatively at times, to affirm, refusing to retreat to the solitude of mere negation.

Moreover, we must acknowledge that Wiesel's greatest strength is with the anecdote, briefly related without elaboration or commentary. Thus it is perhaps unfortunate that a recurring convention in his longer narratives, beginning with the final pages of *The Town Beyond the Wall,* is to bring the teacher into the story and to provide him a platform from which to attempt an answer to the questions posed in the narrative.[26] In the structure of the story, the speeches sometimes unhappily intrude as appendages to the narrative movement. While the drama of interrogation provides the movement and energy to the stories of Wiesel, the moment of answering the questions often mars aesthetic power and narrative effectiveness. "Art," Samuel Beckett has commented, "is pure interrogation, rhetorical questioning, less the rhetoric."[27] Wiesel's art occasionally edges toward the rhetorical; in doing so, the rhetoric threatens to break precisely the interrogative engagement which the stories themselves might effect. Moral outrage tempts Wiesel at times to do too much for the reader, to tell all, instead of narrating and allowing the interrogative process to wend its way in the silence.

These demurrers aside, the final weight of Wiesel's storytelling is aesthetic, not narrowly moral; it is interrogative, not obstinately declarative or imperative. His storytelling gains its ethical intensity in part because it does precisely that which the aesthetic intends: it awakens the sense of surprise. Pedro accents this motif in *The Town Beyond the Wall:* "Blessed is he capable of surprising and being surprised. If I had a prayer to address to God, it would be, 'O God, surprise me. Bless me or damn me: but let thy benediction or thy punishment be a surprise'" (*TBW* 133). Indifference is that inhibitor of action against which all of Wiesel's literature inveighs, and the antidote to indifference is the capacity of being surprised by lying *and* by truthfulness, by evil *and* by good, by dying *and* by living. We are surprised to find love where we might have foreseen hate, to happen upon hope when we might have anticipated despair, to come upon evil when we might have predicted good, to find destiny when we might have expected mere chance.

Through awakening the sense of surprise, which in many respects is the same as eliciting an interrogative vision, Wiesel's literature achieves its moments of greatest power. Art, whenever it is in the service of surprise, while fulfilling a noble aesthetic function, is at the same time initiating that interrogative drama which is essential to ethical judgments and which best expresses the religious tenor of our time.

Notes

1. Elie Wiesel, *Night,* trans. Stella Rodway (New York: Hill & Wang, 1960), p. 16. Hereafter pagination for quotations from Wiesel's literature is given in parentheses in the text. The following abbreviations and editions are used: *A* = *The Accident,* trans. Anne Borchardt (New York: Avon Books, 1962); *BJ* = *A Beggar in Jerusalem,* trans. Lily Edelman and the author (New York: Avon Books, 1970); *D* = *Dawn,* trans. Frances Frenaye (New York: Avon Books, 1970); *GF* = *The Gates of the Forest,* trans. Frances Frenaye (New York: Avon Books, 1967); *JS* = *The Jews of Silence,* trans. Neal Kozodoy (New York: Signet Books, 1967); *LT* = *Legends of Our Time* (New York: Avon Books, 1970); *N* = *Night; O* = *The Oath,* trans. Marion Wiesel (New York: Avon Books, 1970); *OGA* = *One Generation After,* trans. Lily Edelman and the author (New York: Avon Books, 1972); *SF* = *Souls on Fire,* trans. Marion Wiesel (New York: Vintage Books, 1973); *TBW* = *The Town Beyond the Wall,* trans. Stephen Becker (New York: Avon Books, 1970).

2. For extensive exploration of man as questioner, see Bernard Lonergan, S.J., *Insight: A Study of Human Understanding* (New York: Philosophical Library, 1956). Also see Michael Novak, *The Experience of Nothingness* (New York: Harper & Row, 1971), pp. 44–51.

3. Wiesel remarks, "To transmit is more important than to innovate. Every question a disciple will ask his Master, and that until the end of time, Moses already knew. Yet, we must ask the questions and make them ours by repeating them" (*SF* 257). For a discussion of Wiesel as a "reconstructionist of faith," see Byron L. Sherwin, "Elie Wiesel and Jewish Theology," *Judaism* 18 (1969): 39–52.

4. Paul Tillich, "The Lost Dimension in Religion," in *Ways of Being Religious,* ed. Frederick J. Streng et al. (Englewood Cliffs, N.J.: Prentice-Hall, Inc.), p. 356.

5. *Three American Moralists: Mailer, Bellow, Trilling* (Notre Dame, Ind.: University of Notre Dame Press, 1973), p. 221.

6. In the life story of at least one of Wiesel's protagonists, the question of self-identity is explicitly a pre-Holocaust issue. Kalman, the teacher of Michael in *The Town Beyond the Wall,* instructs his student to question his soul. And Michael records that for weeks he was obsessed with such questions as, Who am I? and What am I? (*TBW* 49). The location of this question prior to the Holocaust is an instance of Wiesel's seeking to discern threads of continuity, fragile as they may appear, between his pre- and post-Holocaust history (see *LT* 215–237).

7. Samuel Beckett, *Three Novels: "Molloy," "Malone Dies," "The Unnamable"* (New York: Grove Press, 1958), p. 10. For discussion of the turn within as an element of modern sensibility, see Erich Heller, *The Artist's Journey into the Interior and Other Essays* (New York: Vintage Books, 1968).

8. The movement from one novel to the next in Wiesel displays the question/ answer dialectic in that each succeeding narrative attempts more fully to answer the question of the previous, while at the same time it questions the answer given by the earlier narrative. See "Against Despair," First Annual Louis H. Pincus Memorial Lecture, United Jewish Appeal, 1974 National Conference, New York, December 8, 1973. There, Wiesel comments: "Somewhere . . . there lives a man who asks a question to which there is no answer; a generation later, in another place, there lives

a man who asks another question to which there is no answer either—and he doesn't know, he cannot know, that *his* question is actually an answer to the first." To this story, Wiesel adds, "To us, however, questions remain questions."

9. *The Oath*, Wiesel's most recent long narrative, is an exception, for its protagonist is the first who is not a survivor of the Holocaust. But, in accord with the pattern I point out here, the protagonist does imaginatively return to his own holocaust, a pogrom which occurred earlier in this century.

10. In his turn to fictionalizing the self, Wiesel's protagonist joins the parade of characters who people the literature of such figures as Gide, Pirandello, and Beckett. For a discussion of the function of masks in the literature of these figures, see Enrico Garzilli, *Circles without Center: Paths to the Discovery and Creation of Self in Modern Literature* (Cambridge, Mass.: Harvard University Press, 1972).

11. Quoted by Frank Kermode, *The Sense of an Ending: Studies in the Theory of Fiction* (New York: Oxford University Press, 1966), pp. 140–141.

12. "The Uses of a Theological Criticism," in *Literature and Religion*, ed. Giles Gunn (New York: Harper & Row, 1971), p. 45.

13. Quoted in N. Jeffares, *W. B. Yeats: Man and Poet* (New York: Barnes & Noble, 1966), p. 38.

14. Wiesel himself suggests that indifference is not only a sin but a punishment in "Storytelling and the Ancient Dialogue," lecture delivered at Temple University, November 15, 1969.

15. T. S. Eliot, "Four Quartets: Little Gidding," in *The Complete Poems and Plays* (New York: Harcourt Brace & Co., 1952), p. 145.

16. For a sensitive discussion of caring, see Milton Mayeroff, *On Caring* (New York: Harper & Row, 1971).

17. Eliot, p. 145.

18. Graham Greene, *The Quiet American* (New York: Viking Press, 1956), p. 230.

19. Jose Ortega y Gasset, "The Self and the Other," trans. Willard Trask, in *The Dehumanization of Art, and Other Writings on Art and Culture* (Garden City, N.Y.: Doubleday & Co., 1956), p. 167. This essay has several parallels with Wiesel in its discussion of the self, thought, and action. Ortega writes: "Unlike all the other beings in the universe, man is never surely *man*; on the contrary, *being man* signifies precisely being always on the point of not being man, being a living problem, an absolute and hazardous adventure, or, as I am wont to say: being, in essence, drama!" And, again: "Man's destiny, then, is primary *action*. We do not live to think, but on the contrary, we think in order that we may succeed in surviving" (pp. 173, 174).

20. Michael evidences this polarity when he speaks: "Mother wants me to be a rabbi. Father would rather have me study for a doctorate in philosophy. . . . My mother lives body and soul for Hasidism: she devotes her actions and thoughts to God. My father adores reason: he devotes all his time to skepticism about the eternal verities. To make peace between them I promised to study religion *and* philosophy" (*TBW* 30).

21. Interview on the "Today Show," NBC television, May 20, 1974.

22. The similarity between Wiesel and Camus, as it is in many ways, is apparent in this judgment on suicide (see Camus, *The Myth of Sisyphus*, trans. Justin O'Brien [New York: Vintage Books, 1955]).

23. For a discussion of the limits of a logical address to certain questions, see *LT*, pp. 215–237. Of attempts to explain the Holocaust, Wiesel writes: "To find one

answer or another, nothing is easier: language can mend anything. What the answers have in common is that they bear no relation to the questions. . . . All the words in all the mouths of the philosophers and psychologists are not worth the silent tears of that child and his mother, who live their own death twice" (*LT* 222–223).

24. Henry James, *The Art of the Novel* (New York: Charles Scribner's Sons, 1939), p. 3.

25. I have in mind the work in hermeneutical theory of such figures as the philosophers Martin Heidegger and Paul Ricoeur and the theologians Ernst Fuchs and Heinrich Ott. For a helpful discussion of these matters, see Nathan A. Scott, Jr., "Criticism and the Religious Horizon," in *Humanities, Religion, and the Arts Tomorrow*, ed. Howard Hunter (New York: Holt, Rinehart & Winston, 1972), pp. 39–60. I am indebted to Scott's essay for the phrase "drama of interrogation" (p. 49). For further consideration of interpretation theory, see Stanley R. Hopper and David L. Miller, eds., *Interpretation: The Poetry of Meaning* (New York: Harbinger, 1967).

26. Wiesel is as much the teacher as he is the artist; as much the guide as the quester. This recognition suggests that the pairs which dominate his literature are two parts of the author himself. Interestingly, Wiesel has recently taken a teaching post at the City College of New York. This reinforces what we already know from his art: that to be a teacher of great power is perhaps a higher calling than to be a "pure" artist. Or, more accurately stated, the highest calling for Wiesel is to be an artist who, through his storytelling, is at the same time a compelling teacher.

27. "Denis Devlin," *Transition* 27 (April–May 1938): 289.

BENJ MAHLE

The Power of Ambiguity:
Elie Wiesel's Night

In teaching *Night*, Elie Wiesel's puissant and often poetic account of his Holocaust experiences, I used to feel a gnawing inadequacy when my ninth grade students would ask questions for which I had no satisfactory responses. "Why," they'd ask, "did the Jews of Sighet not believe Moche the Beadle when he described to them the details of the pogrom he had miraculously survived?" Or, "How could the Nazis dump a truck load of babies into a burning pit, and feel nothing? How could a son attack and kill his own father for a mouthful of bread? How could anyone survive a forty mile march through the freezing night with only snow to eat?" Only recently have I become comfortable with answering "I don't know" or "I'm not sure" when they confront me with questions like those.

This change results from my latest rereading of *Night* wherein I've concluded that Elie Wiesel intended his account to be ambiguous, that he hoped to raise more questions that he would answer.

For example, consider his treatment of the theme of religious faith. In chapter three, the young Elie—heretofore a profound believer—first experiences the atrocities of the Auschwitz camp. Subsequently he declares, "Never shall I forget those flames which consumed my faith forever." *Consumed* suggests total destruction. Yet there are subtle suggestions that at least a flicker of faith remains. For as he details the horrors being perpetrated by men, he

English Journal, Volume 74 (October 1985): pp. 83–84. Copyright © 1985 National Council of Teachers of English.

21

consistently contrasts these with benign, even appealing images of nature. Since we frequently perceive nature as a reflection of God, is it not possible to interpret these images as evidence of God's concern? In this passage Elie is being moved to a new camp (the italics are mine):

> Ten gypsies had come and joined our supervisor. Whips and truncheons cracked around me. My feet were running without my being aware of it. I tried to hide from the blows behind the others. *The spring sunshine . . .*

Later,

> The gypsies stopped near another barracks. They were replaced by SS, who surrounded us. Revolvers, machine guns, police dogs. The march had lasted half an hour. Looking around me I noticed that the barbed wires were behind us. We had left camp.
> *It was a beautiful April day, the fragrance of spring was in the air. The sun was setting in the west.*
> But we had been marching for only a few moments when we saw the barbed wire of another camp. An iron door with this inscription over it: "Work is Liberty"—Auschwitz.

These references to the natural beauty of this day may give support to the notion that God is offering hope. On the other hand, perhaps the author is sarcastically suggesting that God merely deigned to ease their suffering by allowing that it should be done in pleasant weather. Consider another passage from chapter three—Elie's moving and deeply poetic description of his first night in camp:

> Never shall I forget that night, the first night in camp, which has turned my life into one long night, seven times cursed and seven times sealed. Never shall I forget that smoke. Never shall I forget the little faces of the children, whose bodies I saw turned into wreaths of smoke beneath a *silent blue sky*.

Few things in nature stir in us more hope for a fine day than blue skies. Yet I wonder if the contrast here is supposed to provide a suggestion of hope? Is it instead a quiet condemnation of God's apparent silence, represented by the tranquility of nature at a moment when it would seem right that a sudden tempest should douse the flames or the earth should open up and swallow the murderers? Eli Wiesel consistently provides readers with details rather than explanations. And I believe his purpose in providing these contrasting images is appropriately ambiguous.

In the first pages of his book, the author states that his teacher, Moche the Beadle, believed that "every question possessed a power that did not lie in the answer." The questions posed by my students during their reading of *Night* evince a power that has moved many of them to seek more information. Ultimately, in attempting to find their own answers, these students experience shock and revulsion that in the entire history of the human race such questions should ever have needed to be asked. Their curiosity and the complexity of the issues forces them to experience the power of these questions with their hearts as well as their heads.

So, I no longer feel frustration when I don't satisfy the curiosities of my students during their study of *Night* and the Holocaust. For I've concluded that what is important is *not* that all these questions should be answered; what is important is that all of us should continue to ask them. I believe it was to this end that Elie Wiesel created a *poetic* account of awful beauty, ambiguity, and power. He must have sensed that as long as we question the events of the Holocaust, our memory of it—and our outrage—will be an eternal flame within each of us.

SUKHBIR SINGH

The Parable of Survival in Elie Wiesel's Night

In *Night* (1958) Elie Wiesel gives a witness to the massacre of his family, along with thousands of other Hungarian Jews, by the Nazi forces in the concentration camps at Auschwitz and Buchenwald. A reading of this tragic episode opens a dark abyss of absolute evil where "The human creature, outraged and humiliated beyond all the heart and spirit can conceive of, defied a divinity who was blind and deaf."[1] Shaken with fear, the reader desperately needs to know how one could survive as a *human being* under such circumstances of human crisis. Wiesel himself answers this bewildering query by organising his experience of the Holocaust around the parable of survival which normally eludes the attention of the reader in the midst of an overwhelming darkness of the night of death. Wiesel conveys it through his treatment of the father-and-son relationship in the book.

Young Eliezer and his old father have to live under the extreme conditions of life in the Nazi camps. The SS guards torture them mercilessly to break their body and soul. Their prayers for help from the Almighty remain unanswered. But, Eliezer and his father fight against dehumanisation and death in the absence of God by their faith in themselves and in their moral values. The father and the son take it to be their moral obligation to help each other to survive the crisis. The sacred act of fulfilling moral responsibility becomes their life principle. They observe its sanctity in an extreme

Notes on Contemporary Literature, Volume 16, Number 1 (1986): p. 6. Copyright © 1986 *Notes on Contemporary Literature*.

situation where "everyman has to fight for himself and not think of anyone else. Even of his father" (121–122). Eliezer and his father derive necessary physical strength and moral inspiration from the act of fulfilling their moral responsibility to each other. During the process they become "Stronger than cold or hunger, stronger than the shots and the desire to die . . ." (99).

Wiesel communicates the implication of this divine phenomenon as a source of life in an environment of death, in two ways. First, he gives a couple of contrasting instances where sons violate the sanctity of their sacred obligation at the cost of their lives. For example, Rabbi Eliahou's son is missing after he betrays his father "to free himself from an encumbrance which could lessen his own chances of survival" (103). Another son kills his old father mercilessly for a bit of bread. He is immediately killed by other prisoners, in a similar manner, for the same (112–113). Secondly, the author reveals the conflict that arises at times in the most secret region of Eliezer's heart. At one moment Eliezer thinks, "if only I could get rid of this dead weight (his father), so that I could use all my strength to struggle for my own survival, and only worry about myself" (117). At another moment he tells himself, "It's too late to save your old father . . . You ought to be having two rations of bread, two rations of soup . . . " (122). But, Eliezer immediately feels guilty, and ashamed of himself. His moral ambivalence intimates him that it would be the end of him and his father if he betrays his commitment to his moral obligation. Thereafter, Eliezer promptly makes an atonement to overcome his selfish instincts and helps his father with a renewed sense of respect for his moral principle.

The son helps his old father to survive until he dies of an acute dysentery at Buchenwald. The father dies with his son's name on his lips (123). The son engraves into himself the picture of his dying father—"his blood-stained face, his shattered skull" (123). Subsequently, Eliezer is released from the camp by the Russian forces. The son survives by his dedication to his moral responsibility to his father. The father survives in his son. Hence Wiesel's autobiographical novel carries a parable at its centre that one's commitment to one's moral values in times of human crisis becomes a divine source of physical and moral strength to survive with life and humanity intact.

NOTE

1. François Mauriac, "Foreword" to *Night,* tr. Stella Rodway (Harmondsworth: Penguin, 1981), p. 10. All further references are to this edition.

CARDINAL JEAN-MARIE LUSTIGER

The Absence of God? The Presence of God?
A Meditation in Three Parts on Night

Wiesel remains a man of faith, even when all evidence of God's presence seemed destroyed.

How can one discuss the work of Elie Wiesel without speaking about the man? To separate one from the other would amount to betraying both, for Elie Wiesel is completely in his work. He is one of the great theologians of our century.

Such an assertion may come as a surprise. Elie Wiesel himself will not admit to being a "theologian." He shies away from what those who consider themselves "theologians" call "theological" thinking. He even goes so far as to remind us continually that, strictly speaking, "Jewish theology" does not exist.

Elie Wiesel dismisses the idea that he is a theologian doing theology. Yet, he is certainly cognizant of the theology that talks about God but tends to culminate in a kind of rational and coherent whole leading some people to deny its very object. Those who wrote the "theologies" of the death of God or even the "atheistic theologies" claimed to be "theologians." Elie Wiesel is clearly not a theologian in that sense. "How strange," he wrote in *The German Church Struggle and the Holocaust* (1974), "that the philosophy denying God came not from the survivors. Those who came out with the so-called God is dead theology, not one of them had been in Auschwitz."

America, Volume 159, Number 15 (November 19, 1988): pp. 402–406. Copyright © 1988 America Press, Inc.

But one may also conceive of a theologian in another way: As a person to whom God speaks and who, in turn, speaks to God and then tells the story; as a person whom God seeks and who himself searches for God and then communicates the experience; as a person whom God nourishes with the scroll of His Word, commanding him to utter it. God's Word is as sweet as honey on the tongue, even when it voices "lamentations, wails and reproaches" (Jer. 2 and 3).

In this sense, Elie Wiesel has been a theologian since he was a child, and he has never ceased to be one. He could not help it—even during the dark night of Auschwitz. Quite the opposite is true. He tells us in *Night* that as a child: "I ran to the synagogue to weep over the destruction of the Temple. . . . I wept [when I prayed] because—because of something inside me that felt the need for tears."

When he returns to the devastated sanctuary of his childhood soul, Elie may find there the "gift of tears" that God grants to those He loves. Tears and consolation without previous cause are inexpressible yet certain signs of God's presence. This sanctuary of his childhood was burnt to the ground when Elie witnessed the Germans hurl into the "huge flames" of the furnace a truckload of small children still alive. "Babies! Yes, I saw it—saw it with my own eyes . . . those children in the flames."

The blaze dried his tears. The Word became both silence and absence, and in his exile, which no words can describe, Wiesel wrote: "My eyes were open and I was alone—terribly alone in a world without God and without man." This unimaginable ordeal of faith is part and parcel of the struggle of faith. This is what Elie Wiesel ceaselessly keeps telling us, ever since he recovered the ability to speak the Word. To be a theologian is to chart this path and to struggle continually with God's incomprehensible love for His forsaken and distressed people.

Nor can one ever cease questioning the unfathomable patience of the Almighty. Before Noah, God established an everlasting covenant with all flesh. In His Mercy, God promised that He would never destroy His creation again, even though, strictly speaking, justice might require Him to do so. And yet, why does God allow men to commit the absurd injustice of destroying each other and the earth along with them? And how and when will God fulfill the promise made to Abraham and the oath sworn to David? Yes, whoever questions and even challenges God, all the while desiring to obey His Word and listening to His silence, that person is a theologian.

To be a theologian is to acknowledge how incomprehensible are God's ways, and yet never cease to follow them. Is Elie Wiesel a theologian? Yes, in the same way any Jew is who realizes that he rests in the hand of God, even as he contemplates the history of his people. True theology is a life that is faithful to God. We recognize in the works of writers like Charles Péguy and in the diaries of St. Thérèse of Lisieux, who spent her life in prayer, the great achievements of Catholic theology in this century.

Do not conclude that this definition of the theologian—already given by the Fathers of the Church—is intended to reject as worthless the speculative power of human reason. On the contrary, in the expectation of the Final Judgment, it gives rationality its rightful place. Whoever, in order to justify his avoidance of God, would be tempted to make use of the dreadful confession of the child whose soul was devoured by the black flames (see *Night*, p. 44) ought to ponder the following words: "Anyone who is an obstacle to bring down one of these little ones who have faith, would be better thrown into the sea with a great millstone round his neck!" (Mk. 9:42).

* * *

Elie Wiesel received the Nobel Prize for *Peace,* not the Nobel Prize for Literature. Therefore, it is not his literary oeuvre that has been celebrated, but that to which he himself and his writings bear witness: the fate of the Jewish people recognized as a sign of Peace for all men and women.

The granting of this award is not an expression of atonement for the six million Jews who were slaughtered by the Nazis. In his Nobel acceptance speech, Elie Wiesel told us that the honor bestowed upon him "belongs to all the survivors and their children and, through us, to the Jewish people with whose destiny I have always identified." For the "final solution" was not meant to annihilate some individual Jews but the entire Jewish people. The alleged scientific nature of the racist definitions of the Jewish identity cast the light of the glaring inferno upon God's promise.

In his commentary on the Book of Job, Elie Wiesel writes: "Job was not Jewish; but his ordeal concerns all humanity, just as the suffering of the Jewish people ought to concern all humanity. Will the day ever come when the crimes against the Jews will be considered as crimes against humanity, and the crimes against humanity as crimes against the Jewish people?"

How and why can one claim the privilege of such a mission? Should one support his prerogative by keeping a tally of sufferings, or by measuring abominations, or by computing countless numbers of victims? On what sort of scales could we weigh history and its forgotten crimes? Who would dare explore, for example, the bottomless depths of contempt into which over three centuries the slave trade flung 40 million black Africans? Or was it 60 million? Historians are unable to agree when it comes to these numbers. And yet the Jewish people received this mission against which it struggles but which it will never give up, as Elie Wiesel constantly reminds us. "I had always believed that the mission of the Jews was to be the trembling of History rather than the wind which made it tremble," says Elisha, the hero of Wiesel's second book, *Dawn.*

It is precisely upon this unbearable question that the ovens of Auschwitz cast a somber light. But the answer remains an enigma—a "mystery," as we should say together with Elie Wiesel, who without hesitation uses this word so familiar to Christians. Totalitarian paganism stages an attack on God Himself by striving to annihilate His people. "Why are the nations in turmoil? Why do the people hatch their futile plots? The kings of the earth stand ready and the rulers conspire together against the Lord and His Anointed" (Ps. 2).

Nazi paganism wanted to proclaim the Aryan race as the only human one and the master of all others. But Israel, the elect of God, is the disturbing witness to the truth that God alone is God and He created all humans in His image and likeness. Thus, Nazi ideology did not find a better way to wrest the divine election and messianic mission from the Jewish people than by stripping Jews of their dignity and depriving them of their humanity. "I was a body. Perhaps less than that," Wiesel wrote. Remember these final lines of *Night:* "I wanted to see myself in the mirror hanging on the opposite wall. I had not seen myself since the ghetto. From the depths of the mirror a corpse gazed back at me. The look in his eyes, as they stared into mine, has never left me."

But the test Jews were put to exceeded all measure, not only because of the excess of their suffering, but because of their election by God, who established them as the Jewish people, even if they sometimes dream of becoming at last "a people like any other." When you are a witness of man's humanity, how can you consent to being excluded from the human family? It is unbearable to the point of madness to think that God would allow the worst possible disaster to crush the people He created to bring salvation to all humankind.

Peace is one of the messianic blessings. To honor Elie Wiesel and, therefore, as he himself said, "the entire Jewish people," with the Nobel Prize for Peace, is implicitly to recognize that the destiny of Israel is linked with the messianic salvation of all humankind. On the part of the "nations" (see Ps. 2:1) it is a timid sign of hope, a veiled expression of bashfulness in regard to the Lord and His Anointed. Elie Wiesel hinted at such an insight in his acceptance speech at Oslo, while focusing on negative events ("crimes against humanity, crimes against Israel"). He had gone a few steps further in his novel *Beggar in Jerusalem,* speaking through the character of Kalman, the kabbalist: "The Jews are God's memory and the heart of mankind. We do not always know this, but the others do, and that is why they treat us with suspicion and cruelty. Memory frightens them. Through us they are linked to the beginning and the end. By eliminating us they hope to gain immortality."

In the September 1980 issue of Esprit, A. Derczanski noted quite perceptively, "There is much resignation in Elie Wiesel's endeavor. It is grounded in the election which grabs him by the throat, but he wants to decipher it and figure it out through the Holocaust. He is too self-conscious to raise his people to the level not of the martyred but of the Messiah. Perhaps this is why he leaves us thirsting for more."

Indeed, the underlying question is: What is the relationship between the election, the divine vocation of the Jewish people and the Messiah? And does this messianic vocation provide any significance or justification to the suffering of both the people and the Messiah Himself? The unimaginable event of the Shoah prompts Wiesel to respond: "The further I go, the less I understand. Maybe there is nothing to understand. I still fail to understand what happened— either the how or the why."

The disaster has created "a mystery which overwhelms and subjugates us" *(Le Chant des morts)*. Let us recall Isaiah: "Time was when many were aghast at you, my people; so now many nations recoil at the sight of him, and kings curl their lips in disgust.... His form, disfigured, lost all the likeness of a man, his beauty changed beyond human resemblance" (Is. 52: 14–15; 53: 2).

Both the 52nd and 53rd chapters of Isaiah ought to be quoted entirely here, even though their application to Israel remains so painful—if not downright unbearable. As far as I am concerned, I receive these words unreservedly and yet with the same bewilderment when they refer to Jesus, the Messiah of whom I am a disciple. Why was it necessary for the Messiah to endure such suffering in order to enter into His glory? That remains an unfathomable mystery, a folly and an obstacle for faith. Only the Spirit of the Lord who changes human hearts can reveal the depth of God's wisdom. Yes, the Son walked freely to His death, saying to God, His Father: "Burnt offering and sin offering you have not required, then I said: 'Lo, I come!'" (Ps. 40: 7–8).

After these words of Revelation, all violent sacrifices, all the hatred transferred on any scapegoat are proscribed. What an unbelievable trial this must be when a vast force of destruction comes to crush God's beloved people. It is an unbelievable ordeal. What word can be uttered in front of the bloody furrow ploughed like scourges by Evil through the destiny of all humanity? I can bear the night into which Israel was plunged only by sharing the night into which the Messiah willingly entered in order to open to all the way of Life and to bring forth the light of the world, the light of Resurrection, a light more dazzling than all the suns. When I believe this, I do not consider myself separated before God from Elie Wiesel whom I love as a brother.

* * *

For the Nazis, the *thought* that negates both God and man gives way to a systematic *enterprise:* sending both God and man back to nothingness. This shift to action, this translation of abstraction into destruction is truly an infernal form of nihilism. The young Elie could *see* it even before he left his village. The Hungarian police made the last group of deportees walk faster: "They were our first oppressors," wrote Wiesel in *Night*. "They were the first of the faces of hell and death." Experimental logic did not allow Hitler's plan to remain an abstract generality. Any theory can abstractly deny both God and man. But in order to justify its supremacy, the so-called Aryan race had to eradicate the Jewish people as the one through whom God in history had revealed Himself to man and revealed man to himself. This is how and why men sank into the infernal logic of the camps.

Only those who were plunged down into this abyss know what it was like. They ought to bear witness to it, but such hell is unspeakable, since it is the very negation of the Word. "The language of night was not human, but animal or perhaps mineral: hoarse screams, howls, muffled groans, wild laments, blows with a club. . . . A beast striking out and a body collapsing; an officer raises his arm and a community marches to a common grave; a guard shrugs his shoulders and a thousand families burst to pieces and are brought together again only in death. This was the language of the concentration camp. It substituted itself for all other kinds of expressions and suppressed them all. Rather than a link, it became a wall. Was it possible to get over it? Should the reader be made to overcome it? I knew that the answer was 'no' but I also knew that the 'no' had to be changed to 'yes'" *(Paroles d'étranger)*.

Elie Wiesel brings us to the realization of the infernal character of this moment in our history, in the history of the Jewish people and of all humanity. Had anyone before Wiesel led us so far into the depths of this diabolical enterprise? For Wiesel has remained a man of faith, even when all evidence of God's presence was destroyed. His testimony—all his work—brings us back not to the horror of the past, but to the threshold where our personal responsibility still operates. He warns us about the nature of the danger that can always surface again.

This is Elie Wiesel's mission and what makes his message unique. He did not take it on himself, but he received it from the fervent Jewish saints who preceded us, *tsadikim, hassidim;* he received it from On-High.

He never told us who suggested to him the title of the French edition of his first story. But it seems to me that he gives the key, for the word "night" keeps coming up in these few short pages. Derczanski states that in the work of Wiesel there are "certain marks of a liturgy."

The image of an inverted Passover springs out of Wiesel's sentences; it is an infernal experiment made by the Nazis; no one but a Jewish witness can unmask it. "It was night" is the refrain of a Seder poem that spells out the manifestations of God's power and fidelity. But who is the master of the night of Auschwitz? "Hitler," answers one of the faceless prisoners, to the astonishment of the young Elie. "Hitler has made it very clear that he will annihilate all the Jews before the clock strikes twelve, before they can hear the last stroke. . . . I've got more faith in Hitler than in anyone else. He's the only one who's kept his promises, all his promises, to the Jewish people."

It is an infernal Passover where Hitler wants to show his power by destroying the people created and saved by God. References to the Passover abound throughout the story, beginning with the departure from Sighet. It is an infernal, perverted, inverted Passover that replaces the people's election by God with the selection by the S.S.; the Assembly of the people in the desert, the *Qahal* of the Exodus, is replaced by the roll call for extermination. "I understood," Elie Wiesel is quoted in Brigitte-Fanny Cohen's *Elie Wiesel, qui êtes-vous?* "that evil is frightening, even though it is powerless. In its very essence, it releases a sort of physical terror." This is why Auschwitz has become a symbolic name for hell. It is a place of silence. A place of silence that allows the dark terror of evil to be made manifest. A place of silence that cries out to heaven, like Abel's spilled blood. A place of silence that must master the beast crouching at the door, eager and waiting to turn man into a murderer like Cain (Gen. 4: 7). Because of their vocation, Christians ought to understand what such a silence signifies. The liturgy of the church makes all the disciples of the Crucified face this emptiness. When all is accomplished on Good Friday and until the end of the night of Holy Saturday, we have to survive in God's obscure silence. How could we fail to understand and accept the fact that the Jewish people fulfill their sacred mission to allow humankind to listen to the silence to which it has condemned the people blessed by God? This emptiness of time and place can only be gazed upon "from afar" (Lk. 22: 54) by those whose eyes meet the dereliction of Good Friday before they can turn to the rising Sun of the first Day.

EVA FLEISCHNER

Mauriac's Preface to Night: *Thirty Years Later*

Dear Elie: I have been asked to reflect on François Mauriac's Preface to your book *Night* from a perspective of "30 years later." Let me do so in the form of a letter, a genre that symbolizes the personal dimension in our relationship so dear to me.

Whenever I use *Night* in my classes, I tell my students: "Be sure to read Mauriac's Preface. Not all prefaces deserve to be read, but this one does. It will give you a key to the book." All these years *Night* has remained linked to Mauriac's name. This had always seemed quite normal to me, even fitting. After all, it was Mauriac who, in your own words, had launched you as a writer. I can imagine that it had been an honor for you—at the time a young, unknown Jewish journalist—to have the famous French writer and member of the *Académie Française* introduce your first book, and thus introduce you to the world.

But 30 years have gone by. You no longer need Mauriac to introduce you to the world. The world knows you well. You have written many other books, each new book eagerly awaited. You have received the Nobel Peace Prize. Mauriac is dead. And yet, you have kept his Preface as prelude to *Night*, and thereby as prelude to your entire work. What may have been grateful acceptance on your part 30 years ago has long since become deliberate choice.

America, Volume 159, Number 15 (November 19, 1988): p. 411, 419. Copyright © 1988 America Press, Inc.

35

Could this choice have had its moments of difficulty for you? I wonder about this because of all that Mauriac represents, not only in literature (fame and success), but also in religion (Catholicism). Given the profoundly tragic history of the relationship between your faith and his (and mine), was it really so easy for you to accept the endorsement of your work by France's leading Catholic writer? All the more so because, as you make vividly clear in "An Interview Unlike Any Other," Mauriac's approach to Judaism was cast—at least initially, and quite understandably—in the mold common, prior to Vatican II, even to those Catholics who were sympathetic to Judaism. At best—as you mentioned in *A Jew Today*—they saw Judaism as no more than a prelude to Christianity, as the setting for Jesus: "Every reference led back to him. Jerusalem? The eternal city, where Jesus turned his disciples into apostles. The Bible? The Old Testament, which, thanks to Jesus of Nazareth, succeeded in enriching itself with a New Testament. Mendes-France? A Jew, both brave and hated, not unlike Jesus long ago." You leave no doubt in the reader's mind how deeply these words offended the Jew in you—to the point where, for the first time in your life, you "exhibited bad manners." So great was your anger that it overcame your shyness and you wounded the old man with your words, and he began to weep.

You allowed yourself to be angry, and he allowed himself to weep. Each of you had the courage to be in touch with who you truly were at that moment. And it was this that broke down the wall between you. There is no downplaying of the moment of harshness. Mauriac's humanity made him weep over his insensitivity to you as Jew. Your humanity caused you to be deeply troubled because you had hurt an upright and profoundly moral man.

Your humanity, Elie, has seemed to me to be the constant in your life. No matter how much has changed for you and in you these past 30 years, you are no longer homeless and alone. You have a beloved wife and son; you are revered the world over. This has not changed. If, at times, your judgment of Christianity has seemed harsh to me, in your personal interactions, whether with me or with my students or with the many Christian friends who love you, there has never been anything but gentleness and graciousness.

And is it any wonder that you should judge Christianity harshly? That, even as a child, you would cross the street out of fear whenever you passed a church? No, it is no wonder; it is, alas, all too understandable. For Christians have incurred much guilt toward your people. What is surprising, what is extraordinary, is that you have been able to distinguish between the tradition as a whole, and individual Christians. For this I have long been grateful to you.

Recently, since reading your new book *Twilight,* I am grateful in yet another way. For I sense in this book a change in your attitude. Not only is the hero, Raphael, saved by two peasants "who are good Christians," but in describing the age-old pogroms that used to break out during Holy Week in Rovidok (as in so many other villages and towns of eastern Europe) you speak of the perpetrators as "Christians who were not necessarily followers of Christ."

Why do these few words move me so? Let me try to explain. For us Christians, the sense of guilt at our corporate history of persecution of Jews becomes, at times, almost too heavy to bear. The burden is lightened when we discover, or remember, that there have been through the centuries Christian women and men who did not run with the mob, even—also—during that darkest of times that will forever be known as the Holocaust.

Because of the weight your words carry for millions of people, non-Jews as well as Jews, the text I have quoted can, and I believe will, make a crucial contribution to the reconciliation between our two peoples. Thus, more than ever will you have become the messenger of peace the Nobel Peace Prize citation calls you.

And perhaps, also, your relationship with your old friend François Mauriac will have entered a new phase. Were you to talk once more face to face today, 30 years later, yet another barrier between you would have fallen. Perhaps, indeed, the dialogue continues? After all, both Jews and Christians worship a "God who raises the dead."

Permit me to end these reflections with a wish. Won't you, please, as you promised in *A Jew Today,* publish your conversations with Mauriac, which continued over the years? Then we would know a little more of the relationship between you, of what enabled you both to transcend your religious and political disagreements. Only you can give us the answers to this and, by so doing, shed further light on one of the most remarkable friendships of this century.

Happy birthday, and Shalom!

DAVID L. VANDERWERKEN

Wiesel's Night *as Anti*-Bildungsroman

One of our most familiar fictional forms is the story of a young person's initiation into adulthood. That the form remains rich, inexhaustible, and compelling can be confirmed by pointing to the success of *The World According to Garp,* for one. Although specifically coined to describe a certain tradition of German novel deriving from Goethe's *Wilhelm Meister,* "Bildungsroman"—while untranslatable into English—has become our flexible label for hundreds of works that treat a youth's apprenticeship to life. As Martin Swales has shown in *The German Bildungsroman from Wieland to Hesse,* considerable definitional variance exists even within the German tradition. Jerome H. Buckley's survey of British appropriations of the form, *Season of Youth: The Bildungsroman from Dickens to Golding,* further demonstrates the form's suppleness. The latitude our English usage of the word allows does not mean that the term is so elastic as to be meaningless. Certain general patterns remain constant in works so apparently diverse as *The Autobiography of Benjamin Franklin*, Stendhal's *The Red and the Black,* Chopin's *The Awakening,* or Joyce's *A Portrait of the Artist as a Young Man.* Yet the ways in which *Bildungsromane* adhere to or depart from the patterns generate their variety and interest.

Indeed, many *Bildungsromane,* especially modernist ones, gain power and point by parodying or even inverting the traditional formulae of the

Modern Jewish Studies, Volume 7, Number 4 (1990): pp. 57–63. Copyright © 1990 David L. Vanderwerken.

genre. For an early parody example, Crane's Henry Fleming likely ends up learning nothing of self and world, or the relation of self to world, through the course of his initiatory experiences in *The Red Badge of Courage*. As well, W. Clark Hendley has persuasively argued that Philip Roth's *The Ghost Writer* simultaneously pays homage to and mocks the tradition (89). And no better example of the *Bildungsroman* turned inside out and upside down exists than the story of Eliezer Wiesel in *Night*. In his chapter "The Dominion of Death" in *The Holocaust and the Literary Imagination*, Lawrence L. Langer posits that inversion, reversal, and negation are the overt strategies of much Holocaust memoir writing, skewed *Bildungsromane*, of which *Night* is the most powerful (74–123).

Traditionally, the story of maturation takes a youth through a series of educational experiences, some through books and classrooms, but most not, and exposes the youth to a series of possible mentors and guides who become, as Ralph Ellison puts it in *Invisible Man*, "trustee[s] of consciousness" (69). Of course, Ellison's young man has trouble distinguishing the truth-telling mentors from the liars. Usually, however, such life teachers shape the youth toward a cultural ideal of adulthood. The function of education, Joseph Campbell tells us in *Myths to Live By*, is to shift the "response systems of adolescents from dependency to responsibility" (46). Recall grandfather's speech defining what a gentleman is and does to young Lucius Priest at the end of Faulkner's *The Reivers*. Often the initiation process is worked out on a journey, some movement through space, which has the effect of accelerating the rate of maturation, as in the case of Lucius Priest or Huck Finn. And often the journey implies a spiritual quest. The result is a story of moral, emotional, intellectual, and spiritual growth. Normally, the initiate not only achieves self-definition, but also social definition, ready to assume a role in a community, whether the youth is from the provinces, like Julian Sorel, or remains in the provinces, like Sonny in Larry McMurtry's *The Last Picture Show*. In *Night*, Elie Wiesel inverts and reverses, even shatters, the elements of the traditional paradigm.

The very title itself implies a reversal since the *Bildungsroman* usually opens out into day, illumination, awareness, life. Instead, *Night* leads us into darkness and death. While the traditional raw initiate grows out into a knowledge of the richness, fullness, complexity, and multivariety of life—its open-ended possibilities—*Night* starts out with a sense of richness in heritage and culture that is violently and quickly stripped away, denuded, impoverished. Instead of expanding and ripening, young Eliezer's life narrows, withers, contracts, reduces to enclosure. Instead of finding a self and a place in the world, Eliezer begins with a sense of self, located in a coherent, unified community, and ends up when Buchenwald is liberated alone, isolated, and numb. Instead of becoming aware of his own potential, in touch with resources he was hitherto oblivious of in himself, Eliezer looks in the mirror on the last page and sees a corpse. The pious young boy of Sighet has been incinerated. And the corollary spiritual quest that usually leads to some satisfying accommodation or resolution—witness Hans Castorp's vision in Mann's *The Magic Mountain*—leads in *Night* to the void. Instead of climbing the mountain, Eliezer spirals into hell. And at the bottom lurk only questions, no answers.

The opening chapter introduces us to this pious and spiritual adolescent who lives in the eternal world, who knows more about what happened 5000 years ago than what is occurring in Hungary in 1943. The only son in a family of five, Eliezer has been groomed for a life of study, his future as a Talmudic scholar or rabbi tacitly understood. Now twelve, Eliezer feels impatient to delve into the mystical realm of Judaism, the Cabbala, if he can find a teacher. Although his father refuses Eliezer's request to study Cabbala on the grounds of his youth, precocious or no, Eliezer finds a master in Moche the Beadle, the synagogue handyman. In Moche, Wiesel offers an apparently traditional mentor character, the sage who will guide the initiate through the gates of truth: "It was with him that my initiation began" (14). Moche is a Socratic sort of teacher, asking challenging and paradoxical questions that have no easy answers, if any at all. He tells Eliezer that the answers to all our ultimate questions are within ourselves. As a result of their studies, Eliezer says, "a conviction grew in me that Moche the Beadle would draw me with him into eternity" (14). Suddenly Moche vanishes, deported in a cattle car with other foreign Jews, presumably to a work camp.

Just as suddenly, months later, Moche reappears in Sighet having escaped from the Gestapo, and he no longer talks of "God or the Cabbala, but only of what he had seen" (16). Wiesel now reveals Moche's significance as Eliezer's mentor, neither as tutor of the verities of the ancient sacred texts, nor as agent of Eliezer's developing self-knowledge, but as witness and prophet of the reality of the Holocaust, a reality Sighet is not only oblivious of, but also refuses to believe. Consciousness simply reneges at Moche's preposterous tales of mass murder. The town dismisses him as mad; in Wiesel's withering refrain, "life returned to normal" (17). Although Eliezer continues to pursue the truth of the eternal as Moche-I had taught him, it is the truth of temporal fact taught by the Lazarus-like Moche-II—his insights into *l'universe concentrationnaire,* the kingdom of night—that will prove to be the most imperative, the most influential, perhaps the most authentic in Eliezer's near future.

That, for Wiesel, only the mad could imagine the mad truth finds reinforcement in the figure of Madame Schächter on the train to Auschwitz. In chapter two, her hysterical shrieks of furnaces and flames are received like Moche's stories, an obvious consequence of madness. After all, she has been separated from her family. Finally, some of the people beat her into silence.

Yet as the train nears its destination, she rouses to scream again, "'Jews, look! Look through the window! Flames! Look!'" (38). Eliezer does look and realizes that Madame Schächter's cries all along have been premonitions, not psychotic hallucinations, for now he sees the chimneys of what he will learn are the crematoria. This woman of fifty becomes an indirect mentor who provides Eliezer with another insight into contemporary truth.

Of the other adults that Eliezer encounters in the camps, two stand out in offering contradictory advice on how to survive in hell. The first, the prisoner in charge of Eliezer's block upon arrival, makes a speech to the new arrivals that echoes the sentiments of innumerable, traditional moral sages:

> "Have faith in life. Above all else, have faith. Drive out despair, and you will keep death away from yourselves. Hell is not for eternity. And now, a prayer—or rather, a piece of advice: let there be comradeship among you. We are all brothers, and we are all suffering the same fate. The same smoke floats over all our heads. Help one another. It is the only way to survive." (51–52)

Comforted by this plea for faith, community, interdependence, civilization, Eliezer thinks: "The first human words" (52). Yet are they the "'teachings of our sages'" (41)? For this condition? In Buchenwald two years later, after the death march evacuation of Buna, Eliezer hears another sort of advice from a block leader, at a time when Schlomo Wiesel is dying. This sage counsels Eliezer to look out for number one:

> "Here, there are no fathers, no brothers, no friends. Everyone lives and dies for himself alone. I'll give you a sound piece of advice— don't give your ration of bread and soup to your old father. There's nothing you can do for him. And you're killing yourself. Instead, you ought to be having his ration." (122)

Of course, this is practical wisdom as Eliezer knows, but "I dared not admit it" (122). Yet this is the ethical dictum of hell, into which Eliezer has been fully initiated. No ties are sacred.

Night's most powerful dramatization of an inverted mentor-initiate relationship is that of father and son. Schlomo Wiesel, respected community leader upon whom others rely for guidance and strength, represents the patriarchal Jewish father, a *mensch,* or as Bellow's Moses Herzog puts it, "a father, a sacred being, a king" (147). Normally, the father helps the son make the transition in adolescence from dependence to independence. In the kingdom of night, however, the roles completely reverse; the son becomes the parent. In the end, the man whom others looked to has "become like a child, weak, timid, vulnerable" (117). This reversal of the normal order is prefigured at Birkenau when the veteran prisoner urges father and son to declare their ages to be forty and eighteen, not their actual fifty and fourteen, the better to survive Dr. Mengele's selection. Indeed time itself does warp, becoming nightmare time, accelerating human changes. "How he had changed! His eyes had grown dim" (47), comments Eliezer about his father the first night at Birkenau. As time unfolds, Eliezer takes the ascendancy in the father-son relationship, making decisions, taking charge of their common welfare, even feeling angry at his father for not knowing how to avoid the Kapo's wrath and getting beaten: "That is what concentration camp life had made of me" (66). Although he never abandons his father the way Rabbi Eliahou's son had (104), Eliezer has his mental moments of filial disloyalty and betrayal. When they are temporarily separated during an air alert at Buchenwald, Eliezer thinks "'Don't let me find him! If only I could get rid of this dead weight'" (118), but he immediately feels ashamed. However, when his father is carried away to the crematory in the night, perhaps still alive, Eliezer must face the terrible truth: "And, in the depths of my being, in the recesses of my weakened conscience, could I have searched it, I might perhaps have found something like—free at last" (124). He sees himself, then, as finally no better than Rabbi Eliahou's son.

Just as Wiesel radically overturns the stock *Bildungsroman* pattern of master and apprentice, he alters the traditional process of the evolving self on its way to fulfillment. On the day of deportation, Eliezer looks back at his home where he had spent so many years "imagining what my life would be like" (28). The ancient story of youth's departure from the nest, encountering the world and fleshing out the skeletal self, becomes for Eliezer a story of decomposing flesh, of becoming a skeleton. Literally overnight, Eliezer tells us, his sense of self evaporated: "The student of the Talmud, the child that I was, had been consumed in the flames. There remained only a shape that looked like me" (47). Even the name for the "shape that looked like me" dissolves with the engraving of A-7713 on his left arm. The identity nurtured for twelve years collapses in one day.

Eliezer's sense of self is identical with his spiritual life. The worst of *Night*'s outrages, movingly worded by François Mauriac in the Foreword, is the "death of God in the soul of a child who suddenly discovers absolute evil" (9). Again, the flames of the first night, fueled by the truckload of babies, "consumed my faith forever," "murdered my God and my soul and turned my dreams to dust" (44). The two most powerful dramatizations of the consequences of Eliezer's sundered faith—the faith that had given richness and depth to his living—are the hanging of the boy and the first High Holy Days spent in Buna. For Eliezer, God is "hanging here on this gallows" (76). If God is not dead, then he deserves man's contempt, Eliezer feels.

The bitterness pours forth during Rosh Hashanah and Yom Kippur with the mockery of the prisoners carrying out the forms, the absurdity of the starving debating whether to fast. While thousands pray, Eliezer offers up outraged accusations:

> "But these men here, whom You have betrayed, whom You have allowed to be tortured, butchered, gassed, burned, what do they do? They pray before You! They praise Your name!" (78–79)

Like Huck Finn, Eliezer knows you can't pray a lie:

> My eyes were open and I was alone—terribly alone in a world without God and without man. Without love or mercy. I had ceased to be anything but ashes, yet I felt myself to be stronger than the Almighty, to whom my life had been tied for so long. I stood amid that praying congregation, observing it like a stranger. (79)

Also in this scene of the praying ten thousand, one can see Wiesel's ironic presentation of the community that the prepared initiate is to take his place in upon completion of apprenticeship, the culmination of *Bildungsromane,* public and ceremonial like the ordination of clergy or the commissioning of officers. This is a congregation of the living dead, a community of corpses acting out a charade. This is as anti as a *Bildungsroman* can get. Furthermore, if the Book of Exodus can be described as a *Bildungsroman* on the level of an entire people, *Night* can also be read as an anti-Exodus as Lawrence S. Cunningham has cogently argued: "The life giving biblical myth of election, liberation, covenant, and promise becomes the vehicle for telling the story of the unnatural order of death-domination" (24).

Much Holocaust writing has taken the form of anti-*Bildungsromane.* Kosinski's *The Painted Bird,* for one, comes to mind—harrowingly. It's as if the victims of the people who developed the *Bildungsroman,* yet who denied *Bildung* to millions, find a small measure of revenge by turning the very form back on itself, the endpoint being human emptiness instead of human wholeness. If Wilhelm Meister could look deeply enough into his mirror, perhaps he would see Eliezer Wiesel, his twentieth-century double.

Works Cited

Bellow, Saul. *Herzog.* 1964. New York: Penguin, 1976.

Buckley, Jerome H. *Season of Youth: The Bildungsroman from Dickens to Golding.* Cambridge: Harvard University Press, 1974.

Campbell, Joseph. "The Importance of Rites." *Myths to Live By.* New York: Bantam, 1973. 43–61.

Cunningham, Lawrence S. "Elie Wiesel's Anti-Exodus." *Responses to Elie Wiesel.* Ed. Harry James Cargas. New York: Persea, 1978.

Ellison, Ralph. *Invisible Man.* 1952. New York: Vintage, 1972.

Handley, W. Clark. "An Old Form Revitalized: Philip Roth's *Ghost Writer* and the *Bildungsroman.*" *Studies in the Novel* 16 (1984): 87–100.

Swales, Martin. *The German Bildungsroman from Wieland to Hesse.* Princeton: Princeton University Press, 1978.

Wiesel, Elie. *Night.* 1958. New York: Avon-Discus, 1969.

JOYCE LAZARUS

Elie Wiesel's La Nuit and L'Oublié: In Pursuit of Silence

One of the striking characteristics of the writings of Elie Wiesel is his ambivalent attitude toward language, and the predominant role of silence in his works. For Wiesel, despite his more than thirty books on this subject, the experience of the Holocaust is still inexpressible and beyond language. "Words have lost their innocence and their power"[1] since the Holocaust. Since language was used to implement the Final Solution, words can never again be completely trusted. Yet in his commitment to truth, to bear witness to the millions of victims of the Holocaust, Wiesel finds that language, however imperfect it is, is man's only available tool. Through the right choice of words, there is the hope of sparing future generations the horrors of another Holocaust.

Language in Wiesel's novels is terse, highly condensed, and unadorned by wordplay. Influenced by the writings of the Eastern European World War II ghettos, Wiesel creates a sense of urgency by employing the sparse vocabulary of those living on the edge of existence. Attempting to convey the infinite solitude of victims of persecution, to express the inexpressible, Wiesel introduces the weight of silence in all his writings. In numerous interviews, Wiesel has repeatedly spoken of his preoccupation with silence, and his commitment to it as an aesthetic device.[2]

Essays in French Literature, Volume 28 (November 1991): pp. 87–94. Copyright © 1991 University of Western Australia.

In this essay I hope to analyze the role of silence as a dominant metaphor and structural device in two of Wiesel's novels: *La Nuit* (1958) and *L'Oublié* (1989).[3] I have chosen these two works because, although written more than thirty years apart, they have many of the same themes: the father-son relationship, the experience of religious faith, and the incommunicability of the horror of the Holocaust. By examining the role of silence in these two works, it is possible to study the evolution of this metaphor and aesthetic device across a range of emotional perspectives and a wide span of years.

Elie Wiesel himself, in a 1987 interview with Jean-François Thomas, distinguishes several different types of silence preponderant in his literary works: there is the destructive silence of the ignorant or forgetful; the silence of victims who have chosen to carry their truths with them to the grave, in the face of torture and injustice; the "biblical silence" of Job, Aaron, or Jeremiah, tormented by unanswerable religious and philosophical questions; the silence of the world during the Holocaust, and finally the inexplicable silence of God. Wiesel has attempted to make silence palpable, almost "visible", in order to identify, through his silence, with that of all victims: "Aussi j'essaie non pas de refouler le silence, mais de le récupérer à l'intérieur des mots. J'aimerais pouvoir prendre les paroles et mettre là-dedans autant de silence que possible".[4]

In *La Nuit*, silence is equaled with anguish, despair or death, and has a terrifying, ominous power. Wiesel describes the people of Sighet, Hungary, his native town, who naïvely maintained their optimism that no harm would come to them, in the face of all warnings of their imminent demise. In their refusal to talk about the fate of foreign Jews who had been deported, or to discuss the dire warnings of Moché-le-Bedeau, who had narrowly escaped death at the hands of the Nazis, the community, through its silence, has sealed its own doom:

> Des jours passèrent. Des semaines, des mois. La vie était redevenue normale. Un vent calme et rassurant soufflait dans toutes les demeures. (p. 19)

Wiesel depicts the destructive silence of indifferent neighbours in Sighet, who make no protest at the deportation of Jews, thus aiding the Nazi authorities in liquidating the entire Jewish population. He senses them lurking silently behind shuttered windows, waiting for the moment when, like vultures, they will loot the homes of deported Jews:

> La ville paraissait déserte. Mais, derrière leurs volets, nos amis d'hier attendaient sans doute le moment de pouvoir piller nos maisons. (p. 43)

Throughout *La Nuit,* silence is equated with despair, in the pauses between words or sobs of victims, in the unspoken words understood in gazes or
embraces, and in the anguished silence of victims facing death. Wiesel gives
weight to these pauses and moments heavy with inexpressible feelings. In an
exchange between his father and the townspeople of Sighet, just before their
deportation, the words spoken are less significant than what is implied in the
silent pauses between sentences:

> Des bruits circulent selon lesquels on nous déporte quelque
> part en Hongrie pour travailler dans des usines de briques. La
> raison en est, paraît-il, que le front est trop proche d'ici . . .
> Et, après un moment de silence, il ajouta:
> Chacun n'a le droit d'emporter que ses effets personnels. Un sac
> à dos, de la nourriture, quelques vêtements. Rien d'autre.
> Et, une fois de plus, un lourd silence. (p. 31)

The spoken words of his father repeat the lies which he has been told by the
Nazis, while the silent pauses between words indicate the truth suspected by
all his listeners, which they cannot voice: that they will be murdered.

Victims in *La Nuit* trying to express their thoughts and feelings find
their words choked and their lips paralyzed. The horror of confronting absolute evil is beyond language and can only be intimated by the weight of
silence. Waking up a family friend in the ghetto on the morning of their
deportation, young Eliezer is confronted with an old man with a beard who
stares at him as if the child were mad:

> Ma gorge était desséchée et les mots s'y étranglaient, paralysant
> mes lèvres. Je ne pouvais plus rien lui dire.
> Alors il comprit. Il descendit de son lit et, avec des gestes
> automatiques, il se mit à se vêtir. Puis il s'approcha du lit où dormait
> sa femme, lui toucha le front avec une infinie tendresse; elle ouvrit les
> paupières et il me semble qu'un sourire effleura ses lèvres. (p. 33)

The news of their doom is communicated silently from person to person
by a look or touch; the events unfolding are unspeakable both literally
and figuratively.

In Wiesel's descriptions of his mother and younger sister, marching toward the cattle cars, their silent stares and gestures communicate a depth of
anguish that could not be conveyed through dialogue:

> Ma mère, elle, marchait, le visage fermé, sans un mot, pensive.
> Je regardais ma petite soeur, Tsipora, ses cheveux blonds bien

peignés, un manteau rouge sur ses bras: petite fille de sept ans.
Sur son dos, un sac trop lourd pour elle. Elle serrait les dents: elle
savait déjà qu'il ne servait à rien de se plaindre. (p. 39)

Wiesel seems to draw out silent moments between father and son in *La
Nuit* to give voice to thoughts that can only be suggested, never defined. There
is the unspoken communication of hands and embraces: "Je m'en approchai, lui
pris une main et la baisai. Une larme y tomba. De qui, cette larme? La mienne?
La sienne? Je ne dis rien. Lui non plus. Nous ne nous n'étions jamais compris
aussi clairement" (p. 110); the silent, distant gaze of his father next to him when
his father seems absent from reality: "Comme il avait change! Ses yeux s'étaient
obscurcis. J'aurais voulu lui dire quelque chose, mais je ne savais quoi" (p. 64);
or when his father seems lost to him and to the world near the end of his life:
"Père, où cours-tu? Il me regarda un instant et son regard était lointain, illuminé,
le visage d'un autre. Un instant seulement, et il poursuivit sa course" (p.168).

Behind the words of pretence between father and son, regarding the fate
of their family, are their unspoken thoughts revealing a truth too painful to
express out loud:

> Maman est encore une femme jeune, dit une fois mon père. Elle
> doit être dans un camp de travail. Et Tsipora, n'est-elle pas déjà une
> grande fille? Elle aussi doit être dans un camp . . . Comme on aurait
> voulu y croire! On faisait semblant: si l'autre, lui, y croyait? (p. 77)

What is left unsaid is more significant and more revealing in *La Nuit* than
what can be communicated through language.

Silence can also convey a complete loss of humanity, as in the poignant
description of the narrator's silent confrontation with an SS officer who beats
his fatally ill father:

> L'officier lui asséna alors un coup violent de matraque sur la tête.
> Je ne bougeai pas. Je craiguais, mon corps craignait de recevoir à
> son tour un coup. (p. 173)

Through his terse sentences, his distancing from himself as he describes
the feelings of "mon corps", Wiesel equates silence with a death of will and
spirit. Similarly, the final, terrifying image in the novel of his own silent
corpse gazing at him in the mirror suggests his total dehumanization, his
reduction to an empty hollow shell:

> Du fond du miroir, un cadavre me contemplait.
> Son regard dans mes yeux ne me quitte plus. (p. 178)

Silence is a powerful metaphor in *La Nuit* for the inexplicable response of God to the Holocaust. God is paradoxically both present and absent through *La Nuit*, "murdered" along with the innocent victims in the camps:

> Jamais je n'oublierai ce silence nocturne qui m'a privé pour l'éternité du désir de vivre.
> Jamais je n'oublierai ces instants qui assassinèrent mon Dieu et mon âme, et mes rêves qui prirent le visage du désert. (p. 60)

Though silent, God is present in the prayers of young Eliezer in the camps:

> Et, malgré moi, une prière s'est éveillée en mon cœur, vers ce Dieu auquel je ne croyais plus. (p. 144)

and present as the accused in a silent Job-like interrogation conducted by the narrator:

> Aujourd'hui, je n'implorais plus. Je n'étais plus capable de gémir. Je me sentais, au contraire, très fort. J'étais l'accusateur. Et l'accuse: Dieu. Mes yeux s'étaient ouverts et j'étais seul, terriblement seul dans le monde, sans Dieu, sans hommes. (pp. 109–110)

In the novel *L'Oublié*, the memory of the Holocaust is resurrected a generation after World War II, through the conversations of a survivor, Elhanan Rosenbaum, and his son Malkiel, and through the latter's visit to their native village in Roumania. *L'Oublié* has many echoes of *La Nuit:* in both novels silence is often equated with suffering and martyrdom. In *L'Oublié*, Holocaust victims such as Malkiel's grandfather went to their deaths silently, refusing to divulge the names of other Jews, and refusing to compromise in any way in their faith (pp. 105, 112). Silence in both novels is also associated with the apathy and indifference of those non-Jews who might have prevented the massacre of their neighbours. Elhanan describes the town of Fehérfalu just after its liberation in 1945 as ghost town (p. 185). The silence and emptiness in the town seem to reverberate with the memory of the dead, and with accusations against their uncaring Christian neighbours:

> Partagé entre la colère et l'excès de désespoir, Elhanan se promène dans les rues de sa ville comme un somnambule. Il s'attend à chaque carrefour à tomber sur an ami d'enfance, un cousin, un parent. Il voit constamment son père, sa mère lui fait signe d'approcher . . . Il veut leur parler, mais aucun son ne quitte ses lèvres. Il est seul. Certes, il a des copains, des camarades, et il s'en fera encore plus

dans l'avenir, mais ça n'est pas pareil. Rein ne rompra sa solitude d'orphelin. (p.189)

In *L'Oublié*, Wiesel experiments with new structural and thematic elements of the novel. Abandoning a linear narrative structure in favour of episodic leaps back and forth in time between past and present, Wiesel suggests that human identity is not limited to one's chronological life, but instead incorporates the collective memory of all of one's ancestors:

> Malkiel: J'ai quarante ans. Plus trois mille. (p. 11)
> Elhanan: Lui dirai-je l'amour de son grand-père pour l'ètrange et merveilleuse communauté d'Israel, qui à ses yeux, s'étend de toi jusqu'à Moïse? Et de toi Tamar, jusqu'à Sarah? Grâce à lui, je vivrai: grâce à toi, Abraham vit. (p 317)

To the silence of death of the Holocaust, Wiesel opposes, in *L'Oublié*, the redemptive force of the collective memory of the Jewish people.

For Wiesel, all language has become compromised since the Holocaust; all language is potentially destructive, whereas silence in the Jewish Hasidic tradition is purity. Wiesel illustrates this Hasidic view of silence in *L'Oublié*, by his juxtaposition of dialogue between characters, reduced to its sparse, minimalist form, with unspoken "interior dialogue" (ruminations or prayers) of characters. It is through these silent interior dialogues that the principal character of *L'Oublié*, Malkiel Rosenbaum, finds his roots and his identity.

The spoken exchanges between characters throughout *L'Oublié* are often terse and superficial, or marred by misunderstandings, quarrels, or gaffes. The following exchange between Malkiel and Lidia (his Roumanian guide) illustrates with some humour the difficulties encountered in an attempt to communicate:

> Je vous parlerai de moi si vous me parlez de vous, dit Lidia.
> Et ensuite?
> Ensuite je saurai.
> Vous saurez quoi?
> Ce que vous souhaiteriez que je sache.
> Justement. Je ne veux pas que vous sachiez.
> Elle s'arrête, le toise et émet un petit rire:
> Ce que vous êtes compliqué! (p. 24)

Throughout *L'Oublié*, the failures of spoken communication are illustrated by hostile exchanges and misunderstandings, as those between Malkiel and Lidia (pp. 26–27, 137), with Leila (p. 142), with Tamar (pp. 47–48, 303–305), and with Elhanan (pp. 132–135).

The silent ruminations and prayers of Malkiel, on the other hand, enable him to confront his past and his own identity ("Je sais bien: qui écoute un témoin le deviant à son tour; tu me l'as dit, tu me l'as répété . . . Eh oui, père. Je t'ai entendu. Et, dans cette ville étrangère, je t'entends encore" [p. 194]). Through his experience of reliving vicariously his ancestors' traumatic lives (and of encountering some of the people involved in this trauma), Malkiel is finally restored to present-day life with renewed optimism and hope:

> Devant la tombe de son grand-père, Malkiel revoit Tamar. Au chevet d'Elhanan sans doute. Elle ne punit pas le père pour les péchés du fils. Nous allons nous marier, Tamar. Je veux que mon père nous voie unis.
> . . . Et la mémoire de son père chantera et pleurera dans la mienne.
> Et la nôtre, Tamar, s'épanouira dans celle de nos enfants. (p. 311)

The alternation between silent and spoken dialogue, between silence and speech, becomes in *L'Oublié* a metaphor for the oscillation between hope and despair. Silence has ambivalent connotations in *L'Oublié:* it is paradoxically both constructive and destructive for Elhanan Rosenbaum. His success as a psychologist working with Holocaust survivors has been due largely to his ability to listen compassionately in silence to his patients' tales, enabling them to heal their emotional wounds. Yet his progressive muteness is also the symptom of an incurable memory disease that frustrates his attempt to transmit his life history and his values to his son.

Silence is associated in the novel with the unjust suffering of both biblical and contemporary characters: of the righteous Job, robbed of the ability to answer God (p. 307), of Haskel, the preacher ostracized from society who became mute when not permitted to tell his terrible tale of the Holocaust (p. 155), and of Elhanan, robbed of his memory and speech, whose final message to Malkiel is left as an incomplete sentence: "Et moi qui te parle, je ne pourrais plus parler, car" (p. 318). The recurrence of this tale of the Jew throughout history who is silent against his will, so prevalent in both *L'Oublié* and *La Nuit* (cf. Mme Schachter who is gagged when she tries to voice her prophetic visions of flames to Jews en route to Auschwitz, pp. 49–51), gives it the character of a parable.

Yet *L'Oublié* ultimately conveys hope in the redemptive power of memory to "give voice" to the silent dead and to express the unspoken words of a father to his son. The ghosts in Elhanan's native village knock each night at

the doors of the town's inhabitants, disturbing their sleep forever to remind
them of the victims of the Holocaust (p. 128); the gravediggers Hershel and
his blind companion Ephraim call themselves guardians of the memories of
the dead (p. 255), suggesting metaphorically the redemptive force of literature
to conquer forgetfulness and indifference.

Elhanan's final message to his son is not incoherent language dissolv-
ing into silence (like the "message" of the guest speaker at the end of Eugene
Ionesco's *Les Chaises* [1952]). Six lines before his final silence, Elhanan expresses the conviction that his son will find by himself the truth for which he
is searching:

> Tout en te parlant, je me dis que, par tes propres moyens, tu
> découvriras quand même ce que mes lèvres n'ont pas pu ou su dire.
> (p. 318)

The oscillation in Wiesel's novels between hope and despair, between
silence as redemption and silence as curse, reflect his roots in Hasidic messianism. The elements of messianism—the fervent waiting, the hope for
redemption, the importance of solidarity and love between fellow human
beings as the path to finding God—these elements are all present in *La Nuit*
and *L'Oublié*. Maurice Friedman has described Wiesel's post-Holocaust
faith as the "messianism of the unredeemed":

> Since God has proved an unreliable partner, the Jewish people
> must base their self-affirmation on their choice to remain Jews and
> to assume the past of Jewish history as their own. The three-fold
> elements of this additional covenant are: solidarity, witness and
> the sanctification of life.[5]

Like Sartre and Camus, Wiesel calls on man to invent values and to
affirm meaning in life, despite the absurd, and despite the silence of an uncaring world and of God.

NOTES

1. Elie Wiesel, "An Interview with Elie Wiesel", conducted by Robert
Franciosi and Brian Shaffer, *Contemporary Literature*, 28 (Fall 1987), p. 289.
2. Elie Wiesel in Jean-François Thomas, S.J., "La Vocation d'un Ecrivain:
Dialogue avec Elie Wiesel", *Etudes*, 367 (July–August 1987), pp. 58–59, and in
Robert Franciosi and Brian Shaffer, "An Interview with Elie Wiesel", p. 291. In the
second interview, Wiesel said that all of his books were connected in some way; all
were part of one book which he would entitle "In pursuit of Silence" (p. 300).

3. Elie Wiesel, *La Nuit* (Paris: Minuit, 1958) and *L'Oublié* (Paris: Seuil, 1989). All further references are to these editions.

4. Elie Wiesel, "La Vocation d'un Ecrivain", p. 59.

5. Maurice Friedman, "Elie Wiesel's Messianism of the Unredeemed". *Judaism*, 38 (Summer 1989), p. 316.

JOHN K. ROTH

From Night *to* Twilight:
A Philosopher's Reading of Elie Wiesel

Everything to do with Auschwitz must, in the end, lead into darkness.
—Elie Wiesel

Plato and Aristotle, Hume and Kant, Hegel and Kierkegaard, James, Camus, and Wittgenstein—these great masters of philosophy move me. Philosophically, however, no writer disturbs and provokes me more than one who claims he "never intended to be a philosopher."[1] Whenever I read a book by Elie Wiesel, survivor of the Holocaust, the Nazi attempt to annihilate the Jews, I feel compelled to respond in writing of my own. No other author affects me quite that way. For more than twenty years I have been doing a philosopher's reading of Elie Wiesel. On this occasion I write because I have just reread, as I do annually, his first book, *La Nuit* (1958; translated as *Night*, 1960), and also because his novel *Le Crépuscule, au loin* (1987; translated as *Twilight*, 1988) has been on my mind. *Twilight* complements, not to say completes, a quest begun with *Night* and pursued in everything else that Wiesel has written in between.

The Domain of Madness
Speaking of *Night*, that classic memoir about his entry into and exodus from Auschwitz, Wiesel has said "all my subsequent books are built around it" ("Talking" 269). Spare and lean, that book starts with a boy who "believed

Religion & Literature, Volume 24, Number 1 (Spring 1992): pp. 59–73. Copyright © 1992 John K. Roth.

57

profoundly." It ends with a reflection: "From the depths of the mirror, a corpse gazed back at me. The look in his eyes, as they stared into mine, has never left me" (*Night* 109). In *l'univers concentrationnaire,* as another Holocaust survivor, David Rousset, named it, assumptions treasured and persons loved were stripped away. But the dead left Wiesel behind to wonder and thereby to encounter the living.

L'Aube (1960; translated as *Dawn,* 1961) is Wiesel's second major work. This brief novel portrays Elisha, a young Holocaust survivor who strives to free Palestine from British rule so that a people and a nation can find new life. This, Elisha discovers, is easier said than done. Once the possible victim of an executioner, he must execute a British captain, John Dawson, in retribution for the slaying of an Israeli freedom fighter. "That's it," Elisha says to himself, "It's done. I've killed. I've killed Elisha." Insofar as choosing life requires choosing death as well, dawn may be difficult to distinguish from "the tattered fragment of darkness" that reflects Elisha's face as he gazes through a window at the breaking of a not-so-new day (126–127).

Hitler's "final solution" still seems to mock quests for healing resolutions. Thus, *Dawn's* title is ironic, for after Auschwitz despair coils like a serpent in the heart of being. In Wiesel's third book, *Le Jour* (1961; translated not literally, as *Day,* but as *The Accident,* 1962), despite the fact that he has friends and even a woman who loves him, another survivor, Eliezer, steps in front of a moving car. The "accident" is no accident, and yet life returns to be chosen again. "The problem," Wiesel proposes, "is not: to be or not to be. But rather: to be and not to be" (81). But how best to do so? Wiesel turns to that question again and again.

In *The Accident,* the victim's artist-friend, Gyula, whose name means redemption, urges Eliezer to choose life and put the past behind him. He paints Eliezer's portrait. The eyes are searing, since "they belonged to a man who had seen God commit the most unforgivable crime: to kill without a reason." After showing Eliezer the portrait, Gyula symbolizes the end of the past by setting fire to the canvas. Though he is moved by Gyula's testimony, Eliezer will not be fully healed by it, for the novel's final line states that Gyula departed and forgot "to take along the ashes" (123, 127).

Moving through night into dawn and day, Elie Wiesel's first works travel through the destruction of a supportive universe into a post-Holocaust world of ambiguity and nothingness in which life almost succeeds in fulfilling a desire to cancel itself. Plumbing such depths had to be the prelude to Wiesel's hard-won insistence that the essence of being Jewish is "never to give up—never to yield to despair" (*A Jew Today* 164). That affirmation is one of his categorical imperatives. Keeping it is anything but easy, as *Twilight* shows. Its story does so by asking about "the domain of madness," a realm never far from the center of Wiesel's consciousness. By illuminating, in particular, Maimonides' conviction that "the world couldn't exist without madmen" (202, 9)—it serves as the novel's epigraph—*Twilight* also has much to say about friendship.

Friendship

Arguably Wiesel's most complex novel, *Twilight* defies simple summary. One of its dominant themes emerges, however, when Raphael Lipkin's telephone rings at midnight, This survivor of the Holocaust, now a university scholar, hears an anonymous voice denouncing his friend, Pedro: "Professor, let me tell you about your friend Pedro. He is totally amoral. A sadist. He made me suffer. And not just me, there were many others" (179). Pedro is Raphael's friend indeed. More than once he saved Raphael from the despair that repeatedly threatens to engulf him. He taught the young Lipkin: "It may not be in man's power to erase society's evil, but he must become its conscience; it may not be in his power to create the glories of the night, but he must wait for them and describe their beauty" (118).

The midnight calls keep calling Pedro into question and Raphael into despair. Madness lies in waiting, and, if Pedro were destroyed, Raphael might succumb to it. Recognition of that possibility, recollection that "Pedro taught me to love mankind and celebrate its humanity despite its flaws," renewed realization that Pedro's "enemy is my enemy"—such forces rally Raphael's resistance (201). By reaffirming a summons to save, Raphael's battle against madness that destroys does not ensure a tranquil equilibrium. A different kind of madness, the moral madness without which the world could not exist, is the prospect instead. "The caller tried to drive you out of my life," Raphael tells the absent Pedro. "He failed. Does that mean I've won? Hardly. I cry into the night and the night does not answer. Never mind, I will shout and shout until I go deaf, until I go mad" (202).

Twilight is not the first time a man named Pedro has appeared in Wiesel's novels and provided saving inspiration. Differing from his namesake in *Twilight* because he is not Jewish, another Pedro is a decisive presence in *La Ville de la chance* (1962; translated as *The Town Beyond the Wall*). This book, Wiesel's fourth and fittingly the one most closely linked to *Twilight*, begins with an epigraph from Dostoevsky: "I have a plan—to go mad" (3). It also starts at twilight and under circumstances that can drive one to the madness that destroys.

Once Michael's home, Szerencseváros ("the city of luck") is in the vise of Communist victors over Nazi tyrants. Secretly returning to see whether anyone can be found, Michael stands before his former home. Ages ago a face watched silently there while Jews were sent away. The face, seeking a hatred from Michael to match its own hidden guilt, informs the police. Michael finds himself imprisoned in walls within his past, tortured to tell a story that cannot be told: There is no political plot to reveal; his captors would never accept the simple truth of his desire to see his hometown once more; his friend, Pedro, who returned with him, must be protected. Michael holds out. He resists an escape into one kind of madness by opening himself to another. His cell mate, Eliezer, dwells in catatonic silence. But Michael hears and heeds the advice that he knows his friend Pedro would give him: "That's exactly what I want you to do: recreate the universe. Restore that boy's sanity. Cure him. Hell save you" (182).

What of such a plan? *Twilight*, as well as *The Town Beyond the Wall* and some thirty more of Wiesel's books, follows *Night*. In one way or another, all of *Night*'s sequels explore how the world might be mended. Nonetheless in the order of things dawn, day, and especially twilight leave night close by. Yet even if, as Wiesel contends, "everything to do with Auschwitz must, in the end, lead into darkness," questions remain concerning what that darkness might be and whether the leading into darkness is indeed the end. For if *The Town Beyond the Wall* concludes with Michael's coming "to the end of his strength," it also ends with "the night . . . receding, as on a mountain before dawn" (189). Similarly, as *Twilight* moves toward night, "from far away, a star appears. Uncommonly brilliant . . ." (217).

Twilight and *The Town Beyond the Wall* are both novels about friendship, another theme that is never far from the center of Wiesel's vision. Both Michael and Raphael have friends named Pedro. In each case, Pedro serves as a special kind of teacher. These relationships transcend the physical limits of space and time. Even when absent from *The Town Beyond the Wall* or from *Twilight*, the two Pedros are very much present for their friends. Michael and Raphael take courage from the challenging encouragement that each one's Pedro provides.

Michael and Raphael have learned from their friends named Pedro, What they have discerned resonates with lessons I am trying to learn as I pursue a philosopher's reading of Elie Wiesel. Considering the authorship that moves from *Night* to *Twilight*, with journeys to *The Town Beyond the Wall* and meetings with Pedro among the multitude of encounters in between, reflect on ten of his major insights—two sets of five that focus first on understanding and then on doing. Simple and yet complex, complex and yet simple, each point is central, I believe, to Wiesel's way of thinking and living and to his expression of friendship in particular, None of the insights is an abstract principle; all are forged in fire that threatens to consume. For those reasons these themes from Wiesel have integrity, credibility, and durability that make them worthy guidelines for all seasons.

Understanding

Elie Wiesel seeks understanding—but not too much. While wanting people to study the Holocaust, he alerts them to the dangers of thinking that they do or can or even should know everything about it. While wanting people to meet as friends, he cautions that such meetings will be less than honest if differences are glossed over, minimized, or forgotten. While wanting humankind and God to confront each other, he contends that easy acceptance is at once too much and too little to accept. Wiesel's understanding is neither facile, obvious, nor automatic. Nevertheless its rhythm can be learned. Five of its movements follow.

1. *"The Holocaust demands interrogation and calls everything into question. Traditional ideas and acquired values, philosophical systems and social theories— all must be revised in the shadow of Birkenau"* ("Foreword" ix). Birkenau was the killing center at Auschwitz, and the first lesson Wiesel teaches is that the Holocaust is an unrivaled measure because nothing exceeds its power to evoke the question Why? That authority puts everything else to the test. Whatever the traditional ideas and acquired values that have existed, whatever the philosophical systems and social theories that human minds have produced, they were either inadequate to prevent Auschwitz or, worse, they helped pave the way to that place. The Holocaust insists, therefore, that how we think and act needs revision in the face of those facts, unless one wishes to continue the same blindness that eventuated in the darkness of *Night*. The needed revisions, of course, do not guarantee a better outcome. And yet failure to use the Holocaust to call each other, and especially ourselves, into question diminishes chances to mend the world.

2. *"The questions remain questions"* ("Telling" 1:234). As the first lesson suggests, Elie Wiesel does not place his greatest confidence in answers. Answers—especially when they take the form of philosophical and theological systems—make him suspicious. No matter how hard people try to resolve the most important issues, questions remain and rightly so. To encounter the Holocaust, to reckon with its disturbing Whys?—without which our humanity itself is called into question—that is enough to make Wiesel's case.

Typically, however, the human propensity is to quest for certainty. Wiesel's urging is to resist that temptation, especially when it aims to settle things that ought to remain unsettled and unsettling. For if answers aim to settle things, their ironic, even tragic, outcome is often that they produce disagreement, division, and death. Hence, Wiesel wants questions to be forever fundamental. People are less likely to savage and annihilate each another when their minds are not made up but opened up, through questioning. The Holocaust shows as much: Hitler and his Nazi followers "knew" they were "right." Their "knowing" made them killers. Questioning might have redeemed them as well as their victims.

Wiesel's point is not that responses to questions are simply wrong. They have their place, and can be essential too. Nevertheless questions deserve lasting priority because they invite continuing inquiry, further dialogue, shared wonder, and openness. Resisting final solutions, these ingredients—especially when they drive home the insight that the best questions are never put to rest but keep us human by luring us on—can create friendships in ways that answers never can.

3. *"And yet—and yet. This is the key expression in my work"* ("Exile." 1:183). Elie Wiesel's writings, emerging from an intensity that is both the burden and the responsibility of Holocaust survivors, aim to put people off guard. Always suspicious of answers but never failing for questions, he lays out problems not for their own sake but to inquire, "What is the next step?" Reaching an apparent conclusion, he moves on. Such forms of thought reject easy paths in favor of hard ones. Wiesel's "and yet—and yet" affirms that it is more important to seek than to find, more important to question than to answer, more important to travel than to arrive. It can be dangerous to believe what you want to believe, deceptive to find things too clear, just as it is also dishonest not to strive to bring them into focus. His caution is that it is insensitive to overlook that there is always more to experience than our theories admit, even though we can never begin to seek comprehension without reasoning and argument. So Elie Wiesel tells his stories, and even their endings resist leaving his readers with a fixed conclusion. He wants them instead to feel his "and yet—and yet," which provides a hope that people may keep moving to choose life and not to end it

4. *"There is a link between language and life"* ("Exile" 1:182). The Holocaust was physically brutal. That brutality's origins were partly in "paper violence," which is to say that they depended on words. Laws, decrees, orders, memoranda, even schedules for trains and specifications for gas vans and crematoria—all of these underwrite Wiesel's insistence that care must be taken with words, for words can kill.

Wiesel uses words differently. He speaks and writes to recreate. His words, including the silences they contain, bring forgotten places and unremembered victims back to life just as they jar the living from complacency. Doing these things, he understands, requires turning language against itself. During the Nazi era language hid too much: euphemisms masked reality to lull; rhetoric projected illusions to captivate; propaganda used lies to control. All of those efforts were hideously successful. In our own day, as Wiesel points out, we bid farewell by saying, "Relax." "Have fun." "Take it easy." Seemingly innocuous, such language is certainly a far cry from words possessed by genocidal intent. And yet innocuous words may not be as innocent as they seem. They are likely to distract and detract from needs that deserve concern and care. Language and life are linked in more ways than words can say. Nonetheless, priorities after Auschwitz enjoin that words have to decode words, speech must say what speech hides, writing must rewrite and set right what has been written. None of this can be done perfectly, once and for all.

The task is ongoing, but only as it is going on will lives be linked so that "and yet—and yet" expresses hope more than despair.

5. *"Rationalism is a failure and betrayal"* ("Use" 2:79). Although Elie Wiesel is hardly an enemy of reason and rationality, he does stand with philosophers who believe that one of reason's most important functions is to assess its own limitations, And yet Wiesel's critique of reason is grounded somewhat differently from David Hume's or Immanuel Kant's. Theirs depended on theory. Wiesel's rests on history and on the Holocaust in particular.

The Holocaust happened because human minds became convinced that they could figure everything out. Those minds "understood" that one religion had superseded another. They "comprehended" that one race was superior to every other. They "realized" who deserved to live and who deserved to die. One can argue, of course, that such views undermined rationality and perverted morality. They did. And yet to say that much is too little, for one must ask about the sources of those outcomes. When that asking occurs, part of its search leads to reason's tendency to presume that indeed it can, at least in principle, figure everything out. With greater authority than any theory can muster, Auschwitz shows where such rationalism can lead. Wiesel's antidote is not irrationalism; his rejection of destructive madness testifies to that. What he seeks instead is the understanding that lives in friendship—understanding that includes tentativeness, fallibility, comprehension that looks for error and revises judgment when error is found, realization that knowing is not a matter of fixed conviction but of continuing dialogue.

Doing

Elie Wiesel's lessons about understanding urge one not to draw hasty or final conclusions. Rather his emphasis is on exploration and inquiry. It might be objected that such an outlook tends to encourage indecision and even indifference. However, one of Wiesel's most significant philosophical contributions runs in just the opposite direction. His perspective on understanding and on morality is of one piece. Thus, dialogue leads not to indecision but to an informed decisiveness. Tentativeness becomes protest when unjustified conviction asserts itself. Openness results not in indifference but in the loyalty of which friendship is made and on which it depends. Wiesel's doing is demanding, but it, too, has a rhythm that can be learned. Here are five of its movements.

1. *"Passivity and indifference and neutrality always favor the killer, not the victim"* ("Freedom" 1.210). Elie Wiesel will never fully understand the world's killers. To do so would be to legitimate them by showing that they were part of a perfectly rational scheme. Though for very different reasons, he will not fully understand their victims, either; their silent screams call into question every account of their dying that presents itself as a final solution. Wiesel

insists that understanding should be no less elusive where indifference—including its accomplices, passivity and neutrality—prevails. Too often indifference exists among those who could make a difference, for it can characterize those who stand between killers and victims but aid the former against the latter by doing too little, too late. Where acting is concerned, nothing arouses Wiesel more than activating the inactive.

2. *"It is given to man to transform divine injustice into human justice and compassion"* (*Messengers* 235). Abraham and Isaac, Moses, and Job—these "messengers of God," as Wiesel calls them, understood that men and women abuse the freedom to choose that makes life human. They also wrestled with the fact that human existence neither accounts for nor completely sustains itself. Their dearly earned reckoning with that reality led them to a profound restiveness. It revealed, in turn, the awesome injunction that God intends for humankind to have hard, even impossible, moral work until and through death.

One may not see life the way those biblical messengers saw it. Whatever one's choices in that regard, it is nevertheless as hard as it is inhuman to deny that injustice too often reigns divine and that moral work is given to us indeed. Elie Wiesel presumes neither to identify that work in detail for everyone nor to insist, in particular, where or how one should do it. Those are the right questions, though, and he wants one to explore them. That exploration, he urges, is not likely to be done better than through Holocaust lenses. Enhancing vision sensitively, they can help to focus every evil that should be transformed by human justice and compassion,

3. *"If I still shout today, if I still scream, it is to prevent man from ultimately changing me"* (*One Generation* 95).[2] While "and yet—and yet" may be the key expression in Wiesel's writings, a close contender could be phrased "because of—in spite of." Here, too, the rhythm insists that, no matter where one dwells, there is and must be more to say and do. On this occasion, though, the context is more specific, for the place where "because of—in spite of" becomes crucial is the place where despair most threatens to win. So because of the odds in favor of despair and against hope, in spite of them, the insistence and need to rebel in favor of life are all the greater. And not to be moved by them is to hasten the end.

How this logic works is reflected in a story that Wiesel often tells. A Just Man came to Sodom to save that ill-fated place from sin and destruction. A child, observing the Just Man's care, approached him compassionately:

> "Poor stranger, you shout, you scream, don't you see that it is hopeless?"
> "Yes, I see."
> "Then why do you go on?"

"I'll tell you why. In the beginning, I thought I could change man. Today, I know I cannot. If I still shout today, if I still scream, it is to prevent man from ultimately changing me."

The Just Man's choice is one that others can make as well. Thus, a future still awaits our determination, especially if the rhythm "because of—in spite of" is understood and enacted.

4. *"As a Jew I abide by my tradition. And my tradition allows, and indeed commands, man to take the Almighty to task for what is being done to His people, to His children—and all men are His children—provided the questioner does so on behalf of His children, not against them, from within the community, from within the human condition, and not as an outsider"* ("Trial" 1.176). Some of Elie Wiesel's most forceful writing involves the Jewish tradition known as Hasidism.[3] Many features impress him as he traces this movement from its flowering in eighteenth-century Europe, to its presence in the death camps, and to its continuing influence in a world that came close to annihilating Hasidic ways root and branch. One of the rhythms of understanding and doing stressed by Wiesel derives, at least in part, from a Hasidic awareness of the relationships between "being for—being against."

Hasidism, in particular, combines a genuine awe of God with direct and emotional reactions toward God. It finds God eluding understanding but also as One to whom people can speak. The Hasidic masters argue with God, protest against God, fear, trust, and love God. All of this is done personally and passionately, without compromising God's majesty and beyond fear of contradiction. Levi-Yitzhak of Berditchev, for example, understood his role as that of attorney-for-the-defense, reproaching God for harsh treatment the Jews received. Joining him was Rebbe Israel, Maggid of Kozhenitz, author of one of Wiesel's favorite Hasidic prayers: "Master of the Universe, know that the children of Israel are suffering too much; they deserve redemption, they need it. But if, for reasons unknown to me, You are not willing, not yet, then redeem all the other nations, but do it soon!" (*Souls* 133).

Nahman of Bratzlav holds another special place in Wiesel's heart. Laughter is Nahman's gift: "Laughter that springs from lucid and desperate awareness, a mirthless laughter, laughter of protest against the absurdities of existence, a laughter of revolt against a universe where man, whatever he may do, is condemned in advance. A laughter of compassion for man who cannot escape the ambiguity of his condition and of his faith" (*Souls* 198). And a final example, Menahem-Mendl of Kotzk, embodied a spirit whose intense despair yielded righteous anger and revolt so strong that it was said, "a God whose intentions he would understand could not suit him" (245). This rebel embraced life's contradictions both to destroy and to sustain them. Short of death, he found life without release from suffering. At the same time, he affirmed humanity as precious by living defiantly to the end. Wiesel implies, too, that Mendl hoped for something beyond death. His final words, Wiesel suggests, were: "At last I shall see Him face to face." Wiesel adds, "We don't know—nor will we ever know—whether these words expressed an ancient fear or a renewed defiance" (254).

Anything can be said and done, indeed everything must be said and done, that is for men and women. Wiesel understands this to mean that a stance against God is sometimes enjoined. But he hastens to add that such a stance needs to be from within a perspective that also affirms God. Otherwise we run the risk of being against humankind in other ways all over again. Those ways include succumbing to dehumanizing temptations which conclude that only human might makes right, that there is human history as we know it and nothing more, and that, as far as the Holocaust's victims are concerned, Hitler was victorious.

For . . . against: that rhythm involves taking stands. Spiritually this means to be against God when being for God would put one against humankind. Spiritually this also means to be for God when being against God would put one against humankind by siding with forces that tend, however inadvertently, to legitimate the wasting of human life. Elie Wiesel is fiercely humanistic. His humanism, however, remains tied to God. The lesson here is that, without enlivening and testing those ties and, in particular, their ways of being for and against humankind, a critical resource for saving life and mending the world will be lost.

5. *"By allowing me to enter his life, he gave meaning to mine"* (*Oath* 16). Elie Wiesel's 1973 novel, *Le Serment de Kolvillàg (The Oath),* tells of a community that disappeared except for one surviving witness. It is a tale about that person's battle with a vow of silence. Azriel is his name, and Kolvillàg, his home in eastern Europe, is destroyed in a twentieth-century pogrom prompted by the disappearance of a Christian boy. Ancient animosity renews prejudice; prejudice produces rumor; rumor inflames hate. Accused of a ritual murder, Azriel and his fellow Jews are soon under threat. Moshe, a strange, mystical member of the community, surrenders himself as the guilty party though no crime has been committed. But he does not satisfy the authorities and "Christians" of the town. Madness intensifies. The Jews begin to see that history will repeat, and they prepare for the worst. Some arm for violence; most gather strength quietly to wait and endure. Permitted to speak to the Jews assembled in their ancient synagogue, Moshe envisions Kolvillàg's destruction. He knows the record of Jewish endurance, its long testimony against violence, but this seems to have done little to restrain men and women and even God from further vengeance. So Moshe persuades his people to try something different: "By ceasing to refer to the events of the present, we would forestall ordeals in the future" (239). The Jews of Kolvillàg become Jews of silence by

taking his oath: "Those among us who will survive this present ordeal shall never reveal either in writing or by the word what we shall see, hear and endure before and during our torment" (241).

Next comes bloodshed. Jewish spirits strain upward in smoke and fire. Only the young Azriel survives. He bears the chronicles of Kolvillàg—one created with his eyes, the other in a book entrusted to him for safekeeping by his father, the community's historian. Azriel bears the oath of Kolvillàg as well. Torn between speech and silence, he remains true to his promise. Many years later, he meets a young man who is about to kill himself in a desperate attempt to give his life significance by refusing to live it. Azriel decides to intervene, to find a way to make the waste of suicide impossible for his new friend. The way Azriel chooses entails breaking the oath. He shares the story of Kolvillàg in the hope that it will instill rebellion against despair, concern in the place of lethargy and indifference, life to counter death.

The oath of silence was intended to forestall ordeals in the future. Such forestalling, Wiesel testifies, must give silence its due; it must also break silence in favor of speech and action that recognize the ultimate interdependence of existence. "By allowing me to enter his life, he gave meaning to mine." Azriel's young friend echoes and sums up the insights that Elie Wiesel has shared so generously with those who have read carefully what he has to say. Rightly understood, that understanding becomes a mandate for doing unto others what Azriel did for the boy he saved.

Remembering

As I studied *Twilight* for this essay, I was also rereading an earlier book called *Axis Rule in Occupied Europe*. If the name of its author was not on Wiesel's mind when he wrote *Twilight*, it did keep running through mine as I traced the odyssey of Wiesel's character, Raphael Lipkin. Originally published in 1944, *Axis Rule in Occupied Europe* was written by a Jewish legal scholar named Raphael Lemkin (1901–1959). A resident of Warsaw, Poland, he was wounded during guerrilla fighting outside Warsaw while resisting the German invasion of his homeland in 1939. After weeks of hiding in Polish forests, Lemkin escaped to Sweden by way of Lithuania and the Baltic Sea. There he began to document the Nazis' murderous policies—policies that, at the war's end, would leave him as the sole survivor among some forty of his closest family members.

In 1941 Lemkin found his way to the United States. He taught with distinction at Duke, Yale, Rutgers, and Princeton, and he helped to prepare cases against Nazis who stood trial in Nuremberg after the Second World War. While still at Duke, he published *Axis Rule in Occupied Europe*. In its pages he coined the term *genocide* as he attempted to fathom, while it was still happening, what is now called the Holocaust or Shoah. Four years later, in 1948, Lemkin's leadership was instrumental in obtaining passage for the United Nations' Genocide Convention. These efforts made him a strong contender for the 1950 Nobel Peace Prize.

Like Wiesel's men named Pedro, Lemkin was not without detractors. Some called him a dreamer, others a fanatic. A more apt description makes him a brother to Wiesel's morally sensitive madmen. Like Raphael Lipkin and his creator, Elie Wiesel, Raphael Lemkin worked to forestall ordeals in the future. Thus, it is fitting that the name Raphael links not only the three of them but all who have been and will be touched by the lessons that reading Wiesel has to teach.

Some ancient texts—Tobit and Enoch for example—as well as kabbalistic writings refer to an angel named Raphael. Stories about this angel make clear that Raphael has power to conquer demons. The name, significantly, is a compound of the Hebrew *rapha*, meaning "healed," and *El*, which designates God. Raphael, then, is the Angel of Healing or "God's healing." After Auschwitz, divine powers of that kind may be found wanting, thus making human counterparts to the angelic Raphael all the more important. Without them, God's healing, in all of its varied nuances, may not exist. To conquer demons permanently and forever—that task is more than human energy can accomplish. Nevertheless to resist them and to apply a healing touch wherever and whenever the opportunity arises—that Raphael-like task is one that cannot be shirked with impunity.

If reading from *Night* to *Twilight* drives home Elie Wiesel's insights about understanding and doing, it will still be true that "everything to do with Auschwitz must, in the end, lead into darkness." Nevertheless that end ought not to be the ending. Remembering and acting accordingly could lead beyond. Honesty probably permits no greater optimism in the twilight that forms the post-Holocaust world. And yet some light remains. Though not as much as we need, might it be enough to keep destruction's nighttime madness at bay so that day can dawn again?

Notes

A version of this essay was presented at a symposium held at Webster University, St. Louis, Missouri, on September 29, 1988. Organized by Professor Harry James Cargas, the symposium celebrated Elie Wiesel's sixtieth birthday and the thirtieth anniversary of the French publication of his classic memoir *Night*.

1. Elie Wiesel, "Why I Write" 200. The quotation that serves as this article's epigraph is from "Auschwitz—Another Planet," Elie Wiesel's review of *Auschwitz* by Bernd Naumann (2.293).

2. See also *The Testament* (1981).

3. See, for example, *Souls on Fire: Portraits and Legends of Hasidic Masters, Four Hasidic Masters and Their Struggle Against Melancholy, Somewhere a Master: Further Hasidic Portraits and Legends,* and *Sages and Dreamers: Biblical, Talmudic, and Hasidic Portraits and Legends.*

WORKS CITED

Abrahamson, Irving, ed. *Against Silence: The Voice and Vision of Elie Wiesel.* 3 vols. New York: Holocaust Library, 1985.

Lemkin, Raphael. *Axis Rule in Occupied Europe.* Washington, D.C.: Carnegie Endowment for International Peace, 1944.

Wiesel, Elie. *The Accident.* Trans. Anne Borchardt. New York: Avon, 1970.

———. "Auschwitz—Another Planet." Abrahamson 2:292–294.

———. *Dawn.* Trans. Frances Frenaye. New York: Avon, 1970.

———. "Exile and the Human Condition." Abrahamson 1:179–183.

———. "Freedom of Conscience—A Jewish Commentary." Abrahamson 1:208–210.

———. "Foreword." *Shadows of Auschwitz: A Christian Response to the Holocaust.* Ed. Harry James Cargas. New York: Crossroad, 1990.

———. *Four Hasidic Masters and Their Struggle Against Melancholy.* Notre Dame, Indiana: University of Notre Dame Press, 1978,

———. *A Jew Today.* Trans. Marion Wiesel. New York: Random, 1978.

———. *Messengers of God: Biblical Portraits and Legends (Célébration biblique: Portraits et Legends,* 1975). Trans. Marion Wiesel. New York: Random, 1976.

———. *Night.* Trans. Stella Rodway. New York: Bantam, 1986.

———. *The Oath (Le Serment de Kolvillàg,* 1973). Trans. Marion Wiesel. New York: Random, 1973.

———. *One Generation After (Entre deux soleils,* 1970). Trans. Lily Edelman and Elie Wiesel. New York: Avon, 1972.

———. *Sages and Dreamers: Biblical, Talmudic, and Hasidic Portraits and Legends.* Trans. Marion Wiesel. New York: Summit, 1991.

———. *Somewhere a Master: Further Hasidic Portraits and Legends (Contre la mélancolie: Célébration hassidique II,* 1981). Trans. Marion Wiesel. New York: Summit, 1982.

———. *Souls on Fire: Portraits and Legends of Hasidic Masters (Célébration hassidique: Portraits et légendes,* 1972). Trans. Marion Wiesel. New York: Random, 1972.

———. "Talking and Writing and Keeping Silent." *The German Church Struggle and the Holocaust.* Ed. Franklin H. Littell and Hubert G. Locke. Detroit: Wayne State University Press, 1974.

———. "Telling the Tale." Abrahamson 1:234–238.

———. *The Testament (Le Testament d'un poète juif assassineé,* 1980). Trans. Marion Wiesel. New York: Summit, 1981.

———. *The Town Beyond the Wall.* Trans. Stephen Becker. New York: Avon, 1970.

———. "The Trial of Man." Abrahamson 1:175–178.

———. *Twilight.* Trans. Marion Wiesel. New York: Summit, 1988.

———. "The Use of Words and the Weight of Silence." Abrahamson 2:75–84.

———. "Why I Write." Trans. Rosette Lamont. *Confronting the Holocaust: The Impact of Elie Wiesel.* Ed. Alvin Rosenfeld and Irving Greenberg. Bloomington: Indiana University Press, 1973.

DANIEL R. SCHWARZ

The Ethics of Reading Elie Wiesel's Night

A Dead Child Speaks

My mother held me by my hand. Then someone raised the knife of
parting: So that it should not strike me, My mother loosed her hand
from mine. But she lightly touched my thighs once more And her hand
was bleeding—

After that the knife of parting Cut in two each bite I swallowed—It
rose before me with the sun at dawn And began to sharpen itself in my
eyes—Wind and water ground in my ear And every voice of comfort
pierced my heart—

As I was led to death I still felt in the last moment The unsheathing
of the great knife of parting.

—Nelly Sachs

The survivor [. . .] is a disturber of the peace. He is a runner of the blockade
men erect against knowledge of "unspeakable" things. About these he aims
to speak, and in so doing he undermines, without intending to, the validity
of existing norms. He is a genuine transgressor, and here he is made to feel
real guilt. The world to which he appeals does not admit him, and since
he has looked to this world as the source of moral order, he begins to doubt
himself. And that is not the end, for now his guilt is doubled by betrayal—
of himself, of his task, of his vow to the dead. The final guilt is not to bear
witness. The survivor's worst torment is not to be able to speak

—Terence Des Pres

Style, Volume 32, Number 2 (Summer 1998): pp. 221–242. Copyright © 1998 Northern
Illinois University.

In considering ethical reading, we should differentiate between an ethics of reading and an ethics while reading. For me, an ethics of reading includes acknowledging who we are and what are our biases and interests. An ethics of reading speaks of our reading as if, no matter how brilliant, it were proposing some possibilities rather than vatically providing the solution to Daniel's prophetic reading of handwriting on the wall; it means reading from multiple perspectives, or at least empathetically entering into the readings of those who are situated differently. For me, an ethics while reading would try to understand what the author was saying to her original imagined audience and both why and how the actual polyauditory audience might have responded and for what reasons. An ethics while reading is different from but, in its attention to a value-oriented epistemology, related to an ethics of reading. An ethics while reading implies attention to moral issues; generated by events described within an imagined world. It asks what ethical questions are involved in the act of transforming life into art, and notices such issues as Pound's or Eliot's anti-Semitism and the patronizing racism of some American nineteenth- and early twentieth-century writers. What we choose to read and especially what to include on syllabi have an ethical dimension. Thus, I will choose to select other Conrad works for my undergraduate lecture course than the unfortunately titled *The Nigger of the Narcissus*.

Let me tentatively propose five stages of the hermeneutical activities involved in ethical reading and interpretation. Even while acknowledging that my model is suggestive rather than rigorous, I believe that we do perceive in stages that move from a naive response or surface interpretation to critical or in-depth interpretation and, finally, to understanding our readings conceptually and ethically in terms of other knowledge. Awareness of such stages enables us to read ethically. My stages are:

1. Immersion in the process of reading and the discovery of imagined worlds. Reading is a place where text and reader meet in a transaction. As we open a text, we and the author meet as if together we were going to draw a map on an uncharted space. We partially suspend our sense of our world as we enter into the imagined world; we respond in experimental terms to the episodes, the story, the physical setting, the individualized characters as humans and, the telling voice. While it has become fashionable to speak dismissively of such reading as "naive," or the result of the "mimetic illusion," in fact how many of us do not read in that way with pleasure and delight—and with ethical judgments? Who of us would be teaching and studying literature had we not learned to read mimetically?

2. Quest for understanding. Our quest is closely related to the diachronic, linear, temporal activity of reading. The quest speaks to the gap between "what did you say?" and "what did you mean?" In writing, as opposed to speech, the speaker cannot correct, intrude, or qualify; she cannot use gestures or adjust the delivery of her discourse. Because in writing we lack the speaker's help, we must make our own adjustments in our reading. As Paul Ricouer notes, "What the text says now matters more than what the author meant to say, and every exegesis unfolds its procedures within the circumference of a meaning that has broken its moorings to the psychology of its author" (191). We complete the sign of the imagined world by providing the signified, but no sooner do we complete a sign than it becomes a signifier in search of a new signified. In modern and postmodern texts, our search for necessary information will be much more of a factor than in traditional texts. In this stage, as we are actively unraveling the complexities of plot, we also seek to discover the principles or world-view by which the author expects us to understand characters' behavior in terms of motives and values. Moreover, we make ethical judgments of intersubjective relations and authorial choices.

3. Self-conscious reflection. Reflection speaks to the gap between "what did you mean?" and "what does that mean?" Upon reflection, we may adjust our perspective or see new ones. What the interpretive reader does—particularly with spare, implicatory modern literature—is fill the gaps left by the text to create an explanatory text or midrash on the text itself. As Iser puts it, "What is said only appears to take on significance as a reference to what is not said; it is the implications and not the statements that give shape and weight to the meaning" (Suleiman and Crosman 111). While the reader half-perceives, half-creates his original "immersed" reading of the text, he retrospectively—from the vantage point of knowing the whole—imposes shape and form on his story of reading. He discovers its significance in relation to his other experiences, including other reading experiences, and in terms of the interpretive communities to which he belongs. He reasons posteriorly from effects to causes. He is aware of referentiality to the anterior world—how that world informs the author's mimesis—and to the world in which he lives. He begins—more in modern texts, but even in traditional texts—to separate his own version of what is really meant from what is said, and to place ethical issues in the context of larger value issues.

Here Todorov's distinction between signification and symbolization is useful. "Signified facts are understood: all we need is knowledge of the language in which the text is written. Symbolization facts are interpreted: and interpretations vary from one subject to another" (Suleiman and Crosman 73). A problem is that, in practice, what is understood or judged by one reader as signified facts may require interpretation or a different ethical judgment by another.

4. Critical analysis. As Paul Ricouer writes, "To understand a text is to follow its movement from sense to reference, from what it says to what it talks about" (214). In the process, we always move from signifier to signified; for no sooner do we understand what the original signifiers signify within the imagined world than these signifieds in turn become signifiers for larger issues and symbolic constructions in the world beyond the text. And we respond in terms of the values enacted by the agon and, as with Eliot's and Pound's anti-Semitism, resist where texts disturb our sense of fairness.

While the reader responds to texts in such multiple ways and for such diverse reasons that we cannot speak of a correct reading, we can speak of a dialogue among plausible readings. Drawing upon our interpretive strategies, we reflect on generic, intertextual, linguistic, and biographical relationships that disrupt linear reading; we move back and forth from the whole to the part. My responses to my reading are a function of what I know, what I have recently been reading, my last experience of reading a particular author, my knowledge of the period in which she wrote as well as the influences upon her and her influence on others, and my current values. My responses also depend both on how willing I am to suspend my irony and detachment and enter into the imagined world of the text and on how much of the text my memory retains.

5. Cognition in terms of what we know. Drawing upon our interpretive strategies, we reflect on generic, intertextual, linguistic, and biographical relationships that disrupt linear reading; we move back and forth from the whole to the part. As Ricouer writes: "The reconstruction of the text as a whole is implied in the recognition of the parts. And reciprocally, it is in constructing the details that we construe the whole" (204). We return to the original reading experience and text and subsequently modify our conceptual hypotheses about genre, period, author, canon, themes, and most of all, values. We integrate what we have read into our reading of other texts and into our way of looking at ourselves and the world. Here we consciously use our values and our categorizing sensibility—our rage for order—to make sense of our reading experience and our way of being in our world. In the final stage, the interpretive reader may become a critic who writes his own text about the "transaction" between himself and the text—and this response has an ethical component. Novels raise different ethical questions, ones that enable us to consider not only how we would behave in certain circumstances, but also whether—even as we empathetically read a text—we should maintain some stance of resistance by which to judge that text's ethical implications.

II

Let us now turn to our example. Elie Wiesel begins *Night,* his fictionalized autobiographical memoir of the Holocaust with a description of Moshe the

Beadle, an insignificant figure in a small town in Transylvania who taught the narrator about the cabbala: "They called him Moshe the Beadle, as though he had never had a surname in his life. He was a man of alii work at a Hasidic synagogue. The Jews of Sighet—that little town in Transylvania where I spent my childhood—were very fond of him. He was very poor and lived humbly. [. . .] He was a past master in the art of making himself insignificant, of seeming invisible. [. . .] I loved his great, dreaming eyes, their gaze lost in the distance" (1). But Moshe is expelled in early 1942 because he is a foreign Jew, and is not heard of for several months. He unexpectedly returns to tell of his miraculous escape from a Gestapo slaughter of Jews in the Polish Forests. But no one believes him. Moshe cries: "Jews, listen to me. [. . .] Only listen to me" (5). But everyone assumes that he has gone mad. And the narrator—still a young boy—recalls asking him: "Why are you so anxious that people should believe what you say? In your place, I shouldn't care whether they believed me or not" (5).

Let us consider the significance of Moshe the Beadle. For one thing, Wiesel is using him as metonymy for himself in his present role as narrator who is, as he writes, calling on us to listen to his words as he tells his relentless tale of his own miraculous escape from Nazi terror. Implicitly, he is urging us that it is our ethical responsibility not to turn away from the Witnessing Voice—Moshe, himself, indeed all those who have seen, specifically, the Holocaust, and metonymically, for us, man's inhumanity to man—whether it occurs in Bosnia, Northern Ireland, or Somalia.

Night is a narrative that traces the dissolution of the Jewish community in Sighet, the ghettoes, deportations, concentration camps, crematoriums, death marches, and, finally, liberation. Distilling memoir into narrative form, *Night* traces the growth of adolescent courage and the loss of religious faith. Wiesel's original Yiddish title for *Night* was *Un di velt hot geshvign*, or in English, *And the World Remained Silent*. He distilled 862 pages to the 245 of the published Yiddish edition and Jerome Lindon, the French publisher, further edited it to 178 pages. I am interested not in the indictment of Wiesel for transforming his nominalistic memoir into novelistic form, but in how, in response to publishing circumstances and perhaps his own transformation, he reconfigured an existential novel about the descent into moral night into a somewhat affirmative reemergence to life. While the narrator is a fifteen year old boy, Wiesel was born in 1928 and would have been sixteen for most of the 1944–1945 period. Is not this age discrepancy one reason why we ought think of *Night* as a novel as well as a memoir?

Another more important reason *Night* is a novel is that there was a substantive change from the original Yiddish text submitted in 1954, months before he met Francois Mauriac, and 1958 when the French version was published. In 1956, it was volume 117 of a series on Polish Jews

entitled *Dos polyishe yidntum (Polish Jewry)*. Wiesel's title was *Un di velt*.
Seidman writes:

> What distinguishes the Yiddish from the French is not so much
> length as attention to detail, an adherence to that principle of
> comprehensiveness so valued by the editors and reviewers of
> the *Polish Jewry* series. Thus, whereas the first page of *Night*
> succinctly and picturesquely describes Sighet as "that little town
> in Transylvania where I spent my childhood," *Un di velt* introduces
> Sighet as "the most important city [shtot] and the one with the
> largest Jewish population in the province of Marmarosh." The
> Yiddish goes on to provide a historical account of the region:
> "Until the First World War, Sighet belonged to Austro-Hungary.
> Then it became part of Romania. In 1940, Hungary acquired it
> again." And while the French memoir is dedicated "in memory
> of my parents and of my little sister, Tsipora," the Yiddish names
> both victims and perpetrators: "This book is dedicated to the
> eternal memory of my mother Sarah, my father Shlomo, and my
> little sister Tsipora—who were killed by the German murderers."
>
> The Yiddish text may have been only lightly edited in the
> transition to French, but the effect of this editing was to position
> the memoir within a different literary genre. Even the title *Un di
> velt hot geshvign* signifies a kind of silence very distant from the
> mystical silence at the heart of *Night*. The Yiddish title indicts
> the world that did nothing to stop the Holocaust and allows its
> perpetrators to carry on normal lives; *La Nuit* names no human or
> even divine agents in the events it describes. From the historical
> and political specificities of Yiddish documentary testimony,
> Wiesel and his French publishing house fashioned something
> closer to mythopoetic narrative. (5)

What Seidman calls the "mythopoetic narrative," I would call a novel with a
central agon, a structure of affects, a narrative voice, an imagined narratee,
and an ending that transforms, modifies, and reformulates what precedes.

Whether a novel or memoir, *Night* depends upon and affirms the concept of individual agency, for the speaker tells a wondrous and horrible tale
of saving his life and shaping his role as Witness, perhaps our Daniel. As
Terence Des Pres writes:

> Silence is the only adequate response, but the pressure of the
> scream persists. This is the obsessive center of Wiesel's writing: his
> protagonists desire a silence they cannot keep. [. . .] The conflict

> between silence and the scream, so prominent in Wiesel's novels,
> is in fact a battle between death and life, between allegiance to
> the dead and care for the living, which rages in the survivor and
> resolves itself in the act of bearing witness. [. . .] Silence, in its
> primal aspect, is a consequence of terror, of a dissolution of self
> and world that, once known, can never he fully dispelled. But
> in retrospect it becomes something else. Silence constitutes the
> realm of the dead. It is the palpable substance of those millions
> murdered, the world no longer present, that intimate absence—of
> God, of man, of love—by which the survivor is haunted. In the
> survivor's voice the dead's own scream is active. (36)

In *Night* we see dramatized the process of the narrator's developing into his role of ethical witness in the face of historical forces that would obliterate his humanity, his individuality, and his voice. Notwithstanding the efficiency of Nazi cultural production and the technology of the death camps and gas chambers, the narrator recreates himself through language. In the sense of the technological fulfillment of an ordered state that subordinated individual rights to the national purpose of the State, Nazi ideology has been thought of as a product of modernism. For those, like Wiesel, who have experienced the Holocaust first hand—for whom Auschwitz is not a metaphor but a memory—language is more than the free play of signifiers. For these people and others on the political edge, their very telling—their very living—testifies to will, agency, and a desire to survive that resists and renders morally irrelevant simple positivistic explanations arguing that an author's language is culturally produced. One might ask why Wiesel writes. For one thing, it is to bear witness; for another, it is an act of self-therapy; for a third, it is a kind of transference; and as the dedication stresses ("In memory of my parents and my little sister, Tsipora,") it is an act of homage. Furthermore, in psychoanalytic linguistic terms, the narrator's telling is a resistance to the way in which the word "Jew" was culturally produced to mean inferior people who were progressively discounted, deprived of basic rights as citizens, labeled with a Yellow Star of David, imprisoned, enslaved, and killed. We might recall how all male German Jews were required to take the middle name "Israel," all females the name "Sarah."

Modernism, as James Clifford notes, takes "as its problem—and opportunity—the fragmentation and juxtaposition of cultural values" (117). Wiesel's novel/memoir *Night* is an essentialist rejection of that fragmentation and juxtaposition even while it records the grotesque consequences in Europe of their occurrence. According to Wiesel, "the Holocaust in its enormity defies language and art, and yet both must be used to tell the tale, the tale that must be told" (Muschamp 1). The very opening, "They called him Moshe the

Beadle," is a storyteller's invitation to step into another world. As with any life writing, the selection and arrangement into narrative blur the line between fiction and fact, and the inclusion of dialogue, recalled at an immense distance of years, contributes to the novelistic aspect of his memoir.

Wiesel explains in his essay "An Interview Unlike Any Other" why he waited ten years to write his memoir:

> I knew the role of the survivor was to testify. Only I did not know how. I lacked experience, I lacked a framework. I mistrusted the tools, the procedures. Should one say it all or hold it all back? Should one shout or whisper? Place the emphasis on those who were gone or on their heirs? How does one describe the indescribable? How does one use restraint in re-creating the fall of mankind and the eclipse of the gods? And then, how can one be sure that the words, once uttered, will not betray, distort the message they bear?
>
> So heavy was my anguish that I made a vow: not to speak, not to touch upon the essential for at least ten years. Long enough to see clearly. Long enough to learn to listen to the voices crying inside my own. Long enough to regain possession of my memory. Long enough to unite the language of man with the silence of the dead. (*A Jew Today* 15)

Night is a spare, rough-hewn text that is an eloquent testimony depending on human agency and ethical commitment. *Night* reminds us, too, that the concept of author-function as a substitute for the creating intelligence does not do justice to the way in which language and art express the individual psyche. Readers will recall that the book's signification depends on a taut structure underpinning an apparently primitive testimony, and, depends, too, on its spare, even sparse style. Its eloquence derives from its apparent ingenuousness. Yet *Night* speaks on behalf of meaning, on behalf of will—the will to survive, the will to witness—and on behalf of language's signification. *Night* eloquently reminds us of a grotesque historical irony, namely, that with its use of modern technology and Enlightenment rationality, Western man's progress led to the efficiency of the Nazi transport system, Nazi work camps, and Nazi gas chambers. *Night* is a text that resists irony and deconstruction, and cries out in its eloquence, pain, and anger as it enacts the power of language. The text traces the death of the narrator's mother, a sister, and finally, his father; it witnesses an encroaching horrible moral NIGHT, a night that includes the speaker's loss of religious belief in the face of historical events. Notwithstanding his religious upbringing, Wiesel parts company from those who, as Dawidowicz explains, accept the Holocaust as God's will:

For believing Jews the conviction that their sacrifice was required as a testimony to Almighty God was more comforting than the supposition that He had abandoned them altogether. To be sure, God's design was concealed from them, but they would remain steadfast in their faith. Morale was sustained by rabbis and pious Jews who, by their own resolute and exalted stance, provided a model of how Jews should encounter death. (308)

We should think of the text as a physical object and note its slimness, its titleless chapters, its breaks between anecdotes. We wonder what could be added in those white spaces, whether his loss of faith, for example, is gradual? But the slim volume, the white spaces, become a kind of correlative or metonymy to emptiness, to his "starved stomach" (50). The short paragraphs give a kind of cinematic effect as if the paragraphs are like frames in an evolving film. The very simplicity—the almost childlike quality—of the imagery gives the work its parabolic quality.

Wiesel draws upon a tradition of prophetic hyperbole: "Never shall I forget that night, the first night in camp, which has turned my life into one long night, seven times cursed and seven times sealed. [. . .] Never shall I forget those moments which murdered my God and my soul and turned my dreams to dust. Never shall I forget these things, even if I am condemned to live as long as God Himself. Never" (32). The camps dissolve traditional morality and replace it with extreme conditions that make the struggle to survive the only value. Thus the death of his father "frees" him to save himself; he is at once "free at last" and emotionally anaesthetized: "nothing could touch me any more" (106–107). We might recall the words of Lucy Dawidowicz:

The wish to live, the inability to believe in one's own imminent death, the universal human faith in one's own immunity to disaster—all these factors conspired to make the Jews believe that resettlement, not death, was the fact. "At bottom," wrote Freud, "nobody believes in his own death." Not gullibility, or suggestibility, but universal human optimism encouraged them to believe in the deceptions that the Germans perpetrated. In the process of repressing and denying the overpowering threat that confronted them, perceptual distortion and skewed interpretation based on wishful thinking managed to reconcile the illogic and inconsistencies of their fears and hopes. Without accurate information, without corrective feedback from authoritative sources on the course of events, their isolation helped give credence to their distorted and distorting evaluation of their predicament. This mechanism of denial, this arming oneself against disquieting facts, was not pathological, but,

as psychologists point out, a tool of adaptation, a means of coping
with an intolerable situation in the absence of any possibility for
defensive action. The alternative was despair, the quiet stunned
reaction of the defeated. (306)

Wiesel's text is written in the biblical style in which highlighted moments
full of significance are presented without the careful concatenation of events
we find in the realistic novel. Yet, he has an eye for details that may owe
something to his journalistic career in the years prior to meeting Mauriac. The biblical style owes itself to his being steeped not only in the Old
Testament—a text that pays little attention to background or setting, and
eschews gradual introductions of its heightened and sublime moments—but
also to a Talmudic tradition by which parabolic anecdotes are used to illustrate important themes. Rather than gradual change when he loses faith, a
change developing from the Nazi arrival, he experiences loss of faith as an
epiphanic moment. Unlike the realistic novel or memoir, we cannot relate
his role of passionate witness to a grammar of specific causes such as his
father's tears:

> For the first time, I felt revolt rise up in me. Why should I bless
> His name? The Eternal, Lord of the Universe, the All-Powerful
> and Terrible, was silent. What had I to thank Him for? (31)

Assuming in its form—especially its prophetic voice—an ethical narratee,
Night also demands an ethical response. By that I mean a real attention to
issues that pertain to how life is lived within imagined worlds. Truth in
novels takes place within the hypothesis "as if" which is another way of saying that, as we think about our reading we are never completely unaware of
the metaphoricity of literature. At one time, some critics may have naively
ignored the metaphoricity of language and confused characterization with
actual human character. But have not some theorists reached the other
pole of willfully denying analogies to human life and naively repressing
the possibilities of significance? We shall see that Holocaust fiction—like
Night—has an ethical narrator, demands an ethical narratee, believes at least
hypothetically in essential truths, insists on strong analogies to life lived
within the Holocaust, and has faith that language signifies.

Rereading *Night* is a powerful experience, one that requires self-
conscious reflection about how language can rescue meaning from the moral
vacuum surrounding Holocaust events. What strikes the reader is its efficiency as a work of art. Derived, as we have seen, from a much longer Yiddish typescript, the precise, lucid, and laconic telling is in ironic juxtaposition to the historical complexity in Europe, but appropriate for the simple

cause and effect of annihilating an entire people. Such stark imagery as that with which he described a work detail—"we were so many dried up trees in the heart of a desert"—(*Night* 35) is all the more effective for its spareness. Wiesel has written:

> There are some words I cannot bring myself to use; they paralyze me. I cannot write the words "concentration," "night and fog," "selection," or "transport" without a feeling of sacrilege. Another difficulty, of a different type: I write in French, but I learned the language from books and therefore I am not good at slang.
>
> All my subsequent works are written in the same deliberately spare style as *Night*. It is the style of the chroniclers of the ghettos, where everything had to be said swiftly, in one breath. You never knew when the enemy might kick in the door, sweeping us away into nothingness. Every phrase was a testament. There was no time or reason for anything superfluous. Words must not be imprisoned or harnessed, not even in the silence of the page. And yet, it must be held tightly. If the violin is to sing, its strings must be stretched so tight as to risk breaking; slack, they are merely threads.
>
> To write is to plumb the unfathomable depths of being. Writing lies within the domain of mystery. The space between any two words is vaster than the distance between heaven and earth. To bridge it you must close your eyes and leap. A Hasidic tradition tells us that in the Torah the white spaces, too, are God-given. Ultimately, to write is an act of faith. (*Memoirs* 321)

The English translation of *Night* was published in the U.S. in 1960 by Hill and Wang; it sold only a few thousand copies in its first few years. As Wiesel recalls,

> As for *Night*, despite Mauriac's preface and the favorable reviews in the French, Belgian, and Swiss press, the big publishers hesitated, debated, and ultimately sent their regrets. Some thought the book too slender (American readers seemed to prefer fatter volumes), others too depressing (American readers seemed to prefer optimistic books). Some felt its subject was too little known, others that it was too well known. In short, it was suggested over and over again that we try elsewhere. Refusing to lose heart, Georges [Borchardt, a New York literary agent] kept trying. In the end Hill and Wang agreed to take the risk. (*Memoirs* 325)

Although the basic unit of form is the retrospective memory of the teller who wrote after a ten year hiatus, the book is also organized around a number of motifs. The most important is the loss of faith in the face of evidence that God can do or will do nothing to prevent the Holocaust. Young Wiesel has a transvaluation of faith to disbelief and unbelief. He loses all illusions about a purposeful world. As Naomi Seidman put it:

> In the description of the first night Eliezer spends in the concentration camp, silence signals the turn from the immediate terrors to a larger cosmic drama, from stunned realism to theology. In the felt absence of divine justice or compassion, silence becomes the agency of an immune, murderous power that permanently transforms the narrator. (1)

Let us continue our critical analysis. As if the narrator were struggling to stay alive, as if he were having trouble breathing, the unnumbered and untitled chapters get shorter; the last three of nine chapters take up only seventeen pages. That he moves, on occasion, to a postwar retrospective gives the reader the sense, as in Conrad's Marlow's telling in *Heart of Darkness* that his memory is struggling with the narrative and that at times he needs to avoid the horrors. Wiesel's breaks between anecdotes has the same effect, as if a pithy anecdote was all the narrator could stand to tell before being overcome. The recurring term "empty" reminds us of how, except for the will to live, his life had become a negation—that is, an absence of love, comfort, health, food. But in the retelling it reminds us of how he has become spiritually anaesthetized and how he has left behind everything he had on the written page. The verbal correlatives to "empty" include "Night" and "Never" and of course anticipate the survivors mantra, "Never Again."

> Never shall I forget that night, the first night in camp, which has turned my life into one long night, seven times cursed and seven times sealed. Never shall I forget that smoke. Never shall I forget the little faces of the children, whose bodies I saw turned into wreaths of smoke beneath a silent blue sky.
>
> Never shall I forget those flames which consumed my faith forever.
>
> Never shall I forget that nocturnal silence which deprived me, for all eternity, of the desire to live. Never shall I forget those moments which murdered my God and my soul and turned my dreams to dust. Never shall I forget these things, even if I am condemned to live as long as God Himself. Never. (32)

The observant young boy who at the outset wished to be initiated into the mysteries of the cabbala feels the "void" of unbelief; the void is the alternative to the plenitude of belief (66, 93).

> Why, but why should I bless Him? In every fiber I rebelled. Because He had had thousands of children burned in His pits? Because He kept six crematories working night and day, on Sundays and feast days? Because in His great might He had created Auschwitz, Birkenau, Buna, and so many factories of death? How could I say to Him: "Blessed art Thou, Eternal, Master of the Universe, Who chose us from among the races to be tortured day and night, to see our father, our mothers, our brothers, end in the crematory? Praised be Thy Holy Name, Thou Who hast chosen us to be butchered on Thine altar"?
>
> This day I had ceased to plead. I was no longer capable of lamentation. On the contrary, I felt very strong. I was the accuser, God the accused. My eyes were open and I was alone—terribly alone in a world without God and without man. Without love or mercy. I had ceased to be anything but ashes, yet I felt myself to be stronger than the Almighty, to whom my life had been tied for so long. (64, 65)

III

Our ethics of reading requires that we look back and understand how the themes organize the agon. The title motif of *Night* is moral death, or historical void. Antithetical to light and its association with understanding—the Enlightenment of Europe—and with inner faith and wisdom, "night" is the dominant pattern around which the novel is organized. In *Night*, death is the antagonist, an active principle present at every moment. During the death march from Auschwitz, Wiesel recalls:

> Death wrapped itself around me till I was stifled. It stuck to me. I felt that I could touch it. The idea of dying, of no longer being, began to fascinate me. Not to exist any longer. Not to feel the horrible pains in my foot. Not to feel anything, neither weariness, nor cold, nor anything. To break the ranks, to let oneself slide to the edge of the road. (82)

During the transport to Buchenwald, he remarks:

> Indifference deadened the spirit. Here or elsewhere—what difference did it make? To die today or tomorrow, or later? The night was long and never ending. (93)

Yet, as Des Pres writes, Wiesel's narrative gives the lie to indifference and moral nights:

> Survivors do not bear witness to guilt, neither theirs nor ours, but to objective conditions of evil. In the literature of survival we find an image of things so grim, so heartbreaking, so starkly unbearable, that inevitably the survivor's scream begins to be our own. When this happens the role of spectator is no longer enough. But the testimony of survivors is valuable for something else as well. By the very fact that they came to be written, these documents are evidence that the moral self can resurrect itself from the inhuman depths through which it must pass. These books are proof that human heroism is possible. (Des Pres 49–50)

At first night is juxtaposed to day, but gradually it devours day:

> The night was gone. The morning star was shining in the sky. I too had become a completely different person. The student of the Talmud, the child that I was, had been consumed in the flames. There remained only a shape that looked like me. A dark flame had entered into my soul and devoured it. (*Night* 34)

That last sentence contains a major motif. *Night* becomes something that nullifies and obliterates; finally night overwhelms light, language, and meaning:

> The days were like nights, and the nights left the dregs of their darkness in our souls. The train was traveling slowly, often stopping for several hours and then setting off again. It never ceased snowing. All through these days and nights we stayed crouching, one on top of the other, never speaking a word. We were no more than frozen bodies. Our eyes closed, we waited merely for the next stop, so that we could unload our dead. (94–95)

On the death march, when he recalls that "the night had now set in. The snow had ceased to fall" (88), it is rich with metaphorical meaning. We recall his words as he is leaving Buna:

> The last night in Buna. Yet another last night. The last night at home, the last night in the ghetto, the last night in the train, and, now, the last night in Buna. How much longer were our lives to be dragged out from one "last night" to another? (79)

Night threatens everything, even the cosmos:

> Night. No one prayed, so that the night would pass quickly. The stars were only sparks of the fire which devoured us. Should that fire die out one day, there would be nothing left in the sky but dead stars, dead eyes. (18)

An important image is that of fire and burning. When during the death march, he feels his infected foot "burning," we recall Madame Schächter's prophetic delirious nightmare on the train to Auschwitz:

> "Jews, listen to me! I can see a fire! There are huge flames! It is a furnace!"
>
> It was as though she were possessed by an evil spirit which spoke from the depths of her being. (23)

Note how fire and death are associated with night. Her words turn out to be all to true:

> "Jews, look! Look through the window! Flames! Look!"
>
> And as the train stopped, we saw this time that flames were gushing out of a tall chimney into the black sky.
>
> Madame Schächter was silent herself. Once more she had become dumb, indifferent, absent, and had gone back to her corner.
>
> We looked at the flames in the darkness. There was an abominable odor floating in the air. Suddenly, our doors opened. Some odd-looking characters, dressed in striped shirts and black trousers leapt into the wagon. They held electric torches and truncheons. They began to strike out to right and left shouting:
>
> "Everybody get out! Everyone out of the wagon! Quickly!"
>
> We jumped out. I threw a last glance toward Madame Schächter. Her little boy was holding her hand.
>
> In front of us flames. In the air that smell of burning flesh. It must have been about midnight. We had arrived—at Birkenau, reception center for Auschwitz. (25–26)

Within Wiesel's dramatization of Madame Schächter's psyche are the warnings of Moishe, the rumors of cremation, the anxiety about the two sons and husbands being deported early. But she also is part of the prophetic and mystical tradition when she foresees the fire. Of course, the very meaning of the word Holocaust is the complete destruction of people or animals by fire, and an offering the whole of which is burned.

As in other Holocaust texts, hunger is a dominant theme in Auschwitz. The narrator recalls he soon

> took little interest in anything except my daily plate of soup and my crust of stale bread. Bread, soup—these were my whole life. I was a body. Perhaps less than that even: a starved stomach. The stomach alone was aware of the passage of time. (50)

After a hanging he recalls: "I remember that I found the soup excellent that evening" (60). Or, after another hanging,

> Behind me, I heard the same man asking:
>   "Where is God now?"
>   And I heard a voice within me answer him:
>   "Where is He? Here He is—He is hanging here on this gallows [. . .]"
>   That night the soup tasted of corpses. (62)

We might ask whether the last sentence is a metaphor or a searing actuality? Is "soup" that "tasted of corpses" a tactile transference of his feelings to his senses or vice versa? We recall Des Pres's words about how survival depended on fulfilling basic needs at the loss of ethics:

> To oppose their fate in the death camps, survivors had to choose life at the cost of moral injury; they had to sustain spiritual damage and still keep going without losing sight of the difference between strategic compromise and demoralization. Hard choices had to be made and not everyone was equal to the task, no one less than the kind of person whose goodness was most evident, most admired, but least available for action. (131)

Another motif is the father-son tie, one that is so essential in Jewish life. Within the horrors of the Holocaust, these bonds threaten to dissolve. In an awful scene after the evacuation of Auschwitz, when he and his father are being transported to Buchenwald, a son fights his father for bread:

> "Meir. Meir, my boy! Don't you recognize me? I'm your father [. . .] you're hurting me [. . .] you're killing your father! I've got some bread [. . .] for you too [. . .] for you too. [. . .]"

He collapsed. His fist was still clenched around a small piece. He tried to carry it to his mouth. But the other one threw himself upon him and snatched it. The old man again whispered something, let out a rattle, and died amid the general indifference. His son searched him, took the bread, and began to devour it. He was not able to get very far. Two men had seen and hurled themselves upon him. Others joined in. When they withdrew, next to me were two corpses, side by side, the father and the son.

I was fifteen years old. (96)

On another occasion, a son—a pipel, that is, a boy belonging to the Kapo—beats his own father for not making his bed well (60). Whenever Wiesel thinks fleetingly of his father as a burden, he feels pangs of guilt. Indeed, his loyalty to his father is among the text's most touching motifs. He rejects the terrible advice of "the head of the block" (104).

"Don't forget that you're in a concentration camp. Here, every man has to fight for himself and not think of anyone else. Even of his father. Here, there are no fathers, no brothers, no friends. Everyone lives and dies for himself alone. I'll give you a sound piece of advice—don't give your ration of bread and soup to your old father. There's nothing you can do for him. And you're killing yourself. Instead, you ought to be having his ration."

I listened to him without interrupting. He was right, I thought in the most secret region of my heart, but I dared not admit it. It's too late to save your old father, I said to myself. You ought to be having two rations of bread, two rations of soup. [. . .]

Only a fraction of a second, but I felt guilty. I ran to find a little soup to give my father. But he did not want it. All he wanted was water. (105)

By contrast to Wiesel's devotion to his father, the son of another inmate, Rabbi Eliahou

wanted to get rid of his father! He had felt that his father was growing weak, he had believed that the end was near and had sought this separation in order to get rid of the burden, to free himself from an encumbrance which could lessen his own chances of survival. (87)

While Wiesel's narrative is informed by retrospective guilt, we ask what more could Wiesel, the son, have done? Isn't Wiesel's guilt disproportionate to his behavior? In a way, the father represents the tradition for which he has departed, the man he would have been. His early perceptions are informed by his Jewish upbringing. Describing the SS Officer when he arrived at the barracks, he writes as if the German were stamped with the mark of Cain, who would kill his brother:

> An SS officer had come in and, with him, the odor of the Angel of Death. [. . .] A tall man, about thirty, with crime inscribed upon his brow and in the pupils of his eyes. He looked us over as if we were a pack of leprous dogs hanging onto our lives. (35–36)

His father is the eternal flame to which he returns as a boy and his memory returns in the telling.

One terrible irony is that the bad luck of a choice he and his father made is a cause of their worst days:

> I learned after the war the fate of those who had stayed behind in the hospital. They were quite simply liberated by the Russians two days after the evacuation. (78)

But how could he and his father have known that if they had stayed behind in the hospital as they could have, that they could have been liberated two days later and that his father would have lived. The dramatic action is filled with missed chances; the opportunity of emigrating to Palestine (6); the missed warning by the Hungarian police inspector because they didn't open the window in time: "It was not until after the war that I learned who it was that had knocked" (12); the maid Martha who could have hidden them in her village, and of course Moshe's warning. Palestine becomes the anti-tale, the Utopian alternative. He meets two brothers in Auschwitz:

> Having once belonged to a Zionist youth organization, they knew innumerable Hebrew chants. Thus we would often hum tunes evoking the calm waters of Jordan and the majestic sanctity of Jerusalem. And we would often talk of Palestine. Their parents, like mine, had lacked the courage to wind up their affairs and emigrate while there was still time. We decided that, if we were granted our lives until the liberation, we would not stay in Europe a day longer. We would take the first boat for Haifa. (48)

Transformation is as much a theme here as it is in Kafka. By showing us how life was in Sighet at the outset, we can see the terrible transformation in young Wiesel and his father. When he writes of the masquerade of clothes before the death march, we think of the clown motif in Picasso and the grotesque carnival in James Ensor:

> Prisoners appeared in strange outfits: it was like a masquerade. Everyone had put on several garments, one on top of the other, in order to keep out the cold. Poor mountebanks, wider than they were tall, more dead than alive; poor clowns, their ghostlike faces emerging from piles of prison clothes! Buffoons! (79)

When we see his father as a virtual corpse—broken in spirit, a musulman—before dying, we realize how little time had passed since he was a respected fifty year old senior member of his village.

> My father was a cultured, rather unsentimental man. There was never any display of emotion, even at home. He was more concerned with others than with his own family. The Jewish community in Sighet held him in the greatest esteem. They often used to consult him about public matters and even about private ones. (2)

As in Primo Levi's *Survival in Auschwitz*, recurring memorable characters, employed in relationship to the evolving plot give the text unity: Juliek, the violinist who plays Beethoven—in violation of the German prohibition of Beethoven—when they arrive in Gleiwitz; and who is dead in the morning.

> I could hear only the violin, and it was as though Juliek's soul were the bow. He was playing his life. The whole of his life was gliding on the strings—his lost hopes, his charred past, his extinguished future. He played as he would never play again (90);

Madame Schächter with her prophetic nightmares; Idek the psychotic kapo; Rabbi Eliahou; Meir Katz, the healthy giant who finally gives up and dies; the faceless cynic in the hospital who says: "I've got more faith in Hitler than in anyone else. He's the only one who's kept his promises, all his promises, to the Jewish people" (77).

Wiesel occasionally moves to the present as when he tells us what he learned after the war about the liberation of Auschwitz, when he speaks of the man who knocked on the window to warn his family, or the women throwing coins to the poor in Aden, or when he concludes his testament with a searing bridge across time:

One day I was able to get up, after gathering all my strength. I wanted to see myself the mirror hanging on the opposite wall. I had not seen myself since the ghetto.

From the depths of the mirror, a corpse gazed back at me.

The look in his eyes, as they stared into mine, has never left me. (109)

The mirror as a reflection of the inner self—the other self—is the recurring image in modernism, but the mirror is also a traditional image of realistic representation in the Western tradition. By his act of writing, Wiesel rejects the corpse as his double. In both cases, he makes a rhetorical gesture that positions himself within Western culture and away from his iconoclastic position as witness or as one of the humble anonymous Lamed Vov or Just Men. As Seidman puts it,

In the final lines of *Night* when the recently liberated Eliezer gazes at his own face in a mirror, the reader is presented with the survivor as both subject and object, through his inner experience and through outward image of what he has become. (3)

But when we note how different this is from the original ending, we begin to place our reading in the context of what we now know. In his 1995 *Memoirs: All Rivers Run to the Sea*, Wiesel recalls the original ending before Lindon edited it:

The book ended this way (I only quote it for its relevance today):

I looked at myself in the mirror. A skeleton stared back at me.

Nothing but skin and bone.

It was the image of myself after death. It was at that instant that the will to live awakened within me.

Without knowing why, I raised my fist and shattered the glass, along with the image it held. I lost consciousness.

After I got better, I stayed in bed for several days, jotting down notes for the work that you, dear reader, now hold in your hands.

But [. . .]

Today, ten years after Buchenwald, I realize that the world forgets. Germany is a sovereign state. The German army has been reborn. Ilse Koch, the sadist of Buchenwald, is a happy wife and mother. War criminals stroll in the streets of Hamburg and Munich. The past has been erased, buried.

Germans and anti-Semites tell the world that the story of six million Jewish victims is but a myth, and the world, in its naivete, will believe it, if not today, then tomorrow or the next day.

So it occurred to me that it might be useful to publish in book form these notes taken down in Buchenwald.

I am not so naive as to believe that this work will change the course of history or shake the conscience of humanity.

Books no longer command the power they once did.

Those who yesterday held their tongues will keep their silence tomorrow.

That is why, ten years after Buchenwald, I ask myself the question, Was I right to break that mirror? (*Memoirs* 319–320)

He questions whether his breaking the mirror as an affirmation of his decision to live is appropriate. Seidman comments:

By stopping when it does, *Night* provides an entirely different account of the experience of the survivor. *Night* and the stories about its composition depict the survivor as a witness and as an expression of silence and death, projecting the recently liberated Eliezer's death-haunted face into the postwar years when Wiesel would become a familiar figure. By contrast, the Yiddish survivor shatters that image as soon as he sees it, destroying the deathly existence the Nazis willed on him. The Yiddish survivor is filled with rage and the desire to live, to take revenge, to write. Indeed, according to the Yiddish memoir, Eliezer began to write not ten years after the events of the Holocaust but immediately upon liberation, as the first expression of his mental and physical recovery. In the Yiddish we meet a survivor who, ten years after liberation, is furious with the world's disinterest [sic] in his history, frustrated with the failure of the Jews to fulfill "the historical commandment of revenge," depressed by the apparent pointlessness of writing a book. (7–8)

But should we not also notice how Seidman, too, especially in the last of the above sentences, appropriates Wiesel for her own purposes, namely to indict Wiesel and his successors for eschewing a rhetoric of revenge. As Seidman puts it, "*Un di velt* does not spell out what form this retribution might take, only that it is sanctioned—even commanded—by Jewish history and tradition" (6).

IV

We continue to our final phase of hermeneutics—cognition in terms of what we know—when we turn to the introduction to the French edition. Originally, when Wiesel was a young unknown, Francois Mauriac, a French Catholic Nobel Laureate, not only helped him get his book published in France but also wrote the introduction which with its Christian meditation on the narrator's loss, became part of the text:

> And I, who believe that God is love, what answer could I give my young questioner, whose dark eyes still held the reflection of that angelic sadness which had appeared one day upon the face of the hanged child? What did I say to him? Did I speak of that other Jew, his brother, who may have resembled him—the Crucified, whose Cross has conquered the world? Did I affirm that the stumbling block to his faith was the cornerstone of mine, and that the conformity between the Cross and the suffering of men was in my eyes the key to that impenetrable mystery whereon the faith of his childhood had perished? Zion, however, has risen up again from the crematories and the charnel houses. The Jewish nation has been resurrected from among its thousands of dead. It is through them that it lives again. We do not know the worth of one single drop of blood, one single tear. All is grace. If the Eternal is the Eternal, the last word for each one of us belongs to Him. This is what I should have told this Jewish child. But l could only embrace him, weeping. (*Night* x–xi)

The introduction frames the book in a Christian context and implies a different set of beliefs. Mauriac was the kind of cultural icon who gave legitimacy to the novel. It were as if a young writer were now being published under Wiesel's auspices. In 1963, as Wiesel notes in his *Memoirs*, Mauriac wrote in his newspaper column:

> Someday Elie Wiesel will take me to the Holy Land. He desires it greatly, having a most singular knowledge of Christ, whom he pictures wearing phylacteries, as Chagall saw him, a son of the synagogue, a pious Jew submitting to the Law, and who did not die, "because being human he was made, God," Elie Wiesel stands on the borders of the two testaments: he is of the race of John the Baptist. (271)

There can be no doubt that Mauriac's introduction shapes the response of some readers into a more Christian reading. For example, when a child is among three condemned prisoners, Christian students see the parallel to a crucifixion scene, and see the longer and slower death of "a child with a refined and beautiful face" as a Christ figure (*Night* 60). Yet, didn't Wiesel mean the scene as a challenge to the original Christian readers—whether Poles or French, most of whom had—while night engulfed Europe—either remained silent or done far worse? In his memoir he distances himself from Mauriac's teleology:

> Where I come from and from where I stand, one cannot be Jew and Christian at the same time. Jesus was Jewish, but those who claim allegiance to him today are not. In no way does this mean that Jews are better or worse than Christians, but simply that each of us has the right, if not the duty, to be what we are. (*Memoirs* 271)

But has he written a novel that fulfills the paradigm of rebirth and resurrection to use Mauriac's words "of a Lazarus risen from the dead" and does he really speak to us not as a twenty-six year old adult but as a child, as Mauriac contends?

The child who tells us his story here was one of God's elect. From the time when his conscience first awoke, he had lived only for God and had been reared on the Talmud, aspiring to initiation into the cabbala, dedicated to the Eternal. Have we ever thought about the consequence of a horror that, though less apparent, less striking than the other outrages, is yet the worst of all to those of us who have faith: the death of God in the soul of a child who suddenly discovers absolute evil? [...] It was then that I understood what had first drawn me to the young Jew: that look, as of a Lazarus risen from the dead, yet still a prisoner within the confines where he had strayed, stumbling among the shameful corpses. (*Night* viii–ix)

Is Mauriac's construction not only a Christian appropriation of *Night*'s angst, but, no matter how well meant, an ethical transgression? It is as if, for Mauriac, Wiesel were the Christ child, an archetype for all victims whose suffering was redemptive. Seidman writes:

> The friendship between the older Christian and younger Jew began, then, with Wiesel relinquishing his aim of manipulating Mauriac for Jewish purposes and turning, in all sincerity, to the man himself. With the psychological shift, Wiesel began his transformation from Hebrew journalist and (still unpublished) Yiddish memoirist to European, or French writer. [...] The French reworking of *Un di velt hot geshvign* and Mauriac's framing of this text together suggest that *La Nuit*—read so consistently as authentically Jewish,

autobiographical, direct—represents a compromise between Jewish
expression and the capacities and desires of non-Jewish readers,
Mauriac first among them. (13, 14)

She concludes:

Was it worth "unshattering" the mirror the Yiddish Eli breaks,
reviving the image of the Jew as the Nazis wished him to be, as the
Christians prepared to accept him, the emblem of suffering silence
rather than living rage? In the complex negotiations that resulted
in the manuscript of *Night*, did the astonishing gains make good
the tremendous losses? It is over this unspoken question that the
culture of Holocaust discourse has arisen and taken shape. (16)

V

What is the grammar of cause and effect within Wiesel's testament? To a
contemporary reader, historical ironies abound. Why did the Germans continue to persecute Jews when they needed every resource to stem defeat? Was
it an attempt on the part of a compulsive if not psychotic collective group
psychology—or should we say psychopathology?—to shift blame and erase
evidence? Why did they use Jewish slave labor mostly for useless tasks and
systematically starve that labor? As Des Pres puts it,

But here too, for all its madness, there was method and reason.
This special kind of evil is a natural outcome of power when
it becomes absolute, and in the totalitarian world of the camps
it very nearly was. The SS could kill anyone they happened to
run into. Criminal Kapos would walk about in groups of two
and three, making bets among themselves on who could kill a
prisoner with a single blow. The pathological rage of such men,
their uncontrollable fury when rules were broken, is evidence of
a boundless desire to annihilate, to destroy, to smash everything
not mobilized within the movement of their own authority. And
inevitably, the mere act of killing is not enough; for if a man dies
without surrender, if something within him remains unbroken
to the end, then the power which destroyed him has not after all
crushed everything. (59)

By confronting the horrors of the Holocaust and insisting on bearing
witness (and resisting Mauriac's Christian gloss), Wiesel's text is an antidote
to the way that Anne Frank's story had been manipulated to "glorify," as Bru-

no Bettelheim puts it, "the ability to retreat into an extremely private, gentle, sensitive world, and there to cling as much as possible to what have been one's usual attitudes and activities, although surrounded by a maelstrom apt to engulf one at any moment" (*Survivors and Other Essays* 247). In the play and film, we hear Anne's voice from beyond saying, "In spite of everything, I still believe that people are really good at heart," but Bettelheim argues passionately that this statement is not supported or justified in Anne's diary:

> This improbable sentiment is supposedly from a girl who had been starved to death, had watched her sister meet the same fate before she did, knew that her mother had been murdered, and had watched untold thousands of adults and children being killed. This statement is not justified by anything Anne actually told in her diary. (Bettelheim 250)

But, of course, we see Anne's last word as ironic because she has been killed. Bettelheim is quite harsh in his judgments:

> Those Jews who submitted passively to Nazi persecution came to depend on primitive and infantile thought processes: wishful thinking and disregard for the possibility of death. Many persuaded themselves that they, out of all the others, would be spared. Many more simply disbelieved in the possibility of their own death. Not believing in it, they did not take what seemed to them desperate precautions, such as giving up everything to hide out singly; or trying to escape even if it meant risking their lives in doing so; or preparing to fight for their lives when no escape was possible and death had become an immediate possibility. (251)

In an essay entitled "Freedom From Ghetto Thinking" Bettelheim defines "Ghetto thinking": "to believe that one can ingratiate oneself with a mortal enemy by denying that his lashes sting, to deny one's own degradation in return for a moment's respite, to support one's enemy who will only use his strength the better to destroy one. All that is part of Ghetto philosophy" (*Freud's Vienna and Other Essays* 261). For him the Franks embody ghetto thinking:

> The Frank family created a ghetto in the annex, the Hinter Haus, where they went to live; it was an intellectual ghetto, a sensitive one, but a ghetto nevertheless. I think we should contrast their story with those of other Jewish families who went into hiding in Holland. These families, from the moment they dug in, planned

escape routes for the time when the police might come looking for them. Unlike the Franks, they did not barricade themselves in rooms without exits; they did not wish to be trapped. In preparation, some of them planned and rehearsed how the father, if the police should come, would try to argue with them or resist in order to give his wife and children time to escape. Sometimes when the police came the parents physically attacked them, knowing they would be killed but thus saving a child. (*Freud's Vienna* 270)

Bettelheim, who himself committed suicide, writes in his essay "Surviving" how the survivor "knows very well that he is not guilty, as I, for one know about myself, but that this does not change the fact that the humanity of such a person, as a fellow being, requires that he feel guilty, and he does. This is a most significant aspect of survivorship" (*Surviving* 297). Bettelheim reminds how, while the foremost condition for survival was luck, other factors helped, such as, to quote Bettelheim, correctly assessing one's situation and taking advantage of opportunities, in short, acting independently and with courage, decision and conviction. [. . .] Survival was, of course, greatly helped if one had entered the camps in a good state of physical health. But most of all, as I have intimated all along, autonomy, self-respect, inner integration, a rich inner life, and the ability to relate to others in meaningful ways were the psychological conditions which, more than any others, permitted one to survive in the camps as much a whole human being as overall conditions and chance would permit. ("Owners of their Faces," *Surviving* 109)

Whether we agree with Bettelheim and whether we chide him for letting his rage distort and appropriate Anne Frank's text as Mauriac and Seidman have appropriated Wiesel, his words give us some sense of how difficult it is for us readers of Holocaust texts to respond ethically to such a searing and heart-rendering narrative of memory, trauma, and literary imagination as *Night*.

WORKS CITED

Bettelheim, Bruno. *Freud's Vienna and Other Essays*. New York: Vintage, 1991.
———. *Surviving and Other Essays*. New York: Vintage, 1980.
Clifford, James *The Predicament of Culture: Twentieth-Century Ethnography, Literature, and Art*. Cambridge, Mass.: Harvard University Press, 1988.
Dawidowicz, Lucy. *The War Against the Jews, 1933–1945*. New York: Bantam, 1986.
Des Pres, Terence. *The Survivor: An Anatomy of Life in the Death Camps*. New York: Oxford University Press, 1970.
Muschamp, Herbert. "Shaping a Monument's Memory." *New York Times* 1993: 1 (Art and Leisure).

Ricouer, Paul. "The Model of the Text." *Social Research* 5.1 (Spring 1984): 185–218.

Sachs, Nellie. "A Dead Child Speaks." Trans Ruth and Matthew Mead. *Holocaust Poetry*. Ed. Hilda Schiff. New York: St. Martin's Press, 1995. p. 67.

Seidman, Naomi. "Elie Wiesel and the Scandal Rage." *Jewish Social Studies: History, Culture and Society* 3.1 (Fall 1996): 1–19.

Suleiman, Susan, and Inge Crossman, eds. *The Reader in the Text: Essays on Audience and Interpretation*. Princeton: Princeton University Press, 1980.

Wiesel, Elie. *A Jew Today*. Trans. Marion Wiesel. New York: Random House, 1978.

———. *Memoirs: All Rivers Run to the Sea*. New York: Knopf, 1995.

———. *Night*. Trans. Stella Rodney. New York: Bantam, 1960.

SAMUEL TOTTEN

Entering the "Night" of the Holocaust: Studying Elie Wiesel's Night

Never shall I forget that night, the first night in camp, which has turned my life into one long night, seven times cursed and seven times sealed. Never shall I forget that smoke. Never shall I forget the faces of the little children, whose bodies I saw turned into wreaths of smoke beneath a blue sky.

Never shall I forget those flames which consumed my faith forever.

Never shall I forget that nocturnal silence which deprived me, for all eternity, of the desire to live . . . Never shall I forget these things, even if I am condemned to live as long as God himself. Never.

—Wiesel, 1969, *Night*, p. 44.

Many powerful and thought-provoking works—diaries, memoirs, historical studies, novels, short stories—have been written about the Holocaust, but few seem to so thoroughly engage secondary-level students as Elie Wiesel's *Night*. It is a memoir about a young boy's horrific experiences as he, his family, his community, and people are ripped from their homes, transported to Auschwitz, and brutalized and murdered in ways that are difficult for the "average" person to fathom. For many, it seems to be a story that penetrates to the core of one's being, never to leave, never to dissipate.

As with any work of literature—be it a diary, a memoir, a short story, a novel, or a play—there are innumerable ways to teach *Night*. What is delineated here comprises a combined literary and historical approach. Prior

Teaching Holocaust Literature, ed. Samuel Totten (Boston: Allyn and Bacon, 2001): pp. 215–242. Copyright © 2001 Pearson Education.

to discussing the aforementioned approach, a summary of Elie Wiesel the person, the activist, and the author is provided.

Elie Wiesel: "A Messenger to Humanity"

Born in 1928, Elie Wiesel grew up in a remote area of Transylvania—in the small town of Sighet in Rumania, a Hungarian-speaking town in the Carpathian mountains—in a highly Orthodox Jewish family. Sighet was part of the Northern Transylvania region of Romania that became part of Hungary in 1940 as a reward to the Hungarians for their alliance with Germany. Immersed in the religious life, he began the study of the Torah and the Talmud at a tender age. At the age of 12 he also began to immerse himself in the study of the Zohar, cabbalistic books, and Jewish mysticism. All of that ended abruptly in 1944, during Passover week, when he, his immediate family, and approximately 15,000 fellow townspeople, were herded onto boxcars and transported to Auschwitz.[1] His mother and youngest sister were immediately murdered in a gas chamber. Following a series of harrowing experiences, he and his father, along with many other prisoners, were forced on a death march to Buchenwald, shortly after which his father perished in Elie's arms. In Auschwitz, Elie Wiesel not only lost his youth but came out doubting both God and life. In regard to the loss of his youth, he has said: "When I was 18 . . . I was not 18. I was an old man. What I knew then, the teachers of my teachers [of the Talmud and other religious works] never knew. What I lived in an hour people don't live in a generation." (quoted in Freedman, 1983, p. 35). As for his relationship with God, he has observed that "Usually, we [Jews] say, 'God is right,' or 'God is just'—even during the Crusades we said that. But how can you say that now, with one million children dead [as a result of the Holocaust]?" (quoted in Freedman, 1983, p. 68). Elsewhere, and mirroring his assertion in *Night*, he has stated that "I [never] denied God's existence, but I doubted His absolute justice" (quoted in Eckardt, 1979, p. 18).

Following his liberation, Elie refused to be repatriated, and was sent to France. There, he was eventually reunited with an older sister. Stateless, he chose to remain in France.

He has observed that, "So heavy was my anguish that in the spring of 1945 I made a vow: not to speak, not to touch upon the essential for at least ten years. Long enough to unite the language of humanity with the silence of the dead" (Kanfer, 1985, p. 78). Here one is reminded of Goethe's statement that when one is in pain one becomes mute because of that pain.

From 1948 to 1951 he studied philosophy at the Sorbonne, where he read and was influenced by the writings of the French existentialists Albert Camus and Jean Paul Sartre. In 1949, he became chief foreign correspondent for the Israeli daily *Yedioth Ahronot* and then in 1957 he also began writing for the New York-based *Jewish Daily Forward.*

Eventually, Wiesel began to write of his ordeal. He published *Night*, his first book, in French, in 1958. In addition to *Night* and numerous novels (including *Dawn, The Accident, The Town Beyond the Wall, The Gates of the Forest, A Beggar in Jerusalem, The Oath, The Fifth Son*), he has written numerous collections of essays, a cantata *(Ani Maamin)*, two Plays (*Zalmen, or The Madness of God* and *The Trial of God*) and books on a wide range of topics, from *The Jews of Silence: A Personal Report on Soviet Jewry* to *Souls on Fire: Portraits and Legends of Hasidic Masters*. In all, he has written over 30 books. "I really believe I have to write," he has said. "There's a certain compulsion. I owe it to everybody but myself. I owe it to the dead. I owe it to the living" (quoted in Freedman, 1983, p. 36). In a similar vein, he has said that, "I feel that having survived, I owed something to the dead. That was their obsession to be remembered. Anyone who does not remember betrays them again" (Berger, 1986, p. 4).

Wiesel eventually moved to the United States, where he became a U.S. citizen in 1963. A long-time resident of New York City, he first began teaching at the City University of New York and now teaches at Boston University. For many years Wiesel was also the chairman of the United States Holocaust Memorial Council, the body that created the United States Holocaust Memorial Museum in Washington, D.C.

An indefatigable human rights activist, Wiesel has traveled to and spoken out about human rights violations and tragedies in Biafra, Lebanon, Vietnam, Cambodia, South Africa, Central America, Bosnia, Rwanda, and Kosovo. Writing about what drives Wiesel to speak on the behalf of the oppressed around the globe, Christian theologian Robert McAfee Brown (1979) has observed that:

> [T]he opposite of participation and mutuality is not only isolation; it is also the spectator role, so chillingly embodied in the observer at the window in [Wiesel's novel] *The Town Beyond the Wall*, the man who feels nothing as Jews are taken to the camps, the one who does nothing, but actually by his doing nothing sides with the executioners rather than the victims. He is the most complicit of all human beings, worse even than the executioner. His is a voluntary withdrawal from participation and abdication of personhood. (p. 23)

In recognition of his life-long work on the behalf of others around the globe, Wiesel was awarded the Nobel Prize for Peace in 1986. In awarding Wiesel the Nobel Prize, the Nobel committee statement observed that

"Wiesel's commitment, which originated in the suffering of the Jewish people, has been widened to embrace all oppressed peoples and races" (Markham, 1986, p. 4).

A man of remarkable eloquence and a prolific writer who is driven to tell the story of the Holocaust, Wiesel has been referred to over the years as "a messenger to all humanity," "the conscience of a people's anguish and a people's hope," and "chronicler of the Holocaust." Ultimately, Wiesel is a witness and a teacher. In regard to his role—and that of other survivors—as a writer and a witness, he has said: "If the role of the writer may once have been to entertain, that of the witness is to disturb, alert, to awaken, to warn against indifference to injustice—any injustice—and above all against complacency about any need and any people" (Wiesel, 1979, p. 36). As for his role as a teacher, he has said of himself and other survivors who tell their stories and write about the Holocaust, "[T]he survivors chose to teach; and what is their writing, their testimony, if not teaching?" (Wiesel, 1978, p. 267).[2]

Developing a Cluster around the Term "Holocaust": A Preassessment Activity

Prior to having the students read *Night*, I have each student develop a cluster (also frequently referred to as a mind-map or conceptual map) around the "target word" Holocaust. A cluster has been defined as "a nonlinear brainstorming process that generates ideas, images, and feeling around a stimulus word until a pattern becomes discernible" (Rico, 1987, p. 17). More graphically, teacher Michael O'Brien (1987) has defined clustering in the following manner: "Think of them as flowers. Clusters do, after all, resemble flowers whose petals burst forth from the central corolla. Note that clusters do beautifully in both remedial and advanced classes . . . " (p. 25).

To develop a cluster, I inform my students, they need to place the term *Holocaust* in the center of a piece of paper (at least as large as 8½" x 11"), circle it, and then draw spokes out from the circle on which they attach related terms or ideas. Each time a term is added, they need to circle the term and connect it, with a simple line, to those other terms and/or concepts that are related to it. Each new or related idea should lead to a new clustering of ideas. As Rico (1987) points out: "A cluster is an expanding universe, and each word is a potential galaxy; each galaxy, in turn, may throw out its own universes. As students cluster around a stimulus word, the encircled words rapidly radiate outward until a sudden shift takes place, a sort of 'Aha!' that signals a sudden awareness of that tentative whole . . . " (p. 17). Furthermore, "Since a cluster draws on primary impressions—yet simultaneously on a sense of the overall design—clustering actually generates structure, shaping one thought into a starburst of other thoughts, each somehow related to the whole" (Rico, 1987, p. 18).

Clustering (or mind-mapping or webbing) is a more graphic and, generally, easier and more engaging method to use to delineate what one knows about a topic than, say, outlining a topic.[3]

In order to make sure that my students know exactly what I mean by clustering, and as a way to illustrate that which constitutes a more complex cluster versus one that is simplistic, I demonstrate the development of, first, a very simple cluster of a topic (on one other than the Holocaust, e.g., the school's sports program), and then take that simple cluster and turn it into a more complex one. I use the two clusters to model; first, a nonexemplar (e.g., the simplistic cluster) and then, second, an exemplar (the more complex cluster). The reason it is important for the teacher to *avoid* developing a cluster on the Holocaust is that many students may be tempted simply to copy what the teacher has done; that is, use the exact same information and make the same sort of connections that the teacher has made in his or her cluster.

In giving directions for the development of the cluster, I encourage my students to develop the most detailed, comprehensive and accurate cluster they possibly can. At the same time, I encourage them to make a Herculean effort to carefully delineate the connections, when appropriate, between and amongst the various and separate items/concepts/events/ideas.

Once each student has completed his or her cluster, I place the students in groups of three and four and have them share and discuss their individual clusters. I tell them that it is an imperative that each and every student be allotted time to succinctly explain his or her cluster (1 to 3 minutes should be ample). Each student should address the following: a quick overview of key points, a rationale as to why he or she included certain ideas, and a brief explanation of the connections between and amongst various ideas. At this time I also note that after every student has presented his or her cluster, each person in the group should add, if he or she so wishes, items from other members' clusters to his or her own cluster. *In adding the new information, he or she should use a color other than the one he or she used in his or her original cluster.* This will simply indicate the type and number of ideas borrowed from others.

Finally, at the end of this session, I ask them to sign their own cluster. Finally, we tape the clusters to the walls around the classroom. The purpose of the latter is to allow us to revisit the clusters, if the need arises, during the course of our study of *Night*.

Having the students develop clusters serves a number of purposes: first, students actually depict for themselves what they know and don't know about the subject; second, as a teacher, I gain a concrete illustration of both the students' depth of knowledge as well as the sophistication of their conceptual framework of a subject; and third, I am able to ascertain the accuracy of students' knowledge as well as any inaccuracies, misconceptions, and/or myths they may hold about a topic. Basically, then, such an exercise serves as

a powerful preassessment exercise. Over and above that, clustering provides
the students with a unique method to express their ideas; and in doing so, it
allows them to tap into an "intelligence" (e.g., spatial) other than the typical one of writing ("linguistic"), to borrow a concept from Howard Gardner
(1983; 1993).[4]

As will be discussed below, I have my students read *Night* twice during
our unit: the first time allows them to become familiar with the work and to
engage in a reader response activity; while the second time around, we analyze
the work from both a historical and literary perspective. At the conclusion
of our *first reading* of *Night*, I have the students complete a second cluster.
Doing so provides us with a vivid sense as to the students' new insights, the
new connections they make between and amongst key topics, and/or whether
their newfound knowledge is couched in a more sophisticated understanding
of the topic of the Holocaust. Finally, after the students have read *Night* for
the second time and we've conducted the historical/literary study of the work,
the students develop a third and final cluster, which they then compare and
contrast with both their initial and second clusters. After developing their
second and third clusters, the students are required to address one or more
key points. For example, What is the most pronounced difference between
the two clusters, and what does this tell you about your knowledge base in
regard to the Holocaust? and/or, Are there any items on your last cluster that
you feel are absolutely imperative for someone to include on such a cluster,
and why?

After the development of each and every cluster, I have my students
develop a working definition of the Holocaust based on their most current
knowledge base.

Using the Cluster/Mind-Map to Develop a
Working Definition of the Holocaust

Next, using the information (facts, concepts, connections) the students have
included in their initial cluster, each student develops a working definition
of the Holocaust. In doing so, they are advised to examine carefully all of the
components of their cluster and then make every effort to develop the most
comprehensive and accurate definition they possibly can. I also tell them
that as they go about developing their definition, if they discover they have
left out key facts or concepts or have failed to make certain connections, they
are free to add those to their clusters, but that they should use a different
color than they have previously used. Likewise, I tell them that they need to
add the new color and its purpose to the legend of their cluster.

Once everyone has developed his or her definition, the students are
placed in small groups (a maximum of three to four people) where they share
their definitions. The groups can be comprised either of the same students as

or different ones than the last small group exercise; it doesn't really matter. Again, I tell them that every member of the group should share his or her cluster, that once a person has shared his or her cluster with the group a short discussion should ensue in regard to any questions or concerns that other group members have, and that someone should take down the most salient points during the course of the discussion of the various definitions.

At the conclusion of the small group discussions, we hold a general discussion in regard to what the students learned during this activity, and we also place any questions or points they are unsure about on sheets of butcher paper with the heading, "Holocaust: Issues to Examine in More Detail." I explain that as we proceed with our study of *Night* we will return to these questions/concerns and attempt to answer them. In doing so, I explain, we will attempt to clarify our understanding of what the Holocaust was (and/or wasn't) as well as come to a more comprehensive and accurate definition of the historical event now referred to as the Holocaust.

Simply to provide the students with an accepted definition of the Holocaust (e.g., the one used by the United States Holocaust Memorial Museum) would be much easier and faster but it would not be the most pedagogically sound approach. In using the method I've described, the students are able to construct their new insights and knowledge of the Holocaust by reexamining their previous ideas against the new information and insights they are gleaning during the course of the study. In that way, they are more likely to come to a more in-depth and lasting understanding of how and why scholars wrestle over definitions and why such definitions are so important in framing an understanding of complex issues and events.

This process, of course, does not preclude, at some point, the examination of different scholars' definitions of the Holocaust. On the contrary, comparing their definition to those of scholars deepens the students' thinking about the historical process as well as their understanding of the Holocaust.

From the outset, the development of definitions by the students provides me with unique insights into their understanding of the Holocaust as well as their misunderstanding, misconceptions, inaccurate information, and so on. This, of course, serves as another powerful preassessment exercise.

What follows is a sample of some of the many initial definitions that a class of high school students came up with at the outset of a study of *Night*. The examples are purposely grouped according to the types of information found in them.

The initial grouping includes those definitions that were the *least* inaccurate among the definitions developed by the students. The wording "least accurate" is deliberately used here for the express purpose of highlighting the fact that *all* of the following definitions are bereft of key information in regard to *why* the Holocaust was perpetrated.

Holocaust: When the Nazis decided the Jews were the cause of Germany's problems. In WWII the Nazis tortured and killed Jews. The Nazis wanted a genocide of the Jews.

Holocaust: To gain political power, Hitler blamed the Jews for Germany's hardships after WWI. This created much of the negative sentiment necessary for Hitler to come to rule Germany. He began imprisoning Jewish people in concentration camps. Eventually millions were murdered and treated like animals.

Holocaust: The persecution and/or extermination of people of primarily Jewish background by the Nazis during WW II, involving the creation of Jewish ghettos, forced labor forces and concentration camps.

Holocaust: Persecution of Jews during 1940s in Germany and near areas of Europe; led by Adolf Hitler a Nazi dictator; took place during WWII; many Jews died in concentration camps due to crowded housing and gas chambers. They were cremated.

Holocaust: A time during WWII when Hitler's Nazi party punished the Jews for "causing all of Germany's problems." The Jews were forced to wear the yellow star of David and had virtually no rights. Many were sent to concentration camps, and many died.

Holocaust: Hitler forced Jews into hiding and killed 6 million Jews in concentration camps. Jews were forced to wear the Star of David, and be segregated from others because Hitler believed that the Germans were the supreme race.

When comparing the above definitions with the one used by the U.S. Holocaust Memorial Museum (1994), one can readily ascertain the gaps in the students' definitions: "The Holocaust refers to a specific event in 20th-century history: the state-sponsored, systematic persecution and annihilation of European Jewry by Nazi Germany and its collaborators between 1933 and 1945. Jews were the primary victims—six million were murdered; Gypsies, the handicapped, and Poles were also targeted for destruction or decimation for racial, ethnic, or national reasons. Millions more, including homosexuals, Jehovah's Witnesses, Soviet prisoners of war, and political dissidents, also suffered grievous oppression and death under Nazi tyranny" (p. 3). In addition to leaving out a good number of the aforementioned concerns, very few of the students' definitions take into consideration the major historical trends that contributed to the Holocaust. As scholar Donald Niewyk (1995) has pointed out: "A number of historical trends combined to make the Holocaust possible: anti-Semitism, racism, social Darwinism, extreme nationalism, totalitarianism, industrialism, and the nature of modern war. The absence of any one of these trends would have made the genocide of the Jews unlikely"

(p. 175). Also obvious is the fact that some students confused "concentration camps" with "death camps," or at least didn't seem to differentiate the major differences between the two. That said, the students who developed the above definitions were at least on the right track in regard to what Nazi Germany was about and who was victimized. Still, obviously, the students had a tremendous amount to learn in regard to why and how the Holocaust was perpetrated.

The next set of definitions not only are bereft of key information but are flawed in various and major ways. More specifically, many include major inaccuracies and misconceptions:

> Holocaust: The destruction of an entire race by a pathological maniac who felt he was in his right as playing God destroying one race and creating a better one.
> Holocaust: The Germans boycotted the Jews and Adolf Hitler had his army ship them off to concentration camps where they were starved to death.
> Holocaust: Discrimination against Jews by Germans in which they were forced into concentration camps, tortured, murdered, gassed, and it caused a world war. Hitler ran the Nazis [sic] party.
> Holocaust: A time in history many of us wish we could forget. The Nazi German type of people were beaten, raped, murdered, put in concentration camps and shot just because they look [sic] different or other things.
> Holocaust: The Holocaust was between 1939–1945. It was when Hitler gathered people (mostly Jews) and put them into death camps, or just killed them. Jews were educated people, and when they started taking most of the jobs, that's when the trouble started. Millions of people died and families were torn apart.
> Holocaust: During WWI Nazi Germany had a problem with Jews. The Holocaust was when the Nazis killed 45 million Jews during that time period.

As one can ascertain, the inaccuracies and misconceptions of some of the students are, to say the least, glaring. More specifically, in some instances, the students referred to the Jews as a race (which they are not, though the Nazis referred to them as such; for a discussion of the fallacious concept of race, see Montagu, 1964 and Gates, 1997); insinuated that the Holocaust was the result of one man's efforts (when, in fact, it involved the Nazi hierarchy, the SS which ran the camps, and tens of thousands of others who contributed in various ways); that the destruction of the Jews was *the* cause for the world to go to war (it wasn't the persecution of the Jews, but rather

the bellicosity of the Germans and Japanese); and that the Jews were pros-
pering in Germany while no one else was and/or at everyone else's expense
(both of which are simply flat-out wrong). Another student was under the
impression that the Nazis killed 45 million Jews (when in fact, they killed
approximately six million Jews and millions of other people). One student
was under the misconception that the sole mistreatment of the Jews was their
starvation by the Nazis (when the fact is that they were killed in numerous
ways, including being shot, hanged, starved to death, beaten to death and, of
course, gassed). The most glaring misconception is the student who totally
misconstrues who the victims and perpetrators were (e.g., "the Nazi German
type of people were beaten, raped, murdered, put in concentration camps
and shot just because they look [sic] different or other things"). Again, it is
worth noting that not a single student mentioned the issue of antisemitism,
let alone the rabid and deadly form of antisemitism practiced by the Nazis.
Nor did any mention the racism of the Nazis.

After the development of each cluster, the students are required to develop a new definition of the Holocaust and to compare and contrast, in writing, their latest definition with their earlier definition(s).

The First Reading: A Reader Response Approach

As previously mentioned, when I teach *Night* to high school students—and
I have done so numerous times—I generally have them read it twice. The
first time they are told simply to read it through in the course of one or two
sittings. This is to introduce them to the memoir in such a way that they
become immersed in it without interruption, to allow them to respond to
it in their own personal way without the superstructure of a deeper historical or literary analysis, and to provide them with an opportunity to soak
the story in on their own and without any "interference" on my part or
the part of their fellow students. The second reading involves, for lack of
a better term, a more *historical/literary* approach, where the students gain
an overview of the history of the Holocaust period and are encouraged to
delve into the story in a more analytical fashion; that is, one in which they
consider Wiesel's experiences in light of the history of the period along
with an examination of such literary concerns as biblical allusions and
inverted symbolism.

Initially, I assign *Night* to my students on a Thursday and ask them
to complete it by Sunday evening, or at least prior to class the following
Monday. It is a relatively short book of 127 pages, and so engaging that even
those who generally do not like to read find it extremely engaging and hard
to put down.

Prior to making the assignment, I provide what should be a "refresher"
mini-lesson on the differences between fiction and nonfiction (including the

distinctions between a diary, an interview, a memoir, and a novel). Unfortunately, many teachers teach *Night* as a novel, when in fact it is a memoir. Concerned about this issue himself, Wiesel (1995) emphatically states, in *All Rivers Run to the Sea: Memoirs,* that "*Night* is not a novel" (p. 271). It is at this juncture that I broach and teach them about the use of heightened language (including metaphorical language), and "invented dialogue" for later discussions. The latter is particularly significant to address since *Night,* which includes a large amount of dialogue, was written a good number of years after the incidents took place.

The assignment that accompanies the reading of *Night* is as follows:

During this unit of study you will read Elie Wiesel's *Night* twice; once simply to become familiar with it and to react to it in the most personal of ways. The second time, you shall be reading it more closely; and in doing so, you shall take into account the history of the period and also examine it from a more literary point of view.

Thus, for this first reading, you should simply do the following: Read *Night* through quickly, noting when applicable, those images, incidents, words, sentences, thoughts that most move you and/or provide you with telling insights into what the Jews, and particularly Elie and his family, experienced during the Holocaust. Once you have concluded the book, take your notes and write a letter to Elie. In your letter, which should be a very personal letter from you, write exactly what you wish about the book. More specifically, you may write anything you wish about the memoir. You may tell the author how his story made you feel, offer your own insights into any aspect of his story, posit any questions you may have about his story or any of the various situations he faced, inquire about anything you still don't understand, or comment on whether you would recommend the book to others or not. The point is, you may approach it in any way you wish. It is your perspective, your point of view that is important. Do not write this for me, the teacher, write it for yourself in which you present your most honest response to the memoir.

Once all of the questions students may have about the directions for the assignment are addressed, I have found that it is a good idea to ask, What does every letter begin with (the students will generally answer "the date" and "a salutation or greeting"). The students should also be asked, And what do letters generally conclude with? Here the students usually answer with "a closing" and "your name." If the teacher does not ask such questions, many students will neglect to set up the assignment in letter format.

During the first class session after the students have read *Night*, I place them in groups of three and provide them with the following directions: "Initially, each person should simply read his or her letter while the rest of the group listens. Once everyone has read his or her piece, each person should read his or her letter again. This time, however, after each person reads his or her letter, a discussion should ensue. During the course of the discussion, the other members of the group are free to ask questions and make comments about the other person's letter; and in doing so, one may corroborate certain points by drawing on thoughts and feelings reflected in one's own letter and/or play the devil's advocate by questioning and probing. As you discuss the ideas in the various letters, be sure to keep returning to the memoir in order to substantiate and clarify your ideas. As soon as the discussion of one person's letter wanes, the next person in line should read his or her letter and the process of discussion should begin anew." While this exercise would work with groups of four, I have found that three in each group is really the optimal number. That is due primarily to the fact that many of the students' letters to Wiesel are rather lengthy, and with four or more students in a group, the activity consumes an inordinate amount of time and some students tend to lose focus.

I further explain that in order for the class to conduct a large-group (e.g., class) follow-up discussion, it will be necessary for each group to have a recorder who jots down the most pertinent points made during the course of the small-group discussion. Since that is the case, I ask each group to decide quickly who the recorder is going to be, and I ask for that individual to raise his or her hand. The latter ensures that each group has a recorder. After all of the recorders have been duly noted, I tell the students that during the general discussion the onus will not be on the recorder to carry the discussion for his or her group, but rather it will be the responsibility of the entire group to expound on their collective ideas. Thus, while the recorder will initially relate the key points that have been made in his or her group, any subsequent discussion of the group's points should be a group effort.

As the small groups engage in the aforementioned work, I circulate from, group to group, and as a rule, I listen to the discussion and refrain from making any comments. However, if an individual or an entire group is at a standstill and asserts something along the lines of "We've covered everything. We're through," I generally ask them if they have any lingering questions about the book, and if so, what they are. Then I encourage them to probe those. If there are none, then I may ask them to consider why Wiesel entitled his book *Night*, and what is the significance of such a title. Initially, I will listen to the outset of their discussion and then come back to see where the discussion has gone. If the discussion has waned again, I may ask the individual members of the group each to come up with a title of their own for the memoir and a rationale as to why they would attach such a title to the work. And once again, I would encourage them to discuss their different ideas.

If, however, a group is stuck on a point—for example, in one group a student was arguing that in Auschwitz Wiesel had forsaken his God, while another argued that God had forsaken the Jews, and yet still another remarked that Elie reminded him of Job—I offer the following advice and encouragement: "OK, that's a good starting point. Now each of you needs to go to the text and provide evidence for your case, and then there needs to be a group discussion around those points. And go to Job in the Bible and read that out loud in order to compare and contrast Job's revolt with that of Wiesel as spelled out in *Night*. See where that discussion goes."

Also, as I move from group to group, I prod the students to *really* wrestle with each student's point and, in doing so, to tie it directly to the memoir and/or to refer to the text in order to corroborate, contest, or expand on the point. With some groups it takes more encouragement and prodding than others, but by gently prodding and urging them to go with their initial reactions and then examine and wrestle with those, the students inevitably come up with remarkably interesting, if not perspicacious, insights.

It is during this initial assignment and during the course of the small group discussions that the students raise a host of questions and issues vis-à-vis various aspects of the Holocaust (e.g., What are Fascists?; What is Passover?; Why did the Jews have to wear a star?; Over and above what the citizens of Sighet heard about the mass killings from Moché the Beadle, which they didn't believe, what did the Hungarian Jews really know about the death camps in 1944?; What did nations outside the Nazis' sphere know about the mass killings and what did they do to help or warn the Jews?; When the Jews were rounded up to be deported, why didn't they resist?; How could anyone live through something like that or even want to live through it?), and questions about Wiesel's style of writing (When was *Night* written and how could he [Wiesel] remember all of those conversations?; There is an eerie cadence to the words when he says "Never shall I forget . . ." over and over again, but at the same time it reminds me of certain passages in the Bible). Many of the issues broached and discussed in the small groups were subsequently discussed in the large group discussions. Furthermore, the issues and students' comments were duly noted by me for the express purpose of revisiting and expanding upon them during the class discussion following the second reading of *Night*.

It is both during the small group and large group discussions that the real work of the teacher begins. If handled with care and skill, the large group discussion becomes extremely rich, informative, and enlightening. By having visited and listened in on the small groups and having jotted down notes about what the students were discussing and wrestling with, the instructor is able to help make connections between various students' comments during the large group discussion. Furthermore, the instructor is able to broach issues that were discussed in small groups that might not, for whatever reason, be brought back up in the large discussion group. Both of these strategies assist in maintaining the flow of the discussion, deepening the discussion, and challenging the students to play off of one another's ideas and to consider various and, sometimes radically different, points of view. I have found that during those few class sessions that I neglected to take notes and/or did not broach issues that generated heated discussion in the small groups, the large group discussions were often not as dynamic, interesting, or thought-provoking as they could or should have been.

Included below are a few excerpts from the students' initial response to *Night* (the letters to Elie Wiesel):

Dear Elie,

Last night I prayed for you, your mother, sisters and father *and for* the world that was silent while you suffered so horribly. I prayed, too, for myself, asking for the strength to not be callous and cold when people are desperate and in need of help.

What I cannot understand is how people—other nationalities, other religions, other races, other backgrounds—can be so cruel to other people. I just cannot understand how a human can hurt another human in the way the Nazis did little babies, children, old people, or anyone for that matter. That's what I feel I need to try to understand. How can such hate be developed in a whole people? How can people be so thoughtless, cruel, horrible to one another. Right now I feel as if I will never be able to understand that. Never! But I will try. (Karen)

Dear Elie,

My heart goes out to you in a way it has never gone out to anyone before. I do not know how you made it through everything that the Nazis put you through and your family through. I could have not made it through.

I thought I knew alot *[sic]* about the holocuast *[sic]* before I read *Night,* your story. Many years ago I had read *The Diary of Anne Frank,* and more recently I had watched some things on the Discovery Channel, and I even saw Schindler List *[sic]* twice, but what you experienced and what you wrote about and how you wrote about it left me feeling that I had no real idea what the holocaust *[sic]* was about.

I don't know what got me most about your story, your experiences—the brutality of the Nazis (which was horrific [sic]) or the fact that no one really tried to help you and your family and community members. (Mike)

Dear Mr. Weisel [sic],
    Over and over again I keep thinking about the first line in your book in chapter 3 that says, "The cherished objects we had brought with us thus far were left behind in the train, and with them, at least, our illusions." As you and your parents and sisters saw the horrer [sic] of Auschwtz [sic] it suddenly hit you what the Nazis were up to. To kill! To wipe out! To torture and murder a hole [sic] people. To turn living people into ash and smoke. To wipe every trace of a persons [sic] life, all Jew's lifes [sic], into nothing. No one could even imigine [sic] that before because it was to [sic] far-featched [sic], to [sic] unbeleiveable [sic], to [sic] crazy to even think about, but not any more. Not anymore. As you also say, "Today anything is allowed. Anything is possible, even these crematories. . . ." (Adam)

Dear Elie,
    . . . I am a very religious person and when you said that "I ceased to pray" (p. 55), tears came to my eyes. You, too, were very religious but what you went through made you Job-like. You say, "I did not deny God's existence, but I doubted His absolute justice" (p. 56). Selfishly, I guess, I am glad you did not deny God's existence, but I do understand, at least to a certain extent, why you doubted His justice. And I can also understand, again, at least to a certain extent, why the men who were forced to watch the hanging of the little boy asked "Where is God? Where is He?" (p. 76). I guess my questions are: Where was the humanity in the Nazis? Where was the humanity in the individual men who ran Auschwitz? And where was humanity, period! [sic] while all of this was going on? And where is humanity today when so many atrocities are being perpetrated across the globe? (Kelly)

As one can ascertain from these few short excerpts, the letters written by the students were thought-filled, compassionate, and thought-provoking. Indeed, collectively, they generated many significant topics that were ultimately examined, analyzed, and debated—initially in small group discussions and then in a large class discussion,
    Among the many questions and issues generated by the above excerpts were: What drives people to commit mass murder? This question spurred a

discussion about the Nazis' propaganda machine and its race policies that perceived Jews as vermin and bacillus that reputedly posed a danger to the "Aryan race"; the silence of the world as the mass murder was committed as well as what the world knew and when; the sheer impossibility, at the time, to imagine that one group of people would actually plan and implement the "manufacture of death" of another group of people; the illusions and false hope that many Jews harbored as the Nazis closed in on and "had their way" with the Jews; and a debate over theodicy (defense of God's goodness and omnipotence in view of the existence of evil).

This initial approach—the writing of the personal letters and the subsequent discussions—is based on reader response theory. As John O'Neill (1994) has written in "Rewriting the Book on Literature: Changes Sought in How Literature Is Taught, What Students Read":

> Basically, reader response theory differs most radically from previous theories about teaching literature in the degree of emphasis placed on the reader's response to an interpretation of the text . . . In reader response theory, the text's meaning is considered to reside in the "transaction" between the reader and the text, not from the text alone. . . .
>
> In practice, reader response theory considers very carefully how students respond intellectually and emotionally to the text . . . By validating students' responses, teachers can spark a lively discussion from which a careful literary analysis will flow. . . Rather than beginning with a discussion of symbolism or metaphor, for example, teachers should allow an exploration of these aspects to develop from students' own observations about the work. . . .
>
> The emphasis on getting students to respond to the literature doesn't mean that any response is as good as another. Students are continuously urged to return to the text to find validation for their views. (pp. 7, 8)

The key is to provide the students with an opportunity to examine literature from their own unique perspective, without imposing either the teacher's or a critic's interpretation on them. It is also a way to avoid having the students attempt to "please the teacher" by coming up with the "single correct answer." As anyone who appreciates the beauty and power of literature knows, good literature is multilayered; and as a result of that, the meaning inherent in a literary work is also multilayered. Thus, when students are prodded—as they often are in the so-called traditional classroom—to come up with the "correct answer" vis-à-vis the meaning of a literary work, the result is, more often than not, a perfunctory study that is bereft of real thinking and engagement by the student, not to mention lacking true insight into the literary work.

This is not to say that the teacher does not have a role in the process. In fact, the role of the teacher, as indicated by the above quote, is critical to the entire endeavor. The teacher's role is to serve as a facilitator of the discussion and to challenge the students to play off of one another's ideas and to plumb the work as deeply as possible by using their personal experiences and background knowledge to elucidate and expand on various points. It is also the teacher's job to introduce new ideas, thoughts, and angles in order to deepen everyone's thinking.

As previously mentioned, following the first reading of *Night*, I required each student to develop a second cluster and definition and that is followed by both small and large group discussions of various facets of the Holocaust and its definition. With very few exceptions, most of the second and third clusters by the students are more detailed, more accurate, and more sophisticated in their depiction of various facets and connections regarding various issues vis-à-vis the Holocaust.

Once the initial session is concluded, the students are required to read *Night* a second time, but instead of doing so in one fell swoop, they are assigned one chapter per evening and asked to examine the chapter more carefully in regard to both historical and literary concerns.

The Second Reading: A Historical/Literary Approach

Based on the inaccurate information and misconceptions (and, in certain cases, myths) evident in many of the students' first clusters (and in the second, to a lesser extent), I have come to the firm conclusion that there is a critical need to provide students with an accurate and fairly thorough historical overview of the history of the Holocaust *at some point during the study of a piece of Holocaust literature.* Without such knowledge, many, if not most students are liable to read a piece of literature and walk away ignorant about the historical context of the piece. The latter situation, of course, also impedes a more complete understanding of the piece of literature.

There are, of course, numerous ways to provide students with key historical background information about the Holocaust and the historical period specifically addressed in the piece of literature. Herein I shall delineate the various ways I have accomplished this task. Since I have generally had ample time (unlike many teachers who face extreme time constraints) to engage my students in such a study—either because I was teaching a semester-long course or engaged in an interdisciplinary unit that spanned 3 to 4 weeks—I have had the opportunity to use a multiple approach during each of my units of study. Those teachers who are facing extremely tight time constraints may choose to implement a truncated version of what I describe herein. That is fine, as long as the approach used is well thought out, thorough, and includes (1) a general overview of the Holocaust and (2) historical information that is germane to the specific literary work under study. In regard to the latter, for example, the teacher could focus on the Nazi policies and actions in the country or countries where the story is set and the reaction(s) of the local populace. Thus, in the case of *Night*, the students would examine the situation in Hungary and Poland in 1944. They might also examine issues that are central to the larger story, such as the difference between concentration and death camps or the purpose and horrific reality of the death marches.

I should note that when I first began teaching *Night* to high school students, which was in 1978, I did very little in the way of preparing the students to understand or appreciate the historical context germane to the period. Rather, during the course of our class discussions I added bits and pieces of information as the need arose. Rather quickly, though, I came to the conclusion that I needed to be more systematic and thorough in providing such a context.

In more recent years, the initial activity my students engage in during this section of the study is an examination of an accurate and comprehensive chronology of the Holocaust period. Useful chronologies for this activity can be found in the *Encyclopedia of the Holocaust*, edited by Israel Gutman (New York: Macmillan, 1990, pp. 1759–1782); *Teaching about the Holocaust: A Resource Book for Educators* (Washington, D.C.: United States Holocaust Memorial Museum, 1994, pp. 111–115); and *Teaching and Studying the Holocaust*, edited by Samuel Totten and Stephen Feinberg (Boston: Allyn and Bacon, 2001). I begin by providing each student with a copy of a chronology (and personally, I prefer the more concise but still fairly comprehensive chronologies such as those found in the latter two works), and ask each student to read carefully over the chronology, noting any *significant patterns* they come across. They are directed to jot down their observations in order to share and discuss them both in small and large groups. After 10 minutes or so, I organize the class into small groups (a minimum of three students, and generally no more than four) and ask each group to share and discuss its insights. Prior to initiating the discussion, I have an individual in each group volunteer to serve as a recorder whose task is to write down the most salient points the group makes and to note agreements, disagreements, and whether the group members come to a consensus or not in regard to whether there are, in fact, any notable patterns. They are also required to discuss the significance of such patterns. Once the small groups have concluded their discussions, we meet again as an entire class and discuss the various groups' findings. Generally, this is done by having one group's recorder report on his or her group's discussion, and as he or she reports, the rest of the class members are free to concur or disagree with a point, posit questions, play the devil's advocate, ask for clarification, and so forth. It is always understood that the recorder is not solely responsible for answering the questions or addressing any challenges but rather that all of the members of his or her group are expected to share the responsibility of engaging in the larger discussion. Once one group has shared its findings and the class discussion is exhausted, we move on to the next group. Invariably, a major finding and discussion point revolves around the incremental nature of the Nazi assault against the Jews, beginning in 1933 and moving inexorably toward ever more drastic measures. We also discuss what such a pattern meant for individual Jews, the community of Jews, non-Jews, and the larger world. In regard to the latter, students begin to discuss the fact that if someone—particularly the leaders and citizens of free nations—had spoken out early on in an urgent and persistent fashion, then possibly something could have been done to have prevented the most drastic actions of all by the Nazis—the mass extermination of millions. This exercise is absolutely essential in setting the stage for what Wiesel, his family and community, and the Jewish people faced in 1944 at the hands of the Nazis. Indeed, it prevents the students from studying the abject horror of the Holocaust in a vacuum in which they may mistakenly be led to believe that the genocide of the Jews by the Nazis simply erupted out of nowhere.

As the students read and discuss the historical essays (see below) and then read *Night* for a second time, they take part in the development of "their own" chronology of the Holocaust period. More specifically, a long piece of butcher paper is stretched along one wall. On the lefthand side of the paper the date 1933 is written (it is important to leave ample space between the edge of the paper and the date, for that way much earlier events, such as the Versailles Treaty of 1919, can be placed on the chart), and on the righthand side is placed the date 1945 (again, it is important to leave space between the date and the very edge of the paper). As various key incidents, events, decisions, promulgations, and dates come up in our discussion (e.g., the Enabling Law, the Nuremberg Laws, Kristallnacht, the Wannsee Conference), the entire class adds them to the chronology, always noting the exact day(s) and year(s). Such a strategy provides the students with a visual aid that assists them to place the events in *Night* and various aspects of the history in a meaningful context. It also provides them with an opportunity to revisit certain key issues throughout the study.[5]

It is during the reading of the historical essays and the second reading of *Night* that the students are required to maintain a "learning log." Succinctly stated, a learning log is a formal running record of the student's thoughts, insights, comments, feelings, and questions vis-à-vis the readings, class discussions, and class activities. Each student is given a copy of the following directions to follow in developing his or her learning log:

As the co-directors of a noted Holocaust education program, Facing History and Ourselves, observe: "Daily . . . writings can chart for each student the process and progress of the course [and] illuminate his or her response to it . . . the journal becomes a means for each student . . . to record ongoing encounters with the many issues that emerge from the course. As students make their way into this history, they will in effect be bearing witness to their own living history, responding to their own growth and change during the course.

"Every individual perceives the world through his or her own experiences and understanding. A student's insights, questions, and memories have an internal reality that is both unique and valuable. If the student can record these perceptions with honesty he or she will have taken an important step toward self-understanding. What the students choose to confront in their journals can tell them much about who they are." (Strom and Parsons, 1982, p. 25)

1. Be sure to place the date and a heading at the top of each response/entry. The heading may simply be a single word that signifies what the entry is about, along with the title of the essay or chapter to which you are responding

2. Keep a daily learning log/journal. In doing so, you may include virtually anything you wish about your study of the Holocaust, in general, and *Night*, in particular. That is, you may focus on anything from what you are learning to your thoughts and feelings about what you are learning. For example, you may wish to: write about something new you learned in class or in a reading; (b) comment on something that took place in class or something you came across in your reading that was particularly thought-provoking or "eye-opening"; (c) remark on new insights you gleaned from a class session or reading; (d) comment on something you do not understand or want to understand in more depth; (e) address something you disagree with that cropped up in your reading, or took place or was commented on in class by the instructor or a fellow student; (f) provide insights as to how a certain class session could have been altered in such a way to have made it more engaging or thought-provoking for you; and (g) reflect on the value of what you are learning. In other words, it is your journal and you are welcome and encouraged to address any issue you wish that is germane to this course and the study of *Night* and the Holocaust.

3. Periodically, Dr. Totten may posit a question regarding some aspect of *Night* or the Holocaust and ask each student to respond to it in his learning log. Likewise, he may write a quote on the board from *Night*—which may stand by itself or be accompanied by a question—and ask each student to respond to the quote and/or the quote and the question. When responding to the quotes, be sure to copy the quote into your learning log and then respond to it. You are free to respond to the quotations or questions in any way you wish, and this may include relating it to other aspects of the memoir or another piece of Holocaust literature, relating it to some aspect of the history we've studied, positing your own questions, etc.

Please note that during the course of reading *Night* for a second time, you will be given six (6) questions per chapter to address in some detail in your log. One question will deal with the history or literary aspects of the memoir and one will require you to respond in a personal way to the information in the chapter.

4. Dr. Totten will read the journals. In doing so, he will write comments in response to your various entries. In certain cases, he may raise a question(s). Once you get your learning log back, you should make a point of answering/addressing the question(s) he raises in a fair amount of detail.

5. Since it is hoped that the learning log will become a reflective experience for you and serve as a means of dialogue between you and Dr. Totten, you should also feel free to raise questions for Dr. Totten to address as well.

6. The emphasis in the learning log should be on quality versus quantity. That is, a shorter entry that reflects high quality of thought and a genuine effort to wrestle with key issues and feelings is more highly valued than a longer entry that is bereft of much thought.

As mentioned above, during the course of reading *Night*, the students are given six questions per chapter to respond to in their log—four of the questions are in the cognitive domain (e.g., posited at the highest levels of the domain—analysis, synthesis, and/or evaluation) and two in the affective domain (e.g., dealing with emotions, feelings, beliefs). Each year, certain questions are culled out and new questions are added; so the set of questions students address from year to year are generally different.

The questions are also used as "discussion starters" during subsequent class sessions. Some of the questions deal with incidents in the story, while others may deal with certain literary conventions such as the previously mentioned issue of heightened language, biblical allusions, inverted symbolism, invented dialogue, etc.

Early on in developing this unit, I decided that it would be both expeditious and valuable to set the stage by giving a short lecture on the whos, whats, wheres, whens, and whys of the Holocaust and the specific situation faced by Hungary and Hungarian Jews during the Holocaust. In general, I avoid lecturing, for I favor a more interactive approach; but since the rest of the unit of study is highly interactive I have no problem giving a lecture in this situation. To prepare the lecture, I generally obtain information from a variety of scholarly books by some of the most noted Holocaust scholars. These include, but are not limited to, Lucy S. Dawidowicz's *The War Against the Jews 1933–1945* (New York: Bantam Books, 1986); *A History of the Holocaust* by Yehuda Bauer (Danbury, Conn.: Franklin Watts, 1982); and Raul Hilberg's *The Destruction of the European Jews* (New York: Holmes & Meier, 1985). While this approach brought about a more informed discussion of *Night*, I still felt that more could and should be done to provide a solid historical context. Thus, during the teaching of subsequent units on *Night*, I combined the aforementioned lecture with the viewing of *Genocide, 1941–1945*. The film addresses the destruction of the European Jewry through the use of archival footage and the testimonies of victims, perpetrators, and bystanders. *Genocide 1941–1945*, which is part of the World at War series, is currently one of the best films available for providing a general overview of the Holocaust. Not only is it readily available, but it is a film that is historically accurate, highly engaging, and readily understood by upper-level secondary-school students. *I should note that I would never be satisfied simply showing this film and skipping the above-mentioned lecture or the readings to which the students read and respond.* That is due to the fact that not only do I wish to provide the students with an overview of the Holocaust (which the film *Genocide* does fairly well), but I also find it crucial to provide the students with specific information regarding the fate of the Hungarian Jews, which Elie Wiesel's family and community were a part of, as well as, for example, specifics regarding the deportations, life and death in Auschwitz, and the death marches. In order to provide the latter information, both the lecture and the readings are a necessity.[6]

Finally, in addition to the aforementioned lecture and the film, I have added another component that requires the students to read and respond to a series of key essays, chapters, and/or articles. Generally, I have the students read and respond to one or two general pieces on the Holocaust and two pieces on the fate of the Jews in Hungary during the Holocaust. These readings are to be completed *prior* to my lecture and the viewing of *Genocide*. Over the years, the exact articles and essays have changed, which is due to the fad that as new books, essays, and articles have appeared, I have made an attempt to locate and use ever more readable pieces that provide a fairly succinct but still thorough overview of major issues vis-à-vis the Holocaust and/or the fate of the Hungarian Jews. Over the years I have used, in various combinations and at different points in time, the following pieces, all of which, "in their own way," have proved useful and informative: Chapter 1, "Precedents" in *The Destruction of the European Jews* by Raul Hilberg (which examines the long, sordid history of antisemitism through time, and the three successive goals of anti-Jewish administrators through the ages: "You have no right to live among us as Jews; You have no right to live among us; You have no right to live" [Hilberg, 1985, p. 8]); "The Evolution of Nazi Jewish Policy, 1933–1938" and "The Final Solution" in *A History of the Holocaust* by Yehuda Bauer; Donald Niewyk's "Holocaust: Genocide of the Jews" (which provides a short but solid overview of key aspects of the Holocaust, including key historical trends that combined to make the Holocaust possible); Randolph L. Braham's "Hungary—Jews During the Holocaust"; György Ranki's "Hungary—General Survey"; and various sections in *The World Must Know: The History of the Holocaust as Told in the United States Holocaust Memorial Museum* by Michael Berenbaum.

In order to allow ample time for the students to read such pieces, I assign them for homework over a 4-day period—Thursday, Friday, Saturday, and Sunday. I inform the students that they are expected to use part of each day, or at least what is comparable time to using a part of all 4 days, to complete the reading assignment.

Teachers who are limited by time need to examine the aforementioned essays as well as others in order to ascertain those that are most ideal for their own situation. That said, if a teacher has a fair amount of time to dedicate to such a study—as well as the financial support to purchase a set of books for the purpose of providing a historical overview—then I strongly recommend that they consider using Michael Berenbaum's *The World Must Know: The History of the Holocaust as Told in the United States Holocaust Memorial Museum* (Boston: Little, Brown, 1993). This book, which was written by the former director of research at the United States Holocaust Memorial Museum, was developed for the general reader and is ideal for use with a secondary level student audience. Not only is it accurate in its portrayal of the history, but it is highly readable, packed with photographs that complement the text, and includes fascinating and informative excerpts from first-person accounts.

Once the students have read the articles, listened to the lecture, and viewed the film, we begin to read and discuss *Night* a second time. As we discuss it, we use the history the students recently learned in order to deepen their understanding of Wiesel's experiences. At one and the same time, we also revisit many of the issues raised during our initial reading of the book. Throughout our discussion, a host of issues, topics, and questions posited by the students provoked deep thought and passionate response. Among some of the many issues and topics that were addressed during one such discussion were the following:

(1) The fact that Wiesel repeatedly mentions that following extremely traumatic incidents, everything in Sighet eventually went back to "normal" (e.g., "Then one day they expelled all foreign Jews from Sighet . . . Several days passed. Several weeks. Several months. Life had returned to normal" [Wiesel, 1969, p. 15]; Moché, a foreign Jew who had been deported, returned to Sighet and reported that "The Jews [who were deported] were made to dig huge graves. And when they had finished their work, the Gestapo began theirs. Without passion, without haste, they slighted their prisoners . . . . Babies were thrown into the air and the machine gunners used them as targets . . . People refused not only to believe his stories, but even to listen to them. . . . That was toward the end of 1942. Afterward life returned to normal") ([pp. 15, 16, 17]). These and other examples of "returning to normality" moved the students to talk about a host of related issues, including the fact that (a) even in abnormal times, many people feel compelled to lead as normal lives as possible; (b) that leading a "normal" life under such circumstances constituted a classic case of denial of the facts; (c) that as long as individuals were not personally attacked, they found a way to inch back to "normalcy"; (d) that seeking "normalcy" was, in part, the downfall of the Sighet Jews; and (e) that the Nazis symbolized "abnormalcy" but few in the world seemed to appreciate just how abnormal their abnormalcy was.

(2) Tied directly to the latter point, almost all of the students were shaken by the following statement in Chapter 1 of *Night:* "Was he [Hitler] going to wipe out a whole people? Could he exterminate a population scattered throughout so many countries? So many millions! What methods could he use? And in the middle of the twentieth century?" (p. 17). Here the students talked about how, at one time in the history of humanity, in fact just under 60 years ago, people could not even imagine something like the mass murder of millions, that of an entire people. What particularly disturbed the students is that today such a horror is "accepted as a given," not even questioned, at least in regard to whether it is possible or not. As one student said, quietly and with sadness, "We live in a very different world today." Here, we also talked about the methods of the mass killing and I gave a mini-lecture on the Nazis' experimentation with mass murder, from the shooting of hundreds of thousands of Jews by the Einsatzgruppen in the Soviet Union beginning on June 22, 1941 to the killing of 600 Soviet prisoners of war on September 3, 1941, in a hermetically sealed cell into which crystals of Zyklon B gas were thrown, to the development and use of gas vans, and finally the refinement of the killing process with the development of the gas chambers and crematoria (Arad, 1990, pp. 461–463). Here, too, we branched off into a discussion of

the concepts of "progress" and "civilized," and what the two mean in a world where weapons of mass destruction are a given and are within an arm's reach of many who distrust, if not detest, "the other."

(3) Speaking about the fate of the Jews at the hands of the Nazis, Wiesel observes early on that "There was no longer any questions of wealth, of social distinction, and importance, only people all condemned to the same fate" (p. 31). This provoked ample discussion about the Nazis' philosophy, goals, and treatment of the Jews. Here I incorporated information about the racial philosophy of the Nazis and the Nuremberg Laws. (For an excellent overview of the racial policies of the Nazis, see "Racism" by George Mosse in the *Encyclopedia of the Holocaust,* and for a succinct but solid overview of the Nuremberg Race Laws, see "Nuremberg Laws" by David Bankier in the *Encyclopedia of the Holocaust.*) During this same discussion, I brought in Wiesel's (1979b) assertion, which he made years after he wrote *Night,* that "While not all victims [of the Nazis] were Jews, all Jews were victims, destined for annihilation solely because they were born Jewish. They were doomed not because of something they had done or proclaimed or acquired but because of who they were: sons and daughters of the Jewish people" (p. iii). I also shared this similar but somewhat different observation of Wiesel's with the students: "Their [the Jews] being was the target to be destroyed. All Jews everywhere shared the same fate, old and young, rich and poor, beggars and princes, children and their grandparents, all had to disappear" (Wiesel, 1977, p. 6).

(4) The issue of the Nazis holding an entire group of people or an entire community responsible for the single action of an individual also resulted in a lengthy discussion. This was prompted by Wiesel's statement regarding the deportations, during which a German officer warned those being crammed into a railway car: "There are eighty of you in the wagon ... If anyone is missing, you'll all be shot, like dogs" (p. 34). This issue of "collective responsibility" and the fear it must have induced in people segued into a discussion about resistance and just how difficult it would be to decide to resist in light of the fact that one's actions could result in the deaths of so many others. Here I introduce the fate of Lidice, a village in Czechoslovakia, 10 miles from Prague, that was completely annihilated by the Germans during World War II. In retaliation for the assassination of Reinhard Heydrich, a high-ranking Nazi, by Czech resistance fighters, "early in the morning of June 10, 1942, all the inhabitants of the village of Lidice were taken out of their homes, and all the men in the village—192 in all—were killed, as were 71 women. The remaining women, numbering 198, were imprisoned in the Ravensbrück concentration camp.... Of the 98 children who had been 'put into educational institutions,' no more than 16 survived.... Lidice was [then] razed to the ground, the official reason being that the villagers had helped the assassins—an allegation that had no basis in fact—and that two men from Lidice serving with the

Czech forces in Britain had assured the parachutists that they could trust the villagers" (Goshen, 1990, pp. 870, 871, 872).

Here, too, I draw the students' attention to the issue of choiceless choices. In speaking of the Holocaust and those options that the victims were given by the Nazis, Langer (1995) describes *choiceless choices* as being one where "whatever you choose somebody loses" (p. 46). Elsewhere Langer (1982) describes *choiceless choices* as those "where crucial decisions did not reflect options between life and death, but between one form of abnormal response and another, both imposed by a situation that was in no way of the victim's own choosing" (p. 72). Such discussions as these serve to complicate, in the best sense of the word, the students' thinking about this history and what it meant to be caught up in the maw of the Nazis.

(5) Throughout the discussion of *Night,* the students, prompted by Wiesel's comments and their own questioning, returned time and again to the issue of "silence"—the silence of the world and the silence of God. Two of the passages that provoked heated discussion were as follows:

> Not far from us, flames were leaping up from a ditch, gigantic flames. They were burning something. A lorry drew up at the pit and delivered its load—little children. Babies! Yes, I saw it—saw it with my own eyes . . . those children in the flames. . . . I pinched my face. Was I still alive? Was I awake? I could not believe it. How could it be possible for them to burn people, children, and for the world to keep silent? (Wiesel, 1969, p. 42)

And:

> For the first time, I felt revolt rise up in me. Why should I bless His name? The Eternal, Lord of the Universe, the All-Powerful and Terrible, was silent. (Wiesel, 1969, p. 43)

(6) After entering Auschwitz, Wiesel states that "I became A–7713. After that I had no other name" (Wiesel, 1969, p. 53). After we discuss what it means to lose one's name and to be referred to as a number, I introduce a poster that is comprised solely of the shoes of hundreds of victims of the Holocaust. It is one poster in a set developed by the United States Holocaust Memorial Museum. I hold the poster in front of the class and ask the students to simply describe what they see. Slowly but then with more confidence as different students share their observations, the students call out such comments as: "All types of shoes!"; "Mounds of shoes"; "Battered shoes, fancy shoes, tiny shoes"; "Men's and women's and baby's shoes"; "Twisted shoes"; "Pairs of shoes and shoes without the other pair"; "Shoes with no feet, no bodies"; "Shoes of rich

people and possibly poor people"; "Shoes with buckles." Next, I ask, "What is the importance of shoes in a person's life?" Here the students respond with comments like: "They tell whether you're 'with it' or 'not'"; "Whether you're a man, woman, teenager, baby or . . ."; "Not always," responds another student, "'cause look at how many old people wear tennis shoes today"; "They tell something about your personality"; "They're individual, like you, as a person"; and so on and so forth. Next, I posit this question: "What do these shoes make you think about when you think about the Holocaust?" Here the students answer with statements like: "The piles of dead in photographs you often see"; "They're discarded, just like the victims were"; "They're all shoes but different types and different ages and different styles, just like the people who were murdered"; "They're without names"; "Just as those murdered in the death camps never received a proper burial, the shoes have just been discarded helter-skelter." This discussion generally spans at least half a period or more, and probes into a host of issues regarding identity and the ramifications of being denied one's identity and why the Nazis set out to accomplish such a goal in the camps.

(7) Ultimately, we confronted the concept of theodicy (e.g., the issue of God's goodness and omnipotence in view of the existence of evil in the world), not a word the students knew but one they broached in their own words, and which at least one student had broached in her letter to Wiesel. An explosion of discussion erupted around this concept when the students read about the hanging of a young boy by the Nazis:

> One day when we came back from work, we saw three gallows rearing up in the assembly place . . . Roll call. SS all round us, machine guns trained: the traditional ceremony. Three victims in chains—and one of the them [a little boy]. The head of the camp read the verdict. All eyes were on the child . . . The three necks were placed at the same moment within the noose . . . "Where is God? Where is He?" Someone behind me asked. . . . I heard a voice within me answer him: "Where is He? Here He is. He is hanging here on this gallows. . . ." (Wiesel, 1969, pp. 75, 76).

The issues mentioned above are just a few of the many issues we addressed as we read and discussed *Night*. To provide a description of the complete discussion would consume a small book. Still, what has been delineated here provides key insights into the issues the students raised and how I made a constant attempt to introduce key aspects of the history in order to deepen the students' understanding of the Holocaust and what the targeted people faced at the hands of the Nazis.

As mentioned earlier, there are, obviously, innumerable ways teachers and their students could approach the study of *Night,* but one method that is particularly intriguing has been developed by Grace Caporino, a long-time Holocaust educator and English teacher at Carmel High School in Carmel, New York. More specifically, she notes that "in searching for a way to help students reach beyond their own immediate worlds and relate to Holocaust readings [not necessarily *Night*], I have delineated five thematic categories that can frame readings and can help them understand the interactions of the different categories. I outline these categories as victim, perpetrator, bystander, collaborator, and rescuer . . . Different works lend themselves to the exploration of the categories" (Caporino, 1999, p. 227). For a discussion as to how Caporino (1999) uses this approach with a poem about the Holocaust, see her essay "Teaching the Holocaust in the English Classroom." Obviously, teachers will have to adapt such an approach in various ways to make it useful for teaching a memoir.

Dr. William Fernekes, a social studies supervisor and teacher at Hunterdon Central Regional High School in Flemington, New Jersey has his students, in part, examine works of literature via the history of antisemitism and the four stages of destruction of the Jews that historian Raul Hilberg (1985) delineates in his *The Destruction of European Jewry:* definition, expropriation, concentration, and annihilation. Writing about the issues of definition, expropriation, concentration, and annihilation in his book *The World Must Know: The History of the Holocaust as Told in the United States Holocaust Memorial Museum,* Michael Berenbaum notes that:

> First Jews were categorized; then civil liberties were restricted and property confiscated. Next, Jews were dismissed from universities and civil service jobs, which often included school teaching, and were barred from the professions. Jewish businesses were taken over and Aryanized. Jews were then isolated, forced to wear the Jewish star and forbidden to use public facilities.
>
> Finally, Jews were assembled, first, in large cities and then in transit camps. From 1942 on, they were deported from these transit camps to the death camp in the east. (p. 68)

To deepen one's understanding and key insights into the four stages, teachers should obtain copies of the student edition of Hilberg's *The Destruction of European Jewry* or the complete three-volume set by the same name. Again, Michael Berenbaum's *The World Must Know: The History of the Holocaust as Told in the United States Holocaust Memorial Museum* is worth consulting as well, particularly in light of the fact that it delineates the four stages in a highly readable manner and in a way that is understandable to most upper-level secondary-level students.

Concluding Activities

For those teachers and students who have the time and inclination, there are numerous concluding and/or extension activities that can further the students' understanding both of Elie Wiesel's work and of the Holocaust. What is highlighted here are two activities that the author has used with a great deal of success.

A final essay examination could require students to respond to one of the following quotes by Elie Wiesel:

> The Nazis' aim was to make the Jewish universe shrink—from town to neighborhood to street, from street to house, from house to room, from room to garret, from garret to cattle car, from cattle car to gas chamber.
>
> And they did the same to the individual—separated from his or her community, then from his or her family, then from his or [sic] identity, eventually becoming a work permit, then a number, until the number itself was turned into ashes. (Wiesel, 1984, p. 1)

> It was easier for a camp inmate then to imagine himself or herself free than for a free man or a free woman to imagine himself or herself today in the victim's predicament. Imagination fails us. Usually in literature imagination precedes reality, but this time reality preceded imagination. (Wiesel, 1978, p. 270)

> I've got more faith in Hitler than in anyone else. He's the only one who's kept his promises, all his promises, to the Jewish people. (Wiesel, 1969, p. 92, *Night*)

> Let us remember that what Nazism did to its Jewish victims was considered to be legal. It was legal to imprison political adversaries, it was legal to practice euthanasia on mentally retarded patients, it was legal to hunt down and execute resistance-fighters, it was legal—and commendable—to push Jews into ghettos to torment them, to torture them, to gas them, to burn them: everything was done with so-called due process, according to German law. That means: the Nazis had corrupted the law itself. They made it into a weapon against humanity. Remember that it can be done—for they did it. The law itself became immoral. Inhuman. (Wiesel, 1982, p. 9)

In responding to one of the quotes, the students could address the validity and significance of the idea expressed in the quote and use specific examples and additional quotes from Wiesel's *Night* to support their position and arguments.

As an extra-credit extension activity, students could be provided with the opportunity to respond to *Night* in an artistic manner. They should be informed that their response could take any form they wish, including but not limited to the following: a musical composition, a painting, a drawing, a choreographed dance, a collage, a piece of sculpture, a mobile, a bulletin board display, or a mural.[7]

Conclusion

It is a cliché that each time a reader returns to a good piece of literature he or she discovers new and different insights; but I must say that—at least for me—in the case of *Night*, it is the truth. Indeed, each and every time I reread *Night* and assist my students in grappling with Wiesel's story and the ramifications that the Holocaust has for humanity today, I leave with a greater appreciation of the work.

Both during and following each reading I am left pondering a whole host of issues, my mind swimming with thoughts about that which makes us human and inhuman, that which constitutes a truly civilized society, and what it means to live in a world where genocide is a "fact of life." The latter invariably finds me pondering Wiesel's comment, not made in *Night* but elsewhere: "The opposite of goodness is not evil; it is indifference to evil." Ultimately, it is my ardent hope that my students also leave the study pondering—hard and long—their own musings.

Notes

1. Though Hungarian Jews faced discrimination and persecution, Hungarian Jews escaped the "final solution" (e.g., systematic killing) until the Germans invaded in March of 1944. In April the Jews were ghettoized and between May 15th and July 8th, 1944—a full eighteen months after the destruction of Polish Jewry—437,402 Jews were deported on 148 trains to Auschwitz. Wiesel and his family were among the deportees.

2. Readers interested in learning more about Wiesel's life should read his *All Rivers Run to the Sea: Memoirs*. New York: Schocken Books, 1995. Another book that provides valuable insights into Wiesel as a person and a writer is *Harry James Cargas in Conversation with Elie Wiesel*. New York: Paulist Press, 1976.

3. For some excellent and thought-provoking discussions by classroom teachers concerning the clustering method, see Carol Booth Olson's *Practical Ideas for Teaching Writing as a Process*. Sacramento, Cal.: California State Department of Education, 1987.

4. For an interesting discussion of how to incorporate multiple intelligences into the classroom, also see Thomas Armstrong's *Multiple Intelligences in the Classroom*. Alexandria, Va.: Association for Supervision and Curriculum Development, 1994.

5. This idea was originated by Stephen Feinberg, a long-time history teacher at Wayland Middle School, who now works at the United States Holocaust Memorial Museum.

6. *Genocide, 1941–1945* is available from Arts and Entertainment, 800-423-1212 or write A & E Home Video, P.O. Box 2284, South Burlington, VT 05407. An excellent annotated bibliography for locating historically accurate films on a wide range of issues germane to the Holocaust is the United States Holocaust Memorial Museum's (USHMM) *Annotated Videography*. For a copy, contact the USHMM's Education Department at 100 Raoul Wallenberg Place SW, Washington, D.C. 20024.

7. For additional ideas for extension activities, see. Samuel Totten's "Teaching Holocaust Literature" in Samuel Totten and Stephen Feinberg (Eds.), *Teaching and Studying the Holocaust* (Boston: Allyn and Bacon, 2001.)

WORKS CITED

Arad, Yitzhak. (1990). "Extermination Camps." In Israel Gutman (Ed.), *Encyclopedia of the Holocaust* (pp. 461–463). New York: Macmillan Publishing.

Armstrong, Thomas. (1994). *Multiple Intelligences in the Classroom*. Alexandria, Va.: Association for Supervision and Curriculum Development.

Bankier, David. (1990). "Nuremberg Laws." In Israel Gutman (Ed.), *Encyclopedia of the Holocaust* (pp. 1076–1077). New York: Macmillan Publishing.

Bauer, Yehuda. (1982). *A History of the Holocaust*. Danbury, Conn.: Franklin Watts.

Berger, Joseph. (1986, October 15). "A Witness to Evil: Eliezer Wiesel." *The New York Times*, p. 4.

Braham, Randolph L. (1990). "Hungary—Jews During the Holocaust." In Israel Gutman (Ed.), *Encyclopedia of the Holocaust* (pp. 698–703). New York: Macmillan Publishing.

Braham, Randolph L. (1981). "What Did They Know and When?" In Yehuda Bauer and Nathan Rotenstreich (Eds.), *The Holocaust as Historical Experience: Essays and a Discussion* (pp. 109–131). New York: Holmes & Meier Publishers. [A more detailed version of this essay appears in Braham's *The Politics of Genocide*. New York: Columbia University Press, 1981.]

Brown, Robert McAfee. (1979, Spring). "The Moral Society and the Work of Elie Wiesel." *Face to Face: An Interreligious Bulletin* (Special Issue: "Building a Moral Society: Aspects of Elie Wiesel's Work"). Volume 6, pp. 22–27.

Cargas, Harry James. (1976). *Harry James Cargas in Conversation with Elie Wiesel*. New York: Paulist Press.

Caporino, Grace. (1999). "Teaching the Holocaust in the English Classroom: Hearing the Voices, Touching the History," In Carol Danks and Leatrice B. Rabinsky (Eds.), *Teaching for a Tolerant World: Grades 9–12: Essays and Resources* (pp. 218–234). Urbana, IL: National Council of Teachers of English.

Dawidowicz, Lucy S. (1986). *The War Against the Jews 1933–1945*. New York: Bantam Books.

Eckardt, Alice L. (1979, Spring). "Rebel Against God." *Face to Face: An Interreligious Bulletin* [Special Issue: "Building a Moral Society: Aspects of Elie Wiesel's Work"]. Volume 6, pp. 18–20.

Ezrahi, Sidra DeKoven. (1982). *By Words Alone: The Holocaust in Literature*. Chicago, IL: The University of Chicago Press.

Freedman, Samuel. (1983, October 23). "Bearing Witness: The Life and Work of Elie Wiesel." *The New York Times Magazine*, pp. 32–36, 40, 65–69.

Gardner, Howard, (1983). *Frames of Mind: The Theory of Multiple Intelligences*. New York: Basic Books.

Gardner, Howard. (1993). *Multiple Intelligences: The Theory in Practice*. New York: Basic Books.

Gates, E. Nathaniel. (Ed.) (1994). *The Concept of "Race" in Natural and Social Science*. New York: Garland Publishing.

Goshen, Seev. (1990). "Lidice." In Israel Gutman (Ed.), *Encyclopedia of the Holocaust* (pp. 870–872). New York: Macmillan Publishing.

Hilberg, Raul. (1985). *The Destruction of European Jewry*. "Revised and Definitive Edition." Three Volumes. New York: Holmes & Meier.

Hilberg, Raul. (1985). *The Destruction of the European Jews—Student Edition*. New York: Holmes & Meier.

Kanfer, Stefan. (1985). "Author, Teacher, Witness; Holocaust Survivor Elie Wiesel Speaks for the Silent." *Time*, March 18, pp. 79, 90.

Langer, Lawrence L. (1982). *Versions of Survival: The Holocaust and the Human Spirit*. Albany: State University of New York Press.

Langer, Lawrence L. (1995). *Admitting the Holocaust: Collected Essays*. New York: Oxford University Press.

Markham, James M. (1986, October 15). "Elie Wiesel Gets Nobel for Peace as 'Messenger'." *The New York Times*, pp. 1, 4.

Montagu, Ashley. (1964). *Man's Most Dangerous Myth: The Fallacy of Race*. Cleveland and New York: The World Publishing Company.

Mosse, George. (1990). "Racism." In Israel Gutman (Ed.), *Encyclopedia of the Holocaust* (pp. 1206–1217). New York: Macmillan Publishing.

Niewyk, Donald. (1995). "Holocaust: Genocide of the Jews." In Samuel Totten, William S. Parsons, and Israel W. Charny (Eds.), *Genocide in the Twentieth Century; Critical Essays and Eyewitness Accounts* (pp. 167–207). New York: Garland Publishing, Inc.

O'Brien, Michael. (1987). "Propagating Clusters." In Carol Booth Olson (Ed.), *Practical Ideas for Teaching Writing as a Process* (p. 25). Sacramento, CA: California State Department of Education.

O'Neill, John. (1994). "Rewriting the Book on Literature: Changes Sought in How Literature Is Taught, What Students Read." *ASCD Curriculum Update* (June): 7, 8.

Parsons, William S., & Totten, Samuel. (1993). *Guidelines for Teaching About the Holocaust*. Washington, D.C.: United States Holocaust Memorial Museum.

Ranki, György. (1990). "Hungary—General Survey." In Israel Gutman (Ed.), *Encyclopedia of the Holocaust* (pp. 693–698). New York: Macmillan Publishing.

Rico, Gabrielle. (1987). "Clustering: A Prewriting Process." In Carol Booth Olson (Ed.), *Practical Ideas for Teaching Writing as a Process* (pp. 17–20). Sacramento, CA: California State Department of Education.

Rosenfeld, Alvin, and Greenberg, Irving. (Eds.). (1976). *Confronting the Holocaust: The Impact of Elie Wiesel*. Bloomington: Indiana University Press.

Strom, Margot Stern, & Parsons, William S. (1982). *Facing History and Ourselves: Holocaust and Human Behavior*. Watertown, MA: Intentional Educations, Inc.

United States Holocaust Memorial Museum. (1994). *Teaching About the Holocaust: A Resource Book for Educators*. Washington, D.C.: Author.

Wiesel, Elie. (1969). *Night*. New York: Avon Books.

Wiesel, Elie. (1977). "The Holocaust as Literary Expression." Speech. 15 pages.

Wiesel, Elie. (1978, April). "Then and Now: The Experiences of a Teacher." *Social Education*, Volume 42 Number 4, pp. 266–271.

Wiesel, Elie. (1979a, Spring). "A Personal Response." *Face to Face: An Interreligious Bulletin* [Special Issue: "Building a Moral Society: Aspects of Elie Wiesel's Work"]. Volume 6, pp. 35–37.

Wiesel, Elie. (1979b). "Preface." *Report to the President*. Washington, D.C.: President's Commission on the Holocaust.

Wiesel, Elie. (1982, May-June). "Address of the Chairman of the U.S. Holocaust Council." *Martyrdom and Resistance*, p. 9.

Wiesel, Elie. (1984, August 19). "All Was Lost, Yet Something Was Preserved. A Review of The Chronicle of the Lodz Ghetto, 1941–1944." *The New York Times Book Review*, p. 1.

Wiesel, Elie. (1990). *From the Kingdom of Memory: Reminiscences*. New York: Schocken Books.

Wiesel, Elie. (1995a). *All Rivers Run to the Sea: Memoirs*. New York: Schocken Books.

Wiesel, Elie. (1995b, August 27). "The Decision—An Excerpt from *All Rivers Run to the Sea*—From the New Autobiography by Elie Wiesel." *Parade Magazine*, pp. 4–6.

SARA R. HOROWITZ

Boyhood Unraveled: Elie Wiesel's Night (1960)

A slender but powerful volume, Elie Wiesel's autobiographical *Night* recounts the details of life and death during the Holocaust from a teenage boy's perspective. One of the most widely read books about the Nazi genocide, *Night* begins in 1941, when Eliezer was a child of twelve living in the Transylvania region of what was then Hungary, and concludes with his liberation from Buchenwald. The memoir focuses on one year's passage—from the spring of 1944, when Germany invaded Hungary, until the German defeat in the spring of 1945, and liberation.

The German entry into Sighet catapulted Eliezer from an ordinary life into a nightmarish world of ghettos, slave labor, concentration camps, and death. Early on, Wiesel makes clear the role that gender played for Jews during the Holocaust. On the one hand, Jewish men and women were equally targeted by Nazi genocide. Enduring or perishing under inhumane conditions, both faced the privations of the ghetto, the degradation of the camps, and the death sentence. On the other hand, men and women suffered in different ways, with different chances for survival. Upon being herded out from the trains, the Jews are divided according to gender, men separated from women. Abruptly and brutally, the boy loses contact with his mother. As Eliezer's father takes his son's hand, the boy sees her walk off with his younger sister. "I did not know that in that time, at that place, I was parting

Women in Literature: Reading through the Lens of Gender, eds. Jerilyn Fisher, and Ellen S. Silber (Westport, Conn.: Greenwood Press, 2003): pp. 211–214. Copyright © 2003 Greenwood Press.

from my mother and Tzipora forever" (27). Indeed, he later learns, they were taken immediately to the gas chambers and murdered.

This separation by gender begins the process called *selection*, in which Nazi S.S. officials "select" which Jews are to be killed, and which will be subjected to hard labor and unspeakable conditions until they die. Only those arrivals who appear strong enough to endure slave labor are left alive. One's chances of surviving the first selection were linked to both age and gender. A seasoned prisoner tells Eliezer and his father to lie about their ages. Eliezer must say he is eighteen, rather than fifteen, and his father must say he is forty, rather than fifty. Younger boys and girls are deemed not fit for work, and hence not fit for living. They accompany their mothers, and—along with women who arrive pregnant—are sent directly to the gas chambers. Thus, as Eliezer's mother is led away with her youngest daughter, the two elder ones join the women's camp (and survive the war, as Wiesel indicates elsewhere). Ironically, this unimaginably painful separation saves the boy's life.

In *Night*, segregation by gender plunges the boy into a womanless world, a world where men vie with one another for the scarce resources necessary to survival. Some Holocaust scholars note that writing by women survivors emphasizes cooperative efforts among women and formation of family-like groups, while men's writing emphasizes individual struggles and competition for survival. They link this difference with the nurturing roles women frequently assume, and the competitive behavior men often exhibit. Teachers might ask students to what extent the behavior of Eliezer, his father, and other males in the book uphold, refute, or complicate this idea.

The contrast between traditional gender roles at the opening of *Night*, and the later upheaval of roles, puts into powerful relief the ways in which Nazi atrocity affected its victims on a personal level. Students might reflect on whether life in the camps, as depicted in *Night*, challenges or reinforces conventional masculinity. For example, during his childhood, Eliezer remembers his father as a "cultured, rather unsentimental man. There was never any display of emotion, even at home" (2). The elder Wiesel, deeply involved in community affairs, was held in great respect. But clearly, Wiesel's mother was the household's emotional center. Thus, the absence of women amidst the prisoners' extremely harsh realities influences the relationship between father and son. When his son's care is thrust upon him in Auschwitz, Eliezer's father struggles to sustain the boy emotionally, and to protect him from Nazi cruelties—to be both father and mother, in the book's terms.

Soon it becomes evident that the adolescent is better able than his father to withstand the crushing labor, beatings, epidemics, and starvation. Eliezer watches as the older man deteriorates physically, unable to do what fathers do in his culture: provide for and keep their families safe, ensure religious continuity. In stark contrast to his prior role as community leader, the older man loses control even over his own body, passively accepting beatings and obeying orders. In a reversal of the father-son relationship characteristic of Holocaust narratives, Eliezer assumes the role of protector, sharing his limited food ration with the weakened older man.

As a male in an Orthodox Jewish household, Eliezer has already embarked upon study of sacred texts and daily prayer by the time the Nazi genocide intrudes upon the life of Sighet Jews. For him, the daily torments of the concentration camp not only threaten his life and assault his human dignity; they also challenge his understanding of the workings of God and God's covenant with the Jewish people. Thus, the narrative presents Eliezer's theological struggle—his crisis of faith. Although Eliezer observes that the loss of faith can lead to disabling despair and death, he himself questions God's silence, even going so far as to proclaim Him dead, "hanging . . . on this gallows" (62). The degeneration of the relationship between father and son—Eliezer's frayed trust in the older man's authority and protection, discerning his father's increasing impotence, and finally outliving the elder Wiesel—parallels the progress of Eliezer's relationship with God, drawing on a traditional Jewish Godlanguage, depicting God as Father.

Because women and men were kept separate, few women appear in *Night*. Those who do appear point to an inversion of gender roles typical of war narratives. Conventional war stories depict heroic men braving danger, defending or victimizing passive and beleaguered women, who remain in the background. Since the Holocaust was not a war fought on battlefields, but an attack upon civilian life waged first in the home, women as well as men fell victim, and also had opportunities to show courage and insight. For example, when the Sighet Jews were already in the box cars, well before their arrival at Auschwitz, Mrs. Schächter wildly anticipates what awaits them, screaming in the darkness about "a terrible fire" (22). The others regard her as mad. But in Wiesel's oeuvre, the figure of the mad(wo)man is elided with the figure of the prophet, or the moral visionary. Indeed, as the narrator acknowledges, Mrs. Schächter's vision proves horribly prophetic. Further, several social historians have noted that the gender roles prevalent in prewar society often enabled women to grasp the gravity of the situation. More attuned to the informal flow of information among neighbors and in the marketplace, women frequently understood what was coming earlier than their husbands, who relied on more official sources of information.

In another reversal, Eliezer encounters a young French woman while assigned to a work detail at a warehouse. Assuming that the two had no common language, he makes no attempt to communicate with her. He suspects her of being Jewish, and only passing as an Aryan laborer. Once, after the boy was brutally beaten by the Kapo, or supervisor of the labor detail, the woman surprises him by risking her life to lift his morale, giving him food, cleaning his wounds, and speaking words of encouragement to him in perfect German, a language she claimed not to understand. At a chance encounter in Paris many years later, she confirms Eliezer's suspicions, telling him of her forged papers, and that speaking more than a few words in German to the young boy "would have aroused suspicion" (51). This episode reverses the gender roles: a boy in distress is rescued by a bold woman willing to put her own life on the line.

Wiesel has repeatedly commented that posing the right questions is far more important than finding the answers, particularly since the answers to certain questions may not exist. The cosmic questions Wiesel raises in *Night*— about the nature of humanity, God, history, and human meaning—are crucial not only in thinking about the Holocaust, but about the postwar legacy, the world we inhabit. In today's classrooms, teachers of *Night* will want students to consider not only life, death, and survival under Nazi atrocity but also the roles, treatment, and courage of men and women in contemporary wartime situations and oppressive regimes, all too immediately with us in the twenty-first century.

WORK CITED

Wiesel, Elie. *Night*. New York: Bantam, 1960.

FOR FURTHER READING

Horowitz, Sara R. "Memory and Testimony in Women Survivors of Nazi Genocide." *Women of the Word: Jewish Women and Jewish Writing*. Ed. Judith Baskin. Detroit: Wayne State University Press, 1994, 258–282.
Ofer, D. and L. Weitzman, eds. *Women in the Holocaust*. New Haven, CT: Yale University Press, 1998.

GARY WEISSMAN

Questioning Key Texts: A Pedagogical Approach to Teaching Elie Wiesel's Night

No work testifying to the horror of the Nazi camps is taught more frequently in American middle schools, high schools, and colleges than Elie Wiesel's *Night*. Indeed, *Night* is the key literary text through which the destruction of the European Jews is contemplated not only by most students of the Holocaust but also by a great many teachers. Consequently, much has been written on teaching *Night*, most of it by and for secondary school teachers, as those in higher education have seldom addressed the practical matter of how to teach this book in the college classroom.[1] Scholars have, instead, produced a vast corpus of commentary on *Night*, much of which describes the book as an incomparable work that resists literary categorization and critical analysis.[2] This scholarship serves foremost to affirm Wiesel's authority as the living memorial to the Holocaust and to elucidate his moral and theological "messages to humanity." It also encourages pedagogical approaches to *Night* that focus on teaching these messages without examining how they are shaped by the act of writing.

This essay proposes that teachers employ a more critical stance when teaching Wiesel's book to college students. It identifies and challenges some assumptions that underlie traditional approaches to *Night*, while describing the alternative path I followed in my literature course Auschwitz Memoirs: Reading and Writing on Holocaust Testimony. Needing to assemble a

Teaching the Representation of the Holocaust, eds. Marianne Hirsch and Irene Kacandes (New York: Modern Language Association of America, 2004): pp. 324–336. Copyright © 2004 Modern Language Association.

137

manageable reading list for this course and wanting to highlight the variety of literary approaches taken to render a shared experience—while emphasizing how vastly different this experience was for Jews and non-Jews, men and women, teens and adults, members of different nationalities, and prisoners assigned to various kinds of work—I decided to limit the readings to six memoirs set largely at Auschwitz.[3] I began the course with *Night* to engage students' prior understanding of how Holocaust memoirs should be read. Because of their familiarity with a conception of the Holocaust that has entered American culture largely through Elie Wiesel, this understanding—that the proper response to survivor memoirs is a kind of self-effacing reverence—was shared even by students who had not previously read *Night*.

Wiesel's influence on Holocaust remembrance is difficult to overestimate, as he has largely defined the terms in which the Holocaust is contemplated and discussed—even establishing *Holocaust* as the common term for the Nazi genocide (Garber and Zuckerman 202). "I remember having chosen the word because of its mystical and religious connotations," he has said (qtd. in Lewis 156). In books, speeches, and newspaper articles, Wiesel describes the extermination of the European Jews as a sacred mystery, central to which is the question of God's role in the tragedy. He contends that the Holocaust transcends history and defies comprehension and comparison to other events; it can be represented through survivor testimony alone, for only the survivors know what it was like, yet even their testimony is incapable of fully revealing the event. The survivors are duty-bound to testify; as for the rest of us, our proper response is one of deferential silence before the ineffable. We are not to understand or explain the Holocaust; we must listen to the survivors and remember.

Even students unfamiliar with Wiesel will have internalized a sense of the Holocaust as an event of intimidating, mystical-religious magnitude. This sense is manifested in students' understanding that survivor memoirs compel an ethical response of awe, grief, or silence. In my classroom the articulation of these responses was the starting point rather than the goal of discussion. Rather than have students respond to writing about the Holocaust as if responding to the Holocaust itself, I wanted them to recognize Holocaust memoirs as writing that can be read critically—in a way that involves not fault-finding but stepping back to reexamine a text from a fresh perspective. This meant putting aside a conception of the Holocaust that grants survivor memoirs the aura of sacred testimony, discouraging inquiry and analysis as irreverent.

James E. Young has persuasively argued that survivor testimony should be valued not for providing factual evidence but for identifying "the kinds of understanding the victims brought to their experiences and . . . the kinds of actions they took on behalf of this understanding" (10). Still, critical readers are faced with an added complexity, for the extent to which survivor memoirs provide historical understanding of how their authors perceived events during the Holocaust is questionable. After all, a survivor's retrospective perception of events may differ substantially from the understanding that shaped his or her comprehension of and response to events as they occurred. Yet, far from detracting from what this literature offers, the fact that the memoirs can testify to how survivors' worldviews have changed since the Holocaust adds a deeply meaningful dimension to what we can learn from reading them. Instead of thinking in terms of "the collective voice of the survivor" (Fine 105), we can explore how surviving victims' distinctive voices continue to develop after Auschwitz, despite many scholars' efforts to ground survivors' world-views and voices in the extreme experience of the Holocaust, making that experience definitive.

As the structure of my Auschwitz Memoirs course suggests, I believe that the Holocaust is best taught not through authoritative key texts but through a number of texts that make smaller claims to being decisive or representative. This view conflicts with a pronounced tendency among Holocaust commentators to lay claim to key texts through which the horror of the Holocaust is laid bare. Not long ago this tendency led to the debacle involving Binjamin Wilkomirski's *Fragments: Memories of a Wartime Childhood*. Praised as a Holocaust memoir on a par with *Night*, *Fragments* accrued numerous awards and speaking engagements for its author before it was revealed to be a fraud, a work of fiction by a Swiss-born, non-Jewish writer impersonating a Holocaust survivor. Early doubts about the veracity of the book were discouraged by suggestions that one would be revictimizing Wilkomirski, impugning the memory of child survivors, and lending credence to deniers by questioning the truthfulness of his memoir (see Eskin 139–153).

The rush to make *Fragments* the newest key text on the Holocaust discouraged critical readings that might have shown that Wilkomirski's book could not be what it professes to be even if its author were a survivor of the Nazi camps. "I am not a poet or a writer," writes Wilkomirski, who claims to recount events not as the survivor-writer remembers them decades later but as they are held in his "child's memory" (4–5). This is the long-silenced, almost preverbal memory of a child so young that little or no social or linguistic understanding predating the camps impinged on his perception of horrific events as they unfolded. In claiming to let this memory speak directly, without the intervention of adult interpretation or the writer's hand, *Fragments* offers readers the fantasy of a Holocaust memoir unmediated by any reshaping of the past.

While as a counterfeit work of Holocaust literature *Fragments* seems an anomaly, it reveals a resistance to critical reading that often accompanies efforts to celebrate key Holocaust texts and defend them against heretical interpretations. This resistance arises from efforts to ground Holocaust testimony in something more authentic and authoritative than writing—which is shaped, on the one hand, by the survivors' subjective and mutable understanding of past experiences and, on the other, by rhetorical decisions regarding such matters as literary approach, narrative voice, and audience. These efforts lead to the creation of mythic origins, such as the grounding of *Fragments* in the unadulterated purity of a child's memory. As the validity of these mythic origins might not stand up to analysis, scholars' commentary on key texts often has the effect of forestalling rather than encouraging critical inquiry. Survivor testimony, when treated as "holy," tends to be read through practices that, as Young has noted, ignore "the ways in which Holocaust literary testimony is . . . constructed and interpretive" and focus instead on "finding meaning in the events it relates" (21–22).

This criticism certainly applies to *Night*, which, more than any other work of Holocaust literature, has given rise to an elaborate mythos regarding its origin. Even readers unfamiliar with commentary on *Night* may encounter it, as my students did, in François Mauriac's foreword, where Wiesel is described as having the look of "a Lazarus risen from the dead,"[4] and in Robert McAfee Brown's preface to the widely available Bantam paperback edition. At the core of this mythos is a mystical-religious sense that the Holocaust has made Wiesel its singular, most authoritative witness. Brown writes, "Among the few who survived . . . was Elie Wiesel, whose deliverance condemned him to tell the story to an unbelieving and uncaring world." He goes on to describe Wiesel as the medium through which we may come closest to the Holocaust, stating that "between us and the fiery furnaces where they burned babies alive stands the presence of Elie Wiesel; his presence casts a shadow from within which we can see, in dimmest outline, the reality he saw and touched and tasted directly" (vi). Here Brown manages to describe how we "see" the Holocaust through Wiesel in terms that make no mention of reading or writing.

Night is, of course, a written text; but myths concerning how *Night* came into being suggest that the book's authenticity lies in its resistance to whatever is potentially distancing and fictionalizing about writing. These myths, often recited by Wiesel and repeated by scholars, base *Night*'s authenticity and authority in the absence of words, in a mystical-religious silence. One myth concerns Wiesel's vow of silence: in 1945 he vowed to wait ten years before writing about the Holocaust, "to be sure that what [he] would say would be true" ("Talking" 274; see also Wiesel, "A Jew Today" 18). Another myth placing the writing of Wiesel's book in the context of a far greater silence involves the paring down of *Night* from eight hundred pages to a slim volume closer to one hundred pages. Wiesel has written:

To bring back at least a certain fragment of the truth the writer becomes responsible not only for the words but for the white spaces between the words, not only for the language but for the silence. Therefore, the less you write, the more true the message and the story. ("How" 65)

One need not refer to noteworthy Holocaust memoirs that are much longer than *Night* or that were written just after the war to cast doubt on these myths of what guarantees truth in representations of the Holocaust; the question is why Holocaust scholars who write on Wiesel have so often embraced the myths. While the young Wiesel may have taken a vow of silence, the story becomes myth when read as evidence of his memoir's truthfulness or authenticity. No doubt there are compelling reasons why he waited years to write about the camps. Perhaps he was too traumatized to dwell on his experiences with the intensity required by writing; perhaps it took him years to feel confident enough as a writer to address them. Such conceivable explanations do not bear on the truth-value of what he eventually did write; instead, they relate to the demands of writing. Surely Wiesel's book is the result not of a purifying ten-year vow of silence but of a complex writing process that began with his decision to write, one day, about the camps. How are students to analyze the book, when the Holocaust's mystical-religious gravity, *Night*'s exalted status as *the* classic memoir of the Holocaust, and Wiesel's stature as *the* survivor of the Holocaust all conspire to dissuade them from considering *Night* as writing that can be read critically?

In my course, students were introduced to the critical reading of Holocaust memoirs through what can be regarded as a heretical reading of *Night:* Naomi Seidman's essay "Elie Wiesel and the Scandal of Jewish Rage." When discussing the essay in class (after we had read and discussed *Night*), many students expressed surprise, if not relief, that a survivor memoir could be closely analyzed and questioned—and without dishonoring the victims or denying the Holocaust. Seidman's essay reintroduced students to *Night* as a text with an elaborate history as a revised, edited, translated, and published piece of writing. It redirects our attention to this writing by comparing *Night* (really *La nuit,* the French work from which *Night* is translated)[5] with an earlier memoir that Wiesel wrote in Yiddish and published in 1956, two years before *La nuit.* This memoir, titled *Un di velt hot geshvign* (And the World Remained Silent), is frequently omitted from discussions of Wiesel's oeuvre and from commentary on *Night,* which is typically referred to as Wiesel's first book. When *Un di velt* is mentioned, it is described in passing as a longer, unrefined version of *Night.* Seidman, by contrast, approaches this "unread ghost" (18) as a book in its own right, a memoir telling a story related to, but different from, the one told in *Night.*

Seidman's critical reading of *Un di velt* is also a critical rereading of *Night*. Her focus is on how Wiesel wrote his memoirs for two different audiences—one of Yiddish-speaking Jews, the other of Christian readers. She finds the differences between the two memoirs best conveyed by the books' contrasting images of the survivor. In *Night* the image is portrayed in the book's oft-cited last lines, where Eliezer, hospitalized in Buchenwald after the camp's liberation, looks in a mirror: "From the depths of the mirror, a corpse gazed back at me. The look in his eyes, as they stared into mine, has never left me" (109). Innumerable scholars have commented on the significance of this image without knowing that it was not Wiesel who chose to end *Night* here but his French editor, Jérome Lindon, who also cut sixty-seven pages from the Yiddish memoir to produce the slim volume he and Wiesel titled *La nuit* (Wiesel, *All* 319; Diamont 260). Whereas *Night* ends with the image of the survivor as corpse, the Yiddish memoir continues: "I saw the image of myself after my death. It was at that instant that the will to live was awakened. Without knowing why I raised a balled-up fist and smashed the mirror, breaking the image that lived within it" (qtd. in Seidman 7).

According to Seidman, the "Jewish rage" that compels the survivor to shatter the reflection of the skeletal camp prisoner also compels him to write about the camps—and "not ten years after the events of the Holocaust but immediately upon liberation as the first expression of his mental and physical recovery" (7). The Yiddish memoir presents an alternative mythic origin for Wiesel's testimony, in which the authenticity of his testimony is based not in silence but in its claim to having originated there in the camps. "I stayed in bed for a few more days, in the course of which I wrote the outline of the book you are holding in your hand, dear reader," writes Wiesel. He sees that "ten years after Buchenwald" the world is forgetting what happened to the Jews and fears that "the naive world" will come to believe the lies of "Germans and anti-Semites" who deny the Holocaust. He concludes, "I thought it would be a good idea to publish a book based on the notes I wrote in Buchenwald" (qtd. in Seidman 7).

Here writing comes across not as a mysterious struggle to represent the unrepresentable but as a practical means of resistance (only later could Wiesel say, "Writing lies within the domain of mystery" [*All* 321]). "The Yiddish survivor is filled with rage and the desire to live, to take revenge, to write," states Seidman (7). The French survivor, by contrast, does not smash the mirror or write notes for a book he will publish to counter the lies of Germans, anti-semites, and a naive world. Why not? Seidman argues that in order to appeal to a wider audience of Christian readers, Wiesel and his French publishers reshaped his story, transforming "the survivor's political rage into his existential doubt" directed at the Jewish God (15).

My point in assigning Seidman's essay was not to replace the mythic reading of *Night* with the "true" reading. In fact, since teaching Auschwitz Memoirs, I have come across a highly negative response to her essay that I would recommend assigning alongside it. The essay, by Eli Pfefferkorn and David Hirsch, "Elie Wiesel's Wrestle with God," sets out to refute what the authors see as "Ms. Seidman's attempt to undermine the authenticity of *Night* as witness testimony" (21). The authors contend that her "revisionist essay," written in both bad faith and righteous fury, grossly exaggerates differences between *Un di velt* and *La nuit* or *Night*. Although I find their arguments largely unpersuasive, their response to Seidman's argument allows students to see the critical reading of *Night* as the subject of an ongoing conversation in which they, too, can take part. Whether or not one agrees with Seidman's reading of *Night*, the real value of her essay for teaching is that it allows students to see the importance of approaching survivor memoirs as texts that are written for specific audiences, that employ various literary strategies, and that express particular interpretations of experience.

Following our discussion of Seidman, and before turning to the memoirs we would read, the class looked at a passage from Wiesel's 1995 memoir, *All Rivers Run to the Sea*, to consider how he might have reinterpreted his experiences since *Night* was published. (A more approachable text may be the 1997 *New York Times* op-ed piece "A Prayer for the Days of Awe," in which Wiesel writes that he now realizes he never lost faith in God, "not even over there," at Auschwitz.) The passage from *All Rivers* describes experiences in Auschwitz that bear no mention in *Night:* Eliezer and his father wake before roll call to strap on tefillin and recite blessings; Eliezer says his prayers every day and hums Shabbat songs on Saturdays (82). Having reexamined *Night* through Seidman's essay, students were prepared to discuss how Wiesel might have reshaped the image of his past, and the image of the survivor, to match his present world-view. That is, they considered how as Wiesel's crisis of religious belief has given way to a growing reaffirmation of Jewish faith, his depictions of Jewish experience at Auschwitz have changed accordingly.

Although I have described an approach using Seidman's essay to introduce students to issues involving the construction and reception of *Night* and of Holocaust memoirs generally, teachers may apply Seidman's insights without necessarily assigning her essay. For instance, teachers can ask students to compare the endings of *Night* and *Un di velt* as well as passages in *Night* and *All Rivers* concerning religious practice in the camp. Through discussion of these passages' stylistic and thematic differences, students may come to their own realization of the complex, nontransparent, evolving relation between experience and writing. In addition to highlighting Wiesel's treatments of certain themes (Jewish identity, the image of the survivor, silence), teachers can ask students to consider how the particular time and language in which each of the three accounts was written bear on the decisions Wiesel made as a writer.

Seidman remarks, "It is a measure of the profundity of the influence of *Night* on the discourse of Holocaust literature that its distinctive tone and approach has come to seem simply inevitable, the only response imaginable" (3). No doubt, *Night*'s mythic status has served to make it a useful tool for teaching the Holocaust to young people, as it encourages teachers to believe that they can adequately cover the Holocaust with this single, short book. In an essay written for teachers, Margaret A. Drew writes that since young people's knowledge of the Holocaust is often limited to what they learn from reading only one book, that text must be "good history as well as good literature" (11). "One of the few books that can meet the criteria in both history and literature is Elie Wiesel's *Night*," she states, adding that it presents "a personal experience that can be multiplied by 6 million" (15–16). Carol Danks similarly recommends *Night* to high school teachers, noting that it "presents accurate historical information, has an authentic narrative voice, seems approachable to students, and can be taught in limited classroom time" (101).

Having been introduced to the Holocaust as a child by reading an autographed copy of *Night*, I can attest to its great educational value. Treated as a window onto the Holocaust, *Night* allows young readers to gain a valuable introductory understanding of what European Jews experienced in the Holocaust. But all texts, and key texts in particular, need to be read differently at different levels. At the college level, *Night* is a key text through which teachers can encourage students to move past an uncritical mystical-religious conception of the Holocaust, toward a deeper understanding of how survivors have translated their experiences into writing. There may be real value in treating Wiesel's book as a text that teaches itself by emotionally affecting younger readers, just as younger students may benefit from reading *Night* as a transparently authentic voicing of accurate historical information, expressing the experience of all victims. But for mature students, a deeper appreciation of Holocaust literature lies precisely in questioning the earlier reading.

Notes

1. Many Web sites offer lesson plans and activities for teaching *Night* to middle and high school students; several can be accessed at *Web English Teacher* (www.webenglishteacher.com/wiesel.html). For published writings see, for example, Danks; Drew; Greenbaum; Totten, "Entering." Totten, a professor of curriculum development, provides one of the more comprehensive guides for teaching *Night*; however, his approach, like many others, suggests that only Wiesel provides the means for "grappling with Wiesel's story and the ramifications that the Holocaust has for humanity today" (239). Totten suggests that students, in addition to "writing a letter to Elie," take a final exam that asks them to respond to the "validity and

significance" of Wiesel's statements by using "examples and additional quotes from Wiesel's *Night* to support their position and arguments" (224, 239). Diamant persuasively argues that for literary scholars as well "it is Wiesel himself who is largely responsible for generating the terms in which he is read" (118).

    2. *Night*'s literary genre is strangely unresolved. "Described as an autobiographical narrative, a fictionalized autobiography, a nonfictional novel, the work defies all categories," writes Fine (114). For a discussion of *Night*'s literary status, see my *Fantasies of Witnessing*. For a brief discussion of the resistance to subjecting *Night* to literary considerations, see Rosen (1321) and Davis, who also offers a valuable discussion of the book's literary construction. For a concise sampling of scholarship on *Night*, see Mass; for a succinct overview of this scholarship, see Rosen (1321–1324).

    3. Besides *Night*, readings included *The Yellow Star*, by Simcha Bunem Unsdorfer; *Auschwitz: True Tales from a Grotesque Land*, by Sara Nomberg-Przytyk; *None of Us Will Return*, by Charlotte Delbo; *Auschwitz: A Doctor's Eyewitness Account*, by Miklos Nyiszli; and *Eyewitness Auschwitz: Three Years in the Gas Chambers*, by Filip Müller. We began with "Auschwitz—an Overview," by Yisrael Gutman. (For more on Delbo, see the essay in this volume by Greenberg.)

    4. For contrasting evaluations of Mauriac's foreword, see Fleischner; Langer (142–144); as well as Seidman's more thorough consideration of Wiesel and Mauriac's relationship.

    5. There are, of course, significant differences between *La nuit* and *Night*, but these fall outside the purview of Seidman's essay. For a consideration of these differences, see Diamant, in which she notes material that has been added to the English translation (287).

Works Cited

Brown, Robert McAfee. Preface. *Night*. By Elie Wiesel. 25th anniversary ed. New York: Bantam, 1986. v–vi.

Danks, Carol. "Using the Literature of Elie Wiesel and Selected Poetry to Teach the Holocaust in the Secondary School History Classroom." *Social Studies* 87.3 (1996): 101–105.

Davis, Colin. "How Wiesel Tells the Story That Can Never Be Told." Mass 78–85.

Delbo, Charlotte. *None of Us Will Return*. Trans. John Githens. Boston: Beacon, 1978.

Diamant, Naomi. "The Boundaries of Holocaust Literature: The Emergence of a Canon." Diss. Columbia Uniterity, 1992.

Drew, Margaret A. "Teaching Holocaust Literature: Issues, Caveats, and Suggestions." Totten, *Teaching:* 11–23.

Eskin, Blake. *A Life in Pieces: The Making and Unmaking of Binjamin Wilkomirski*. New York: Norton, 2002.

Fine, Ellen S. "The Surviving Voice: Literature of the Holocaust." *Perspectives on the Holocaust*. Ed. Randolph L. Braham. Boston: Kluwer-Nijhoff, 1983. 105–117.

Fleischner, Eva. "A Letter to Question *Night*'s Preface." Mass 157–160.

Garber, Zev, and Bruce Zuckerman. "Why Do We Call the Holocaust 'The Holocaust'? An Inquiry into the Psychology of Labels." *Modern Judaism* 9.2 (1989): 197–211.

Greenbaum, Beth Aviv. *Bearing Witness: Teaching about the Holocaust*. Portsmouth: Heinemann, 2001.

Gutman, Yisrael. "Auschwitz—an Overview." *The Anatomy of the Auschwitz Death Camp*. Ed. Gutman and Michael Berenbaum. Bloomington: Indiana University Press; Washington: United States Holocaust Memorial Museum, 1994. 5–33.

Langer, Lawrence L. *Preempting the Holocaust*. New Haven: Yale University Press, 1998.

Lewis, Stephen. *Art out of Agony: The Holocaust Theme in Literature, Sculpture, and Film*. Toronto: CBC Enterprises, 1984.

Mass, Wendy, ed. *Readings on* Night. San Diego: Greenhaven, 2000.

Müller, Filip. *Eyewitness Auschwitz: Three Years in the Gas Chambers*. Trans. Susanne Flatauer. Chicago: Dee, 1999.

Nomberg-Przytyk, Sara. *Auschwitz: True Tales from a Grotesque Land*. Trans. Roslyn Hirsch. Chapel Hill: University of North Carolina Press, 1985.

Nyiszli, Miklos. *Auschwitz: A Doctor's Eyewitness Account*. Trans. Tibère Kremer and Richard Seaver. New York: Arcade, 1993.

Pfefferkorn, Eli, and David H. Hirsch. "Elie Wiesel's Wrestle with God." *Midstream*, Nov. 1997: 20–22.

Rosen, Allan. "Elie Wiesel." *Holocaust Literature: An Encyclopedia of Writers and Their Work*. Ed. S. Lillian Kremer. Vol. 2. New York: Routledge, 2003. 1315–1325.

Seidman, Naomi. "Elie Wiesel and the Scandal of Jewish Rage." *Jewish Social Studies* 3.1 (1996): 1–19.

Totten, Samuel. "Entering the 'Night' of the Holocaust: Studying Elie Wiesel's *Night*." Totten, *Teaching*: 215–242.

———, ed. *Teaching Holocaust Literature*. Boston: Allyn, 2001.

Unsdorfer, Simcha Burem. *The Yellow Star*. New York: Yoseloff, 1961.

Wiesel, Elie. *All Rivers Run to the Sea: Memoirs*. New York: Schocken, 1995.

———. "How Does One Write?" *Against Silence: The Voice and Vision of Elie Wiesel*. Ed. Irving Abrahamson. Vol. 2. New York: Holocaust Library, 1985. 65.

———. *A Jew Today*. Trans. Marion Wiesel. New York: Vintage, 1978.

———. *Night*. Trans. Stella Rodway. Fwd. François Mauriac. New York: Bantam, 1986.

———. *La nuit*. Paris: Minuit, 1958.

———. "A Prayer for the Days of Awe." *New York Times*, 2 Oct. 1997: A16.

———. "Talking and Writing and Keeping Silent." *The German Church Struggle and the Holocaust*. Ed. Franklin H. Littell and Hubert G. Locke. Detroit: Wayne State University Press, 1974. 260–277.

———. *Un di velt hot geshvign*. Dos Poylishe Yidnòtum 17. Buenos Aires: Tsentral-Farband fun Poylishe Yidn in Argentina, 1956.

Weissman, Gary. *Fantasies of Witnessing: Postwar Efforts to Experience the Holocaust*. Ithaca: Cornell University Press, 2004.

Wilkomirski, Binjamin. *Fragments: Memories of a Wartime Childhood*. Trans. Carol Brown Janeway. New York: Schocken, 1996.

Young, James E. *Writing and Rewriting the Holocaust: Narrative and the Consequences of Interpretation*. Bloomington: Indiana University Press, 1990.

FREDERICK L. DOWNING

The Poetics of Memory and Justice: Elie Wiesel and Post-Holocaust Theological Reflection

Like voices from a whirlwind accompanied by a barrage of unanswerable questions cast in the direction of a silent but listening God, the writings of the survivors signal a new era—a period aptly described by what Buber calls the "eclipse of God."[1] Such voices are audible when Elie Wiesel writes in *One Generation After* of the literary evenings that he attended in Buchenwald. There was in that place, Wiesel says, "a veritable passion to testify"—a passion demonstrated through every possible means of expression. What the various testimonies shared was a common desire "to tear from the clutches of night the life and death of what was once a flourishing, vibrant community . . . ." Both haunting and terrifying, these testimonies wavered "between the scream and silent anger."[2]

Elie Wiesel grew up as a God-intoxicated Jewish child in love with God and the Torah. But as a witness to the most profound symbolic confrontation of the twentieth century—the meeting of the human with Auschwitz—Wiesel became convinced of the of the failure of 2000 years of Christian civilization, the defeat of "Meaning," and the death of the idea of the human. For Wiesel, this was part of Buber's "eclipse of God"—a time when the believer must have stopped believing, if only for a moment. Yet convinced that God was revealing something as significant as the giving of the Torah to Moses at

Perspectives in Religious Studies, Volume 35, Number 3 (Fall 2008): pp. 283–300. Copyright © 2008 Baylor University.

Sinai, if only in reverse, Wiesel began to search for an understanding of how to live after the cataclysm that was the Holocaust.[3]

While Wiesel has written many books, the critical methodology for reading those works is still lacking. In an important essay entitled "The Problematics of Holocaust Literature," Alvin Rosenfeld raises questions concerning the nature of Holocaust literature and the work of Elie Wiesel. One of his conclusions is that there is perhaps no greater need for literary scholars than to develop a strategy for reading these texts written under the seal of memory of the most profound confrontation of the twentieth century and inscribed as a tombstone for six million unburied dead.[4] Sixteen years later in his book, *Elie Wiesel's Secretive Texts*, Colin Davis indicates that scholars have not taken up Rosenfeld's proposal. "On the whole," Davis writes, "Wiesel's fiction remains curiously unexplored despite an apparent consensus in France and the United States that Wiesel is one of the most important novelists of the post-Holocaust period." Davis goes on to offer two suggestions as to why there is a critical silence around Wiesel's work. First, there is the understandable fear that by subjecting the Holocaust to literary-critical study one might trivialize the subject—the Holocaust. Second, the ambiguity and difficulty of Wiesel's fiction itself—a theme that Davis goes on to explores.[5] Concerning his attempt, one could say that Wiesel's fiction, like the literature of the Bible, often displays what Robert Alter calls "a certain indeterminacy of meaning."[6]

But if Wiesel's fiction is a part of a larger body of work which needs a strategy for reading, his theology or theological reflection also cries out for more comprehensive analysis. This is especially true in light of the laudatory affirmations often given to Wiesel as a moral spokesperson. He has been called the "most affirmative Jewish voice today," or the "conscience of his generation." By the same token, however, the reluctance to address Wiesel's theology is well-founded. He himself virtually refuses the term "theology." In an interview in 1974, Wiesel says, "I don't like the word 'theologian'; I find it disturbing. What is a theologian, really? Someone who knows things about God. But who knows what God is?" Wiesel goes on to place himself with Kafka who once said: "'Man cannot speak *of* God. If at all, he can speak *to* God.' So I am still trying to speak *to* Him. How can we speak *of* Him?"[7]

If then in Wiesel's view, God cannot be "expressed," only "addressed"—to use Buber's language—how does Wiesel speak *to* God or address God? The thesis of this essay is that while the Holocaust presents Wiesel with an "eclipse of God," he responds in dialogical fashion by creating a "poetics of memory and justice"—as a generative religious personality Wiesel is a contemporary poet who writes himself to prophetic awareness. For Wiesel, narrative becomes a complex dialogue of lament-laden literature presented as "address" to God. Likewise, literature becomes a place to interrogate images of the self and others. Foundational to his dialogue and project are the twin themes of memory and justice especially embodied in the literary forms of autobiography and parable. Therefore, paradoxically while Wiesel may not write or speak "of God," it may be that his entire project is nothing less than an effort—at least on one level—to "address" or dialogue with God in parabolic stories, essays, and speeches. If so, then this dialogue is not only about how to live after the Holocaust, but it is also ironically about God. For as Wiesel says, "What man did to man at Auschwitz could not have been done outside of God: in some way He too was at work—was he questioning man? Was he showing his face?"[8]

I. The Poetics of Memory and Justice

The idea of a "poetics" inevitably turns one's attention to language and one's concept of "words." When Wiesel first began to write, he found himself faced with a fundamental problem: How can one write when language is dead and words are in exile? The "eclipse" that was the Holocaust included a dramatic impact on language. In some profound sense, language died in Auschwitz. This idea of the corruption or death of language is prominent in Wiesel's work.[9] Wiesel learned in his study of the *Zohar* that "when Israel is in exile, so is the word." This means that words could not convey what had happened in the death camps. The writer after Auschwitz had to invent something new or retrieve a model from the past because during the Holocaust word and meaning had been split apart. The language of the death camps negated all other meaning. Now, Wiesel says, "All words seemed inadequate, worn, foolish, lifeless, whereas I wanted them to be searing." Where could a survivor discover a "fresh vocabulary, a primeval language"? Put another way, Wiesel's problem as a survivor was "how to find a secure place, somewhere between memory and imagination, for all those corpses who . . . cry out against the injustice of their end, but for whom no act of vengeance or ritual remembrance exists sufficient to bring them to a peaceful place of rest."[10]

Wiesel eventually concluded that in times of the "eclipse of God" and the death of language one must go back to one's sources, in this case the classical texts like the Bible. From there, Wiesel found that within Judaism there was an age-old tradition of taking significant events from the collective history of the Jewish people and turning those events into paradigms or points of reference in order to measure and understand contemporary events. In joining this quest, Wiesel became heir to a continuous tradition that dates back to the destruction of the first temple. For more than 2500 years Jewish storytellers have sought to document tragedy after tragedy with an unbroken chain of liturgical poems, commentaries, and folk tales. This lamentation literature worked to preserve communal memory in several ways. The poems and stories provided footnotes in Jewish history to chronicle the past, but they also provided a medium and a language by which the contemporary generation could continue to grapple with biblical views of that past and to add new interpretations.[11]

When he writes about such matters himself, Wiesel is ambivalent. There are times when Wiesel wants to warn the reader that survivors speak in a coded language and try as one might, the language will never be understood completely. Between the memory of the survivor and the listener who reflects upon it is a wall that cannot be penetrated. "We speak in code," says Wiesel, "and this code cannot be broken, cannot be deciphered. . . ."[12] Yet there are other times when Wiesel seems to encourage readers to try to understand the language and the code in order to be sensitive and join the number who would fight for justice. In various places and times, Wiesel talks about his own writing and his work as if he is attempting to provide clues for a "true reader." There are also times when he writes about his "code."[13]

Wiesel sums up the issue when he says, "Our problem was and remains what to do with our words, with our tears. Because we did not know how to say certain things, we went back to our sources, to the past."[14] When Wiesel went back to Jewish history to study sources, he found many eloquent voices, but none more so than Jeremiah ben Hilkiah. In a portrait of Jeremiah, Wiesel wrote that he is "the first—and most eloquent—among Jewish writers of all times."[15] Wiesel goes on to write that "We still use his vocabulary to describe our experiences."[16] There is much that commends Jeremiah to the survivor. Perhaps above all, Jeremiah is a link to the Jewish past and the time of the exile. "I love the prophet Jeremiah," Wiesel says, "because he is the one who lived the catastrophe before, during, and after and knew how to speak about it."[17] He also offers the modern reader an "example of behavior" during perilous times. Though Jeremiah is appealing as a writer and as an example, his obsessions and themes are also those of the contemporary survivor: doubt/self-doubt, solitude, despair, protest, testimony, and consolation. Eventually, Wiesel tells his readers that his own code is actually that of Jeremiah.[18]

What does this mean—that Jeremiah provides the literary code for Wiesel? In a literary sense, it must be that Wiesel finds in Jeremiah the inner literary logic, the language, with which to address the crisis brought on by the Holocaust in as much as words can be found to address this profound confrontation. But more than vocabulary, Wiesel found in Jeremiah an example or model figure, a paradigm by which he could at least begin to make some sense of the broken world that now exists.

One could argue that the model which Wiesel found in the portrait of Jeremiah was none other than the formative view of moral transformation and moral character which was emerging in the Jewish community as a response to the disaster that was the Babylonian Exile. Herein, the book of Jeremiah is a "thick" response to the broken world, the "cosmic crumbling." In this thick description, Jeremiah ben Hilkiah is portrayed as the "ideal survivor who relentlessly portrays the poignant nature of this "domain of death." It is from the reading of this portrayal of Jeremiah that the Jewish community first appropriates the new identity of "survivor," so this portrayal of Jeremiah becomes a paradigm for the community to follow. The book's lack of structure forces the community to wrestle with tough questions—to read the abyss of the moment. The very lack of structure in the book of Jeremiah actually introduces or "performs" the collapse of the world in that time is fractured and narrative meaning is ruptured. The book reads the abyss that surrounds the community and forces the group to face the disaster through the proclamation of jumbled narrative. As Kathleen O'Connor writes of the book, "Its mosaic of broken pieces invites the formation of a new text, of a new world, and a new community." Likewise, as Wiesel models his work on Jeremiah, he writes texts that stutter toward a meaning that is never found, and his fiction transmits "a message that it does not know how to formulate." To this extent, Wiesel, like Jeremiah ben Hilkiah, forces his readers to search for a new text, a new vision of community and the world.[19]

If there is a central text in the book of Jeremiah which typifies and summarizes Wiesel's appropriation of a literary logic or code, it is Jeremiah 1:10—the call narrative of the prophet. Here, one can argue, is a comprehensive statement which informs a reading of Wiesel's work, at least on some level. Jeremiah is commanded with six verbs: to pluck up, to pull down, to destroy, to overthrow, and finally to build and to plant. Four of these six verbs are thoroughly negative, and only the last two are positive. Walter Brueggemann summarizes this call to Jeremiah with the two words: "shattering" and "evoking."[20] After reading Jeremiah and Wiesel, one could add a third word which with the previous two becomes the heart of Wiesel's literary logic. That third word is "enacting." Wiesel picks up this theme when he notes that Jeremiah "offers us an example of behavior, not before or after, but during periods of pressure, stress, and peril." Wiesel goes on to write that Jeremiah "defines himself in relation to his fellowmen. . . ."[21] Wiesel is also clear about how the role of public example is also important to him. "Today, I believe, the teacher must give more: he must give an example. I cannot go on writing and teaching one way and behaving another."[22] Wiesel's poetics is therefore comprised of three major components: shattering, evoking, and enacting.[23]

II. Shattering: A Literature of Decomposition

How does Wiesel tell his story? After adopting the "code" of Jeremiah, he appropriates a series of themes and images from the Hebrew Bible and utilizes them together with Jeremiah's language and his own prophetic imagination to construct stories around the Holocaust as an anti-Sinai. He appropriates the central core narrative of Judaism, the story of Moses and the exodus from bondage as a central theme in his re-telling and re-working of the now updated tradition. But Wiesel saw the Holocaust as a reversal of Sinai. So he looked for ways to reverse the core narrative. The *akedah* was also an important story of suffering in Judaism which he thought he could effectively appropriate for his new narrative. It too, however, had to be reversed because of what the Holocaust had done. Each of these narratives were appropriated in a manner that placed them in the service of Jeremiah's literary logic of shattering. Wiesel came to see that Jeremiah's code or literary logic could be useful in telling the story which is still not completely told.[24] His language could be appropriated for this re-telling of the human story. But how could one talk about God and the divine role in this tragic event? Wiesel had heard Buber speak in Paris. He knew that Buber taught that God cannot be expressed, only addressed. Wiesel also knew that the lamentation literature of the Hebrew Bible, which is in part uniquely tied by tradition to Jeremiah, worked to preserve communal memory in poems and stories, and that this literature was addressed to God as well as to others.

Ten years after the Holocaust, when Wiesel began to testify to what he had seen and heard, he found that he had a "given framework"—the paradigm of the prophets of Israel, especially as mediated in the literary framework and paradigmatic model of Jeremiah.[25] The portrait of Jeremiah that Wiesel had found in his Bible during the days of his youth was theologically intentional. It provided a paradigmatic portrait of Jeremiah as poet/prophet. The portrait constructed with words offers to the reader a model of the understanding of the poet/prophet as well as a paradigm of what Israel might become. In adopting Jeremiah's language and ground-plan, Wiesel adopts a similar theological intentionality. The story of his life is now projected as a public persona—a paradigm for "witnessing" to the Holocaust, living as a person of faith in the post–Holocaust age, and eventually modeling what the community of Israel might be like. Just as in the work of Jeremiah, the first of Wiesel's themes is "shattering."

The New Torah: A Second Exodus, An Anti-Sinai

When Wiesel penned *Night*, his narrative opens with a portrayal of Moshe the beadle. The allusion is clear. From the beginning of his story, Wiesel wants the reader to think of the biblical Moshe and his story which was the core narrative of Judaism. Wiesel goes on to characterize Eliezer as a young Jewish boy who "believed profoundly" at the age of twelve. In the beginning, *Night* is a story of a young boy growing up in the midst of Hasidic fervor, in love with his family, his God, and the Torah. But then, at the time of Passover—when in the original core narrative of Judaism, Israel is liberated—Wiesel tells how he and his family are deported from Sighet and taken to the death camps of Birkenau and Auschwitz where his mother and youngest sister are immediately killed, how he and his father struggle through the winter avoiding "selection," and finally after a long forced march in the brutal cold and snow, how his father dies shortly before liberation. As a central framework for his story, Wiesel takes the core narrative of Jewish tradition, the Exodus, and reverses it in order to show the reversal of the classical paradigm of the Exodus/Sinai traditions. As in the first exodus, there is a "going out," but this time the going out is from an ordered land into chaos—a movement from the secure and ordered world of Sighet into the unspeakable horror of the death camps. The season of the year is the same as in the first exodus. Yet this time, the Angel of Death does not spare the Hebrew children. The Jews of Sighet are taken to a place where food tastes like corpses, where gallows are erected to hang young children, and where people ask, "where is God?" Wiesel's autobiography is biography in the sense that he demonstrates that the old order is now no longer. Eliezer and other inmates discover a new history, a new view of God, as well as a new view of themselves and others in the camps.[26]

Tradition Reversed: The Eclipse of God

The original Exodus narrative is a theocentric story of the power and salvation of God who intervenes on behalf of Israel to lead her to the Promised Land. Wiesel's story told in *Night* is a narrative in which the world grows increasingly smaller, far more dangerous, and is characterized by the absence of God. When the doors of the train were shut, the world became a "cattle wagon hermetically sealed." Immediately after his arrival in the reception station of Birkenau, Wiesel writes: "Never shall I forget those flames which consumed my faith forever. . . . Never shall I forget those moments which murdered my God, and my soul and turned my dreams to dust.[27]

What had Eliezer seen and heard? "Men to the left! Women to the right!" As a fifteen year old, he had seen his mother and younger sister taken from him forever. Then he and his father are forced to walk into the "night"— past a burning ditch where a wagon had pulled up to dump its human cargo. The ditch? It was full of burning babies. Eliezer thought that he and his father were going to be marched into such a pit for adults. Eliezer's father began saying *Kaddish*—the prayer for the dead. At that point, Eliezer begins to feel revolt rise up within himself. Was there any reason to bless His name? "The Eternal, Lord of the Universe, the All-Powerful and Terrible was silent." Eliezer asks, why should I give thanks to Him? His father was weeping and his body was trembling. Two steps from the flames they were told to take a right and then were marched into the barracks.[28]

The New Torah as the Akedah in Reverse

In Elie Wiesel's home town of Sighet, the story of Abraham and Isaac was well known. In writing his story to be delivered to Mauriac, Wiesel drew upon this imagery and made the portrayal of the father-son theme reminiscent of the *akedah,* or "binding of Isaac," in Jewish tradition. Early in Wiesel's story, his world is reduced to his relationship with his father. After having been separated from his mother and three sisters on arrival at Birkenau, Wiesel is obsessed with maintaining contact with his father. As the larger story unfolds, one reads a narrative of reciprocal devotion in which each one is committed to saving the other. But the reality of Auschwitz, which is made central to the story, implies that father and son—like Abraham and Isaac before them—stand in front of an altar of death. Yet in Wiesel's story, as Andre Neher points out, the end will reveal a rewriting of the *akedah* and a reversal of the traditional father-son roles.

In Neher's reading of *Night,* the story is the *akedah* "singed" with the fires of a new reality—the reality of Auschwitz. It is the way the story would have been told in the Bible if there were more than a story, and if in its pages Abraham and Isaac—bathed in sweat and blood, and clothed in life and death—could rise up from the literary setting and confront us with the question of "Where is God?" and not, "Where is the ram?" As an *akedah* in reverse, *Night* is the story of a young son dragging an exhausted father to the sacrificial altar, which ironically also brings about the death of the son.[29]

The New Torah as One Unified Outcry

If there is one word which describes the beginning of Wiesel's writing project, it is the word "lamentation." Starting with *Night,* Wiesel seems to give ". . . one unified outcry, one sustained protest, one sobbing and singing prayer."[30] That is, the mood of the lament hangs over all of his early works. As a student of the Hebrew scriptures, Wiesel knew that in the books of Exodus and Deuteronomy, the cry of distress is a part of the narratives of deliverance of ancient Israel. Thus, the lament is a cry from the depths which dates from Jewish antiquity and is therefore a vital and inevitable part of Jewish communion with God.[31]

One of the central questions for Wiesel in *Night* is, "Where is God?" By making this question central to the narrative, Wiesel allows the mood of the personal and communal laments to hover over the entire story. And in this way he shows that his story is, in part, a dialogue with God which has both personal and corporate dimensions. Wiesel's theological intentionality appropriated in the lament seems clear. In composing his testimony to the atrocities, Wiesel knows that the lament has a societal dimension. When Wiesel cast the haunting and dirge-like mood of the lament over his slim volume of testimony, he created not only a cry from the depths directed toward

God, but also a sustained protest against the enemy. Wiesel's testimony, sent to Mauriac in 1955, was a story cast in the Jewish lamentation tradition of how a people of culture turned to genocide, and how the rest of humankind did nothing to prevent it. Yet as a lament, this volume is also a document of faith—protesting faith. The purpose of the lament is to restore the individual to the community through participation in this unique form—the very structure of which places one in bold conversation and dialogue with God. Thus Wiesel's use of the lament form suggests a robust quality to his faith as well as an ability to confront a deep sense of alienation even as he searches for a way to continue dialogue with God.[32]

III. Evoking: Atrocity, Irreality, and a New Universe

Through the literary component of "shattering," Wiesel establishes a postmodern perspective.[33] All the foundational myths of the past are turned upside down, and Wiesel's readers enter into a realm that they did not know existed prior to that moment. *Night* evokes a world in which everything is changed by the Holocaust. The foundations for living are in disarray. *Night* shows that the cataclysm that was the Holocaust is the reverse of Sinai. The Nazis created a new universe in the camps—a universe with its own language, theology, history, literature, and anthropology. Words and the meaning of words were changed indicating the creation of a new vocabulary. Auschwitz is now no longer just a place name for a town in Poland; it is an evocative symbol which conjures up the most profound confrontation of the twentieth century: the meeting of the human with the atrocities of the death camps. The Nazis seized the prerogatives once allotted to God. They became the arbiters of life and death, and assumed the role of God; God and humans changed places. History was reordered. Being became illegal and described as life unworthy of life—a subspecies the killing of which was ordered at whim.

The creation of a new universe was part of the Nazi plot and took place according to Hitler's plan for the coronation of a "master race." Yet this new order was devastating to the survivor. Consequently, Wiesel's literary project began after *Night* as a "literature of testimony," evoking some sense of moral coherence in a world that had been devastated by the Holocaust. As he does so, Wiesel continues to follow Jeremiah's model and style. His literary and spiritual journey is like Jeremiah's—a descent further into darkness. Wiesel knows that he now lives in a time, as did Jeremiah, when the forms of expression are actually breaking up, and that a new literature must be created, and that it must be consistent with the role of the survivor, even that of the ideal survivor. Just as the "confessions" are central for Jeremiah, so is the "literature of testimony" crucial for reading Wiesel. The common theme for both is what Gerhard von Rad calls "questioning reflection." Both Wiesel and Jeremiah take journeys deeper into the religious self. The common pilgrimage is actually a journey into "ever greater despair." "It is a darkness so terrible—that it could also be said that it is something so absolutely new in the dealings between Israel and her God—that it constitutes a menace to very much more than the life of a single man: God's whole way with Israel hereby threatens to end in some kind of metaphysical abyss."[34] With Wiesel as with Jeremiah, the questions which come are not simply personal, but also corporate, involving the nature and destiny of all Israel.

Perhaps under the weight of Jeremiah's code, Wiesel's early literature moves away from realistic fiction to the direction of theological parable with an emphasis on ultimate confrontations wherein the enclosed space becomes the world. While Wiesel's parabolic fiction establishes a contending and protesting faith as the appropriate response for the post-Holocaust era, it begins slowly and tentatively to affirm the sanctity of life, the solidarity of the Jewish people, and to give witness to the enduring qualities of Jewish existence. Yet in the end Wiesel's parabolic fiction, like the work of Jeremiah, is "unreadable" as literature—that is, "it cannot be read sensibly according to our Western habits of coherent literature that make a single, sustained affirmation." Again, as Colin Davis puts it, Wiesel writes texts that stutter toward a meaning that is never found and his fiction transmits "a message that it does not know how to formulate."[35] The end result of Wiesel's work is the creation of a "literature of atrocity" which creates a world of "irreality"—"by design and . . . its very nature, [it] frustrates any attempt to discover a moral reality behind the events it narrates; its questions compel not 'answers,' but a reliving of the nightmare that inspired them." For example, in reading *Night*, one becomes an "initiate into death," pulled into a dark realm of suffering and chaos which convinces the reader that one now inhabits a negative universe.[36] Thus Wiesel's texts, like those of Jeremiah, perform the collapse of the world through the shattering of narrative meaning and the evoking of the abyss. In so doing, Wiesel forces his readers to confront the modern disaster and to join the quest for new understandings.[37]

Unreadable? It is unreadable in the traditional sense because as a "literature of decomposition," as Lawrence Langer puts it, "Wiesel's literary work is a sustained dramatization of counterpositions, a long monologue disguised as a series of dialogues, revealing his own divided self."[38] The problem with which Wiesel deals is not the nature of the Holocaust, but how one should respond to it. Therefore, Wiesel's theme is the quest, and this is why the question is so central to his work. If his work is unreadable in traditional terms and fails to yield a moral reality, how can he render his work as a "literature of testimony" or witness which for him is the new form created by the generation of survivors?[39]

Evoking a New Universe: Israel and Covenant Life

Wiesel's texts are narratives of such intense pain that language cannot express the depth of the experience that it is called upon to convey. Consequently, his narratives communicate the "experience of non-interpretability and chaos," All that the text can do is function as a "metaphor of witness," or, to use Wiesel's language, give "testimony" crying forth the pain and the experience in mystery and inexpressibility. The stories "stutter" in the direction of meaning but cannot find it and finally exist without a sustained affirmation. Thus by its very nature, Wiesel's fractured literature of testimony can contain metaphors of witness or testimony such as memorials to the past and "dangerous memories," subverting the oppressor, but it finally frustrates the effort to find "answers" in the traditional sense.[40]

Through the fictive process of writing his second work entitled *Dawn*, Wiesel recreates the setting for the founding of the modern state of Israel. Within Judaism the rebirth of Israel was celebrated by many as a redemptive event on par with the Exodus and a re-validation of covenant life, though now much more secularized. In writing this novel, Wiesel celebrates the rebirth of Israel and covenant life, but in so doing challenges and questions the nature of both. *Night* had been a book of reversal, as would *Dawn*. The setting reflects a time during which innocence has been lost, and the descendants of the chosen, like the ancestor Jacob, wrestle with extremely difficult questions: Who are we really? How did the Holocaust happen? Why did we not take up arms and resist? How are Jews to live in the new order after the Holocaust? Can Jews take on an identity other than victim? Will they become executioners in the process?

As the story begins, Elisha is living in Paris. He, like the author, is a victim of the Nazi atrocities and is a survivor of Buchenwald. Elisha is obsessed with questions. Where could he find God? When and how is one most truly human? Where does suffering lead? What is the meaning of Hitler's genocidal madness? What is the relationship of victim and executioner? One night a knock at the door interrupted his life and led him to Palestine. Gad had come to recruit Elisha for a paramilitary organization fighting against the British for the freedom and establishment of Israel during the days of occupied Palestine.

Elisha's name means "God is salvation," but this contemporary figure will bring redemption in an ironic way. He will actually reverse the action of his biblical namesake. While the original Elisha brings a person back to life, this contemporary Elisha will take the life of another person at "dawn." Thus the "dawn" to which Wiesel refers is an ambiguous one, and like much of Wiesel's later work is also ironic and moves in the direction of the parabolic.[41] The story is a narrative about the "other" side—an examination of the meaning of killing. Wiesel's autobiographical protagonist is asked to take the role of the executioner of the British prisoner, John Dawson. The parabolic story, set in a house in Palestine, is eventually reduced to a final setting in the cellar where Elisha is alone with the victim. The conventional perspective is embodied by Elisha's colleagues in the movement: "If we must become more unjust and inhuman than those who have been unjust and inhuman to us, then we shall do so," said Gad. Murder would be not only their profession, but also their duty in order that Jews might be truly human.[42]

This was the orientation that young Elisha had come to accept as his own. Yet this perspective is disrupted by Elisha's memories, especially the visitation of his friends and family on the night he was scheduled to kill Dawson. Elisha's own confrontation with his former self on that night and with all those persons who had contributed to the identity of that former self, prevents the easy acceptance of the conventional view of his political action. Consequently, after having killed Dawson, Elisha realizes that he has killed part of himself. Such activity is ruled out in a morally coherent world. In his second literary work Wiesel chronicles the rebirth of the nation of Israel and celebrates the renewal of covenant life in as much as the story describes the remarkable existence of Israel, the solidarity among the people, and in an ironic way the sanctification of life. Israel is established through the use of force and covenant life is resumed with a diminished vision of God, who in some measure depends on the participation of faithful human beings. The ambiguity of this text forces Wiesel's readers to continue to ask questions with him and to search for new answers to questions concerning the relationship of force and violence in a Jewish future, a human future.

Choosing Life: The Accident and the Creation of a Language of Grief
In his next novel, *The Accident,* published in 1961, Wiesel questions the theme of the sanctity of life. Wiesel's protagonist, Eliezer, says, ". . . these people [the survivors] have been amputated; they haven't lost their legs or eyes but their will and taste for life." Consequently, Wiesel pursues an understanding of this "amputation" by exploring the theme of suicide juxtaposed to the theme of self-invention. Next to idolatry, suicide is perhaps the most striking denial of covenant Judaism. But as "amputated" selves, survivors are, for Wiesel, "spiritual cripples" who have lost the will to live and the sense of identity. Eliezer said to the doctor who had saved his life, "You want to know who I am, truly? I don't know myself."[43]

In the camps, the survivor's major defense against the immersion of death is what Lifton calls "psychic numbing," the actual cessation of feeling.[44] Consequently the inmates often become so numb that they can be seen as the walking dead.[45] This is a temporary form of symbolic death which functions in human terms to prevent permanent psychic death. Wiesel tells his readers in *Night* that after his father's death, Eliezer is unable to narrate the story any longer. There are only three pages to tell the events of several months. "I had to stay at Buchenwald until April eleventh," Wiesel writes. "I have nothing to say of my life during this period. It no longer mattered. After my father's death, nothing could touch me any more."[46] Wiesel's other early protagonists are like Eliezer in *The Accident*, "amputated selves" who can neither feel nor enter into positive relationships with others.

Wiesel's early writing, however, narrates the reversal of psychic numbing and lays the foundation for the restoration for some semblance of covenant life. How can a survivor so immersed in death choose life? One of Wiesel's most important achievements in his early writing is the creation of a "poetics of pain," or what Walter Brueggemann calls the "language of grief." It is this language, Brueggemann argues, which alone has the power to cut through the numbness and deathliness of denial. As a poet, Wiesel finds symbols—reactivated from the past—with which he brings to public expression and awareness the fears which terrorize the community. With a "candor born of anguish and passion," Wiesel as a poet/prophet speaks metaphorically about the deathliness that continues to hover over himself and other survivors. In *The Accident*, Wiesel offers to the public a dark symbolic story adequate to the horror of on-going pain. This relentless public expression by Wiesel as a poet/prophet pushes the community to once again engage what has been denied and challenges the community to refuse the realities of the Nazi "royal consciousness" and engage the experience of deathliness that hovers over them.[47]

The Parable of the Choice
Wiesel's own accident in New York City in 1956 becomes the background for his third work set in a New York hospital. The entire novel, except for flashbacks to earlier times and relationships, takes place in the hospital room in which the doctor, Paul Russel, Kathleen, and a friend named Gyula attempt to bring the reluctant patient back to life. Eliezer is aided in his quest for identity by long conversations with each of these three. But the cast which covers Eliezer's body, like the hospital room itself, encloses Eliezer in an impenetrable world and expresses the numbness that covers his being. As a parable, *The Accident* is a story about choosing between life and death. Suicide as a rejection of life is in Jewish tradition a rejection of God and one's human relationships. To investigate this theme, Wiesel makes his protagonist Eliezer like Meursault in *The Stranger* by Camus—they both live with the absurdity of life.[48] This portrayal makes *The Accident* one of Wiesel's darkest and most somber works. For Eliezer, happiness is dead. That is the conventional view of the story as a parable—human existence is without meaning and happiness is not possible. The Holocaust has made it so, and the train cannot move backward.

Yet this perspective which provides Eliezer's orientation throughout the novel is disrupted by Gyula, Eliezer's bantering friend. Gyula barges into Eliezer's room at the end of the novel, completely disregards hospital policy and Eliezer's sense of self-pity. Then Gyula confronts Eliezer with an objective appraisal of the "accident"—it had been an effort to choose death. But "man is alive," Gyula announces. It is so, he affirms, because "he is capable of friendship." Despite Eliezer's continuing pessimism, the parabolic confrontation between the two ways of being in the world have taken place. Eliezer is now aware that friendship is alive. He experiences it in the mature relationship which he shares with Gyula.[49]

A Town Beyond the Walls: Evoking an Alternative Community

In *The Accident,* Eliezer lives with a sense of the absurdity of life. For him, happiness is dead; human existence is without meaning. The Holocaust has made it so. Yet this bitter and pessimistic story is followed by one filled with a passion for justice, the moral courage to withstand a harsh interrogation of the self, a fidelity to friendship, and a claim to human wholeness. What is the difference? How does Michael make the moral journey so far beyond Eliezer? The key comes from Pedro, who, like Gyula, is a teacher/guide and who serves as a link with Wiesel's past. Pedro teaches Michael that "what you must say is 'I suffer, therefore you are.'" As the hero of the novel, Michael is determined to live out this maxim. To that end, he dedicates himself to the overcoming of his hopelessness in prison by saving his catatonic-like cell mate. In the process Michael is able to accept the Talmudic injunction to become partners with God in the on-going process of creation. In living out the maxim: "I suffer, therefore you are," Michael is learning to grieve, which is the only emotion which can penetrate the psychic numbness brought on by the madness of the Holocaust. Ironically, in learning to admit his suffering, he is freed for a survivor mission which goes beyond his own pain.[50]

In learning to grieve, Michael finds the freedom to embrace the politics of confrontation—confrontation with the spectator. As in the Exodus narrative of the Torah, the children of Israel, who feel the weight of their heavy burdens under the oppression of the pharaoh, first "cry" out to God. Then the pharaoh, who wants to continue the "royal consciousness" of the status quo in imperial Egypt, seeks to continue the "politics of oppression." The Israelites eventually learn to demythologize this strategy and proclaim an "alternative consciousness" which frees them from the pharaoh's control.[51] The very title of Wiesel's fourth work, *The Town Beyond the Wall,* is suggestive of the prophetic task to create an alternative community in opposition to forces that oppress and constrict, and implies Wiesel's ever deepening journey into religious selfhood. Michael's embrace of Pedro's dictum, "I suffer, therefore you are," also indicates the transforming power of Wiesel's emerging vision.

The Parable of the Spectator

As a parable, the complex narrative of *The Town Beyond the Wall,* filled with its "prayers" and flashbacks, is a severe testing of Gyula's affirmation in the previous novel. Gyula had virtually shouted to Eliezer that friendship is possible. Now Wiesel examines that proposition. In this story, Michael must act on his friendship with Pedro or his friend will be in great danger. The conventional attitude is embodied by the "spectator" who had witnessed the Jewish departure from Sighet in the spring of 1944. The spectator's position was detached and non-involved, a popular and "safe" existence. Michael as protagonist is led back to Sighet to confront this man and his attitude. This confrontation is one of the most intense in all of Wiesel's work. Michael tells the spectator that to live with indifference is only to subsist on the margins of existence—not really living at all. "You're really a machine for the fabrication of nothingness," Michael tells him. The central position of this confrontation in Wiesel's work is illustrated when Michael says, "I shall return to the life they call normal. The past has been exorcised." It seems to be Michael's own courageous action in confronting the spectator that leads Michael later to attempt to save the life of a cell mate. As a parable, this narrative is a story of courageous action and commitment to friends and the larger human community over against the safe and popular conventional attitude of indifference and non-involvement. Wiesel has evoked a new universe—a new age with a new view of God, the Torah, covenant, and models for living—a journey from numbness, solitude, and indifference to human action and solidarity.

IV. Enacting: A Poet/Prophet for the Nations

In the spring of 1967, Elie Wiesel was invited to give the commencement address for the Jewish Theological Seminary in New York City. Wiesel prepared a speech entitled "To A Young Jew of Today." By the time Wiesel had finished speaking to the "young Jew" that night in June of 1967, it was clear that he had an expanded view of the world and a spiritual geography which was grounded in his understanding of Judaism and its relationship to humanity. There was a creative tension between particularism and universalism—his love for Israel and his commitment to the well-being of human kind. Wiesel now finds it necessary to live out his vision of the ethical that has come down to him through tradition and that he has constructed through fiction and biblical midrash. For Elie Wiesel, life is, at this point, an "enacted word"—an extension of his vocation as a writer. His orientation is that of praxis—the holding together of spoken word and the lived word of action.

Wiesel had begun his career as a writer telling Jewish stories. Yet there came a time when he understood that his vocation was larger than that of a writer. In time, he developed a theory of praxis for his work—the Jewish story is, for Wiesel, the central symbol but appears as a metaphor for the human. Thus by collapsing the conventional categories, Wiesel created a fictive world in which he could envision work for justice and human solidarity. In so doing, he focused on final realities. By telescoping characterization and setting, his localized stories became narratives of the world—a universe in which human community became a possibility and solidarity with victims a foundational premise.

Wiesel's praxis orientation—his life as an enacted word—came as a natural consequence of his literary career and his Jewish background. Following his trip to the Soviet Union in 1965, Wiesel became increasingly involved in public life. The theory of an enacted word which Wiesel described to the "young Jew" as he spoke at the Jewish Theological Seminary demonstrated a praxis orientation that would be the final act of his testimony and the completion of his poetics of memory and justice, all of which provides validation and authenticity to his vision. If Wiesel had taken the time to tell the young Jewish student of the background influences for his speech that night, perhaps he would have said more about Jewish messianism, about the understanding for "doing" *mitsvoth* or about the work of the prophets of Israel especially, Jeremiah.[52]

Beginning in the 1960s Elie Wiesel's life began to move in new directions both in terms of his particularistic devotion to Jews and in later years in more universal directions toward suffering non-Jews. With an eye toward a praxis orientation—and the universal model of the prophet of the nations in Jeremiah—Wiesel saw it necessary to hold faith and practice together. It is this living out of his faith that has pushed him to travel to the jungles of Central America, to the ghettoes of South Africa, and to the borders of Cambodia in Southeast Asia, all of which is the final component of a complex poetics of memory and justice.

V. Conclusion

The centerpiece of Wiesel's literary and theological project is a poetics of memory and justice which grows from his reading and appropriation of the language and logic of Jeremiah ben Hilkiah as his code. I have argued that the central components of his poetics are the ideas of shattering, evoking, and enacting which can be found in Jeremiah's call and are embodied in Wiesel's life and work. Shattering involves the relentless portrayal of disaster—the continual telling of the story which rehearses the decomposition of the world and utilizes primary traditional themes such as the *akedah*, Exodus and Sinai traditions, and the lament. Evoking involves the quest to create a new world, complete with new images of God, Torah, covenant, and models for living. Wiesel involves himself in a drama of interrogation through fiction in which the quest and the question are more prominent than affirmation. In the end, however, Wiesel's fiction is "unreadable" in traditional terms, and he turns to strategies that read the reader, seeking to involve the reader in the on-going quest to bring about justice. Wiesel's final statement is the life that he attempts to live. And as an "enacted word," like Jeremiah, he attempts the role of a survivor who is relentlessly challenging to both humans and to God. Perhaps Wiesel's greatest challenge to contemporary theology comes when he allows the mood of the lament to fall across his entire project addressing both God and humankind; and when his enacted word becomes parabolic, it deforms old stories and projects new ones testifying to the daring conception that now solidarity belongs to the oppressed everywhere.

NOTES

1. See Martin Buber, *Eclipse of God: Studies in the Relation Between Religion and Philosophy* (New York: Harper & Row, 1952), 22–24.

2. Elie Wiesel, *One Generation After* (New York: Random House, 1970), 53.

3. See Lawrence Langer, *The Holocaust and the Literary Imagination* (New Haven: Yale University Press, 1975), 79. See also Elie Wiesel, *Legends of Our Time* (New York: Shocken Books, 1982), 183.

4. Alvin Rosenfeld, "The Problematics of Holocaust Literature," in *Confronting The Holocaust: The Impact of Elie Wiesel* (ed. Alvin Rosenfeld and Irving Greenburg; trans. R. C. Lamont; Bloomington: Indiana University Press, 1978), 10–13.

5. Colin Davis, *Elie Wiesel's Secretive Texts* (Gainesville: University of Florida, 1994), 3, 160.

6. Robert Alter, *The Art of Biblical Narrative* (New York: Basic Books, 1981), 12.

7. Wiesel in an interview with Gene Koppel and Henry Kaufmann, University of Arizona, Tucson, Arizona, April 25, 1973. See also the same interview listed as "A Small Measure of Victory," in Irving Abrahamson, ed., *Against Silence: The Voice and Vision of Elie Wiesel* (3 vols.; New York: Holocaust Library, 1985), 3.217–226.

8. Quoted in Tom Harpur, "A Survivor of Auschwitz Asks Why God Permits Suffering," *Toronto Star,* October 30, 1971, 9. See Also Wiesel quoted in Abrahamson, *Against Silence,* 3.309.

9. See for example: Elie Wiesel interviewed by Lily Edelman, *National Jewish Monthly* (November 1973), reprinted in Abrahamson, *Against Silence,* 2.75–84; Wiesel, *An Address to the International Symposium on the Holocaust,* Cathedral of St. John the Divine, New York, June 3, 1974; reprinted in Abrahamson, *Against Silence,* 2.88–93; and Wiesel interviewed by Robert Cromie, *Book Beat,* December 16, 1978; reprinted in Abrahamson, *Against Silence,* 3.106–111.

10. Lawrence L. Langer, "The Divided Voice: Elie Wiesel and the Challenge of the Holocaust," in *Confronting The Holocaust: The Impact of Elie Wiesel* (ed. Alvin Rosenfeld and Irving Greenburg; trans. R. C. Lamont; Bloomington: Indiana University Press, 1978), 31–48, esp. 33; see also Elie Wiesel, "Why I Write," in *Confronting The Holocaust: The Impact of Elie Wiesel* (ed. Alvin Rosenfeld and Irving Greenburg; trans. R. C. Lamont; Bloomington: Indiana University Press, 1978), 200–206, esp. 201.

11. See James A. Young, *Writing and Rewriting the Holocaust: Narrative and the Consequences of Interpretation* (Bloomington: Indiana University Press, 1988), 95. See also Elie Wiesel, et al., *Dimensions of the Holocaust* (Evanston: Northwestern University, 1977), 6–9. Wiesel writes: "After Auschwitz words are no longer innocent." Based on that premise, Wiesel elaborates the idea that new forms must be created. He writes: " . . . our generation invented a new literature, that of testimony."

12. See Wiesel, *Dimensions of the Holocaust,* 7.

13. See especially Wiesel quoted in Harry James Cargas, *Harry James Cargas in Conversation with Elie Wiesel* (New York: Paulist Press, 1976), 85–86.

14. See Elie Wiesel, *An Address to the National Invitational Conference of Anti-Defamation League of B'nai B'rith and the National Council for the Social Studies* (New York, October 9, 1977), reprinted in Abrahamson, *Against Silence,* 2.151.

15. Elie Wiesel, *Five Biblical Portraits* (Notre Dame: Notre Dame University Press, 1981), 123.

16. Wiesel, *Five Biblical Portraits,* 124.

17. See Elie Wiesel, *An Address to the National Invitational Conference of Anti-Defamation League of B'nai B'rith;* reprinted in Abrahamson, *Against Silence,* 2.151.

18. Elie Wiesel, "The Eternal Flame," (Chicago, October 7, 1976), reprinted in Abrahamson, *Against Silence,* 3.284. Wiesel says, " . . . every writer has his own imagery, has his own vocabulary, his own code, and the code of Jeremiah is actually my code."

19. This reading of Jeremiah is informed by Kathleen M. O'Connor, "'Execute Justice in the Morning': Jeremiah and Moral Character Formation of the Community" (paper presented at the annual meeting of SBL, Toronto, Canada, Nov. 26, 2002). See also Louis Stulman. *Order Amid Chaos: Jeremiah as Symbolic Tapestry* (Sheffield: Sheffield Academic Press, 1998), 57; Davis, *Elie Wiesel's Secretive Texts,* 182. Wiesel also notes in his chapter on Jeremiah that the prophet reaches a time when "language is no longer a vehicle of communication," and that Jeremiah takes up the mode of symbolic action. The unstructured nature of the text is perhaps the final symbolic act when language has failed. See Wiesel, *Five Biblical Portraits,* 113.

20. Walter Brueggemann, "The Book of Jeremiah: Portrait of a Prophet," *Int,* 37 (1983): 130–145.

21. Elie Wiesel, *Five Biblical Portraits,* 121.

22. See Wiesel quoted in Harry James Cargas, *Harry James Cargas in Conversation with Elie Wiesel,* 67.

23. One might question the appropriateness of using Jeremiah as a hermeneutical model for reading Wiesel. There are aspects of Jeremiah's life that do not seem to fit Wiesel's context. Why choose Jeremiah for reading Wiesel? The answer is that Wiesel says that Jeremiah provides the "code" for his work. Since the time of Mowinckel and Duhm, it has been customary to read Jeremiah in terms of

three major sources: A (poetry from Jeremiah), B (biographical prose from Baruch), and C (the prose discourse of Deuteronomic redactors). Why not use these sources in discussing Wiesel's appropriation of Jeremiah? In the first instance, recent scholarship has tended to move beyond these categories to new questions which find focus in ideological and canonical readings. See especially Walter Brueggemann's comments in the preface to *Reading the Book of Jeremiah: A Search for Coherence* (ed. Martin Kessler; Winona Lake, Indiana, 2004), ix. In the second instance, Wiesel's reading of Jeremiah is more canonical and ideological. He does not attempt to read Jeremiah in a historical-critical manner. Rather, Wiesel re-reads biblical texts in light of Holocaust reality. See for example, James A. Young, "The Prophet at the Y," *The New York Times*, October 20, 1991. Young writes that "Wiesel has re-read these stories through the wounded eye of the survivor before retelling them in the remembered images of his own past." In the case of Jeremiah, Wiesel makes Jeremiah into a "survivor." The Holocaust is uppermost in his thinking as he goes to the text of Jeremiah. His Jewish reading of Jeremiah searches for questions that are not in the mind of the typical biblical critic. In fact, Wiesel seems to read Jeremiah with a typology that has recently been found in the Psalms by Walter Brueggemann— orientation, disorientation, re-orientation. The code of "shattering, evoking, enacting," as I have adopted it, addresses this typology. See Walter Brueggemann, *The Message of the Psalms* (Minneapolis: Augsburg Publishing House, 1984), 9–23. Wiesel also tells his own life story in this manner—an idealized portrayal of the past which provides a stark contrast with the horrors of the Holocaust which, in turn, demands a new understanding of the meaning of life and the human. This typology is demonstrated by Wiesel when he writes of Jeremiah: "he alone predicted the catastrophe, experienced it, and lived to tell the tale. . . . we use his words to describe our struggles." Wiesel's readings are more autobiographical and typological than historical. The element of the Babylonian exile seems at first to show that the model of Jeremiah does not work for Jeremiah. Wiesel writes that the reader is disappointed that Jeremiah does not go to Babylon. Wiesel admits that this is an obscure text which one must read again and again. In so doing, Jeremiah becomes an "anti-hero" who elicits conflicting reactions. Yet we begin to like him for his weaknesses. What he sought was to redeem and transform. For example, the letter to the exiles "to build homes" becomes a "blueprint" for life in the Diaspora. Why does Jeremiah insist that Nebuchadnezzar is God's emissary—"because he knows that Israel's suffering is inevitable—and he wants to lend it meaning. Nothing is worse than suffering . . . except meaningless suffering. And the meaning has to be found in the suffering itself." The final question appears to be, can a heuristic model of interpretation based on Jeremiah's call work for reading Wiesel? Wiesel clearly identifies with Jeremiah and uses his "code," and such a thesis seems to add clarity to Wiesel's project when understood in light of his re-reading of the text. See Wiesel, *Five Biblical Portraits*, 97–127. Likewise, see Robert McAfee Brown, *Elie Wiesel: Messenger to All Humanity* (Notre Dame: Notre Dame University Press, 1983, 1989), 12–18. Brown also takes Jeremiah as the proper model for reading Wiesel. He notes that when Wiesel writes about Jeremiah, he is writing about himself.

24. Lawrence Langer describes Wiesel's work as a "literature of decomposition" in which "Every question about the Holocaust contains the seeds of its own contradiction. . . . Wiesel's literary work is a sustained dramatization of counterpositions . . . revealing his own divided self." See Langer, "The Divided Voice," 39–40.

25. See Wolfgang Iser, *The Act of Reading: A Theory of Aesthetic Response* (Baltimore: Johns Hopkins University Press, 1978), 143.

26. See Lawrence S. Cunningham, "Elie Wiesel's Anti-Exodus," in *Response to Elie Wiesel: Critical Essays by Major Jewish and Christian Scholars* (ed. Harry James Cargas; New York: Persea Books, 1978), 23–28.

27. Elie Wiesel, *Night* (trans. Stella Rodway; New York: Hill and Wang, 1960; repr., New York: Bantam, 1980), 32.

28. Wiesel, *Night,* 30–31. Wiesel describes the "eclipse of God" in more narrative and legendary terms at the end of his fourth work, *The Town Beyond the Wall* (trans. Stephen Becker; New York: Holt, Rinehart and Winston, 1964).

29. Andre Neher, *The Exile of the Word: From the Silence of the Bible to the Silence of Auschwitz* (Philadelphia: The Jewish Publication Society of America, 1981), 271.

30. Maurice Friedman, *Abraham Joshua Heschel and Elie Wiesel: You Are My Witnesses* (New York: Farrar, Strauss, Giroux, 1987), 113.

31. One of the unique contributions of Judaism to western culture is the understanding that there are a variety of forms and avenues of approach to God. In ancient times, when God makes the "face" to shine on Israel (when the blessings are manifold), Israel sings the hymns of praise. But when God turned or hid the "face" (when the tragedies of life fall), Israel sings the laments. Consequently, there were songs for orientation, blessing, and security, and then there were songs of disorientation, dislocation, and tragedy. See especially Brueggemann, *The Message of the Psalms,* 9–23.

32. See especially Walter Brueggemann, "From Hurt to Joy, From Death to Life," in *The Psalms and the Life of Faith* (ed. Patrick D. Miller; Minneapolis: Fortress Press, 1995), 3–19; W. Brueggemann, "The Formfulness of Grief," in *The Psalms and the Life of Faith* (ed. Patrick D. Miller; Minneapolis: Fortress Press, 1995), 263–275; Brueggemann, *The Message of the Psalms,* 18; and Claus Westerman, "The Role of Lament in the Theology of the Old Testament," *Int,* 28 (1974): 20–38.

33. Brueggemann writes that "the shattering and forming of worlds is . . . done as a poet 'redescribes' the world, reconfigures public perception, and causes people to reexperience their experience." See Walter Brueggemann, "The Book of Jeremiah," 135.

34. Gerhard von Rad, *Old Testament Theology* (2 vols; New York: Harper & Row, 1965), 2.193, 2.204–205.

35. Colin Davis, *Elie Wiesel's Secretive Texts,* 182; See also Robert Alter, *After the Tradition: Essays on Modern Jewish Writing* (New York: Dutton, 1969), and Walter Brueggemann, "An Ending That Does Not End: The Book of Jeremiah," in *Postmodern Interpretations of the Bible* (ed. A.K.M. Adams; St. Louis: Chalice, 2001), 117.

36. Langer, *The Holocaust and the Literary Imagination,* 75, 120.

37. See O'Connor, "Jeremiah and the Formation of the Moral Community," 12.

38. Lawrence Langer, "The Divided Voice," 40.

39. See Elie Wiesel, et al. *Dimensions,* 9. See also Langer, "The Divided Voice," 40–41.

40. See Robert Detweiler, *Breaking the Fall: Religious Readings of Contemporary Fiction* (Louisville: Westminster/John Knox Press, 1989), 47–48; Robert Alter, *After the Tradition,* 151–160; Johan Baptist Metz, *Faith in History and Society* (New York: The Seabury Press, 1980) 109–110; Elie Wiesel, *Legends of Our Time,* 8.

41. For Paul Ricoeur, a parable is a metaphor with interactive elements in permanent tension: the conventional way of being in the world versus the way of the kingdom. The inter-action between the two viewpoints results in a redescription of the possibilities of human life.

42. See Elie Wiesel, *Dawn* (New York: Hill and Wang, 1961; repr. New York: Avon Books, 1970), 41.

43. See Elie Wiesel, *The Accident* (New York: Hill and Wang, 1962; repr. New York: Avon Books, 1970), 77–79.

44. See Robert Jay Lifton, *Death in Life: Survivors of Hiroshima* (New York: Simon and Schuster, 1967), 480.

45. See especially, Primo Levi, *Survival in Auschwitz: The Nazi Assault on Humanity* (New York: Giulio Einaudi, 1958; repr. New York: Simon and Schuster, 1993), 88–90.

46. Wiesel, *Night*, 107–109.

47. See Walter Brueggemann, *The Prophetic Imagination* (Philadelphia: Fortress Press, 1978), 46–51.

48. A lengthy comparison of Wiesel's work with that of Camus or with the theater of the Absurd is beyond the scope of this article. Yet such a study would be useful. Many of Wiesel's themes parallel those of Camus. It is clear that as Wiesel says, he "was intrigued and stimulated by the intellectual and artistic ferment of Paris" in the post-war years, and that he "read everything by Camus." See Elie Wiesel, *All Rivers Run to the Sea* (New York: Alfred A. Knopf, 1995), 189. For Wiesel, absurdity comes with the Holocaust and the breakdown of covenant life, yielding an unjust and indifferent world devoid of God. The difference with Camus is that for Camus there was no moral order in the beginning.

49. See Wiesel, *The Accident*, 123. The theme of suicide is a personal one for Wiesel. See Wiesel, *All Rivers Run to the Sea*, 156, 178.

50. Elie Wiesel, *The Town*, 118–127,

51. See Walter Brueggemann, *The Prophetic Imagination*, 11–43.

52. See Eugene Borowitz, *A New Jewish Theology in the Making* (Philadelphia: Westminster Press, 1968), 156. Messianic redemption means not only a concern with the self but with others as well. That is, one begins to serve God by learning to serve the children of God. Also in prophetic texts, like Jeremiah, one reads that symbolic action among the prophets was an important function. Such an active demonstration was not a simple effort to reinforce what had been heard, or to create a visual image. As Johanes Lindblom puts it, "such an action served not only to represent and make evident a particular fact, but also to make this fact a reality." See Lindblom, *Prophecy in Ancient Israel* (Philadelphia: Fortress Press, 1962), 172.

NONA FIENBERG

Gazing into the Mirror of Wiesel's Night, Together

I must begin with a confession. When I last taught Literature of the Holocaust, I cut Wiesel's *Night* from the reading list. Teachers are always making hard choices. There's just too much compelling literature to teach in this class. I teach only texts written by survivors. That narrows the field somewhat—so, no Cynthia Ozick, no Anne Michaels, or Ursula Hegi, or Art Spiegelman. I sneak in Nathan Englander's short story "The Tumblers" as end-of-semester reading and for the final exam, but that's a closing flourish. Eliminating *Night* carries a hint of heresy and a measure of guilt. But with Oprah Winfrey as champion, and 10 million copies sold, *Night*'s dominance in discussions of Holocaust literature has long been secured. Less pervasive texts, such as Ida Fink's *A Scrap of Time and Other Stories*, Lore Segal's *Other People's Houses*, Charlotte Delbo's *Auschwitz and After*, Jurek Becker's *Jacob the Liar*, and Imre Kertesz's *Kaddish for an Unborn Child*, claim my class's attention. Perhaps you hear too in the opening of this review of Alan Rosen's edition of essays on Wiesel's *Night*, in the Modern Language Association's series Approaches to Teaching, the echo of Kertesz's 2002 Nobel Prize for Literature lecture, "I must begin with a confession" (604). Kertesz's confessional, analytical literature tackles the need to understand and even explain the Holocaust, as well as the totalitarian oppression to which Auschwitz attests. Wiesel's project is a different one. I seek, in my classroom of about

Pedagogy, Volume 9, Number 1 (Winter 2009): pp. 167–175. Copyright © 2009 Duke University Press.

169

thirty undergraduate students from all disciplinary majors, texts that pose knotty problems for students to untangle, often in small work groups, sometimes using in-class writing followed by problem-solving group exercises. The learning method, a version of think/pair/share, becomes also a model for responsible reading, thinking, and even action on the issues the texts pose. It had been less evident to me that *Night* served as fruitfully for a problem-solving pedagogy.

One small token, then, of the success of Rosen's anthology is Wiesel's *Night*'s place in my syllabus this semester. Rosen has gathered a community of scholars and teachers who together testify to Wiesel's efficacy in the college classroom. Although one might think that teaching Literature of the Holocaust would be a lonely experience, for me and for the colleagues gathered in Alan Rosen's anthology, the moments of solitude are far outnumbered by the shared construction of defiance, resistance, and determination. While *Night* shares with other Holocaust memoirs the thematic of the aloneness of camp experience, Rosen has collected eighteen teachers and scholars who together create a communal intellectual and ethical life. In the voices of the eighteen scholar/teachers, symbolically numbering *Chai,* or life, Rosen's volume breathes new life into the study and teaching of *Night.* Imaginatively, through their vibrant conversations with each other and with the text, they have helped me to understand *Night*'s place in the work of my college classroom.

In my teaching, I collaborate with an interdisciplinary team of Holocaust scholars at Keene State College under the umbrella of the Cohen Center for Holocaust Studies, soon to become the Cohen Center for Holocaust and Genocide Studies. While there can be no denying the pain in these profound texts, as Alan Rosen's introduction attests, the eighteen voices that excavate "Historical and Cultural Contexts," "Literary Contexts," and "Courses and Classroom Strategies" together shed light on the darkest of times. For me, then, because of the challenges and pleasures of teaching together with a team, it is not pain and aloneness that become the greatest classroom challenges in teaching the Holocaust, in particular Wiesel's *Night.* Instead, as Wiesel ages, as the survivors die whose testimony, like that of Congressman Tom Lantos, bears witness, as students look back in alienation to the deep history of anti-Semitism and the mid-twentieth-century history of World War II and the Holocaust, it is critical to answer difficult pedagogical questions. How can teachers and students build bridges to the past and construct bridges to current genocide and future threats? What will make these memories and memoirs live in the twenty-first century as survivors die?

If I felt that other texts provided challenges and responses my students needed to engage these difficult questions, I was in the company Gary Weissman (2004) analyzes in *Teaching the Representation of the Holocaust,* another MLA pedagogy-focused publication, edited by Marianne Hirsch and Irene

Kacandes. Weissman's article "Questioning Key Texts: A Pedagogical Approach to Teaching Elie Wiesel's *Night"* identifies the need Rosen's anthology addresses. What is effective higher education pedagogy for Wiesel's text? Since *Night* has so often been presented and contextualized through high school teaching, its classroom study may have lacked the critical, scholarly rigor it needs. Weissman asks, "How are students to analyze the book when the Holocaust's mystical-religious gravity, *Night*'s exalted status as *the* classic memoir of the Holocaust, and Wiesel's stature as *the* survivor of the Holocaust all conspire to dissuade them from considering *Night* as writing that can be read critically?" (329). Weissman finds one crux, as do a number of authors in Rosen's anthology, in the closing image that so haunts readers. Not Wiesel's chosen close, the English edition ends with Wiesel gazing into a mirror: "From the depths of the mirror, a corpse was contemplating me. The look in his eyes as he gazed at me has never left me" (115). In that image, the mysterious, unexplainable, mystical horror of the Holocaust experience has spoken to generations. Yet not Wiesel but his French editor, Jerome Lindon, ended *La Nuit* with that image. The Yiddish memoir continues, "I saw the image of myself after my death. It was at that instant that the will to live was awakened. Without knowing why I raised a balled-up fist and smashed the mirror, breaking the image that lived within it" (330; quoted in Seidman 1996: 7). As Weissman (2004: 331) suggests, the different ending changes much. In the moment of anger, writing becomes not a mysterious struggle to represent the unrepresentable but a practical means of resistance. I found the first problem-solving exercise for my students in the questions raised by the different endings to Wiesel's *Night.* With such knowledge, scholars can use *Night* as a text to "encourage students to move past an uncritical mystical-religious conception of the Holocaust" (333). What Weissman proposed, Rosen's anthology fulfills.

The first of the essays, in Rosen's opening section, "Historical and Cultural Contexts," is Nehemia Polen's *"Night* as Counternarrative: The Jewish Background" (22–31), which reads Wiesel's memoir of a young man, a scholar of a mystical, transcendent Judaism, as a counter-Torah. In Polen's reading, *Night* echoes Job, Jeremiah, and Psalms ultimately not to praise the triumph of God the father, but to lament the defeat of the father, both as God and as Eliezer's literal father. With Polen's analysis, we see the first of what will become a kaleidoscopic vision of key critical moments. As Weissman predicted, the perspectives in Rosen's anthology reveal themselves through readings of the singular last image in the volume: the survivor of Auschwitz looks in the mirror and sees a corpse contemplating him, in a gaze that has never left him. For his reading, Polen reaches into Talmudic tradition to the story of Simeon the Just, who came to understand that the call to temptation, whether of desire or of despair, might be withstood by telling a tale, since the tale, whether of love or of death, participates in the act of rebuilding. The look in the mirror becomes the metaphor for essential questions of individual identity as well as human identity following the Holocaust. His version of the tale of Simeon the Just places the gaze in the tradition of Narcissus. If you look in a mirror, the temptation is great to love what you see and to live in solipsistic indulgence, perhaps despair. Resistance, in this story, becomes the turning away from the solipsistic gaze and toward a future dedicated to repairing the universe. Here is another set of problems for my students to address in focused freewriting followed by group work. In what contexts is it productive and powerful to read *Night?* What intertexts are useful to bring to bear in the reading of the memoir's close, for example, the Yiddish book's shattered mirror ending?

My approach to Rosen's anthology, then, is to evaluate which essays offer problems my students and I will find engaging and enriching. Which essays pose questions that a class of undergraduates in a general education course will need to address? Which essays exhort students to assume responsibility to construct meaning and, beyond that, to act? Historian Simone Gigliotti, in the second essay of the seventeen in Rosen's anthology, "*Night* and the Teaching of History: The Trauma of Transit" (32–41), considers her challenge as a historian in contextualizing the use of a memoir. When Gigliotti asks how to cross disciplinary boundaries in the teaching of the Holocaust, she also invites students from fields other than English to consider the uses of reading literature. For historians, Holocaust memoirs bring to life the experience of deportation. Gigliotti chooses deportation as a focus that could be treated as "Historical; Aesthetic and linguistic; Corporeal, spatial, geographic; Literary or interpretive; Narrative or (auto)biographical" (39). Gigliotti's interdisciplinary approach confronts historians' concerns about incorporating memoirs into their courses. "The interpretive distinctions between truth and fiction, between historical evidence and fabrication, have proved crucial in the reading of testimonies and memoirs of Holocaust survivors" (39). In contrast to the positivist criterion of writing history as it really was, testimony should not be construed rigidly. Instead, Gigliotti's classes at once "address perceived limitations of emotional, traumatic testimony, and see it as integral to the history of the Holocaust" (40). Read this essay for an inspired teacher's use of Wiesel's account of deportation. For a survivor, memories collapse past and present: "I freeze every time I hear a train whistle" (Wiesel 74). In Wiesel's haunting line, and through Gigliotti's evocative inquiry, teachers of the Holocaust destabilize their own and their students' interest in representing this and other historical representations as "a factually legitimated, ordered, and chronologically constructed event" (34). Instead, students question conventional historical study and investigate trauma, emotion, and sensory evidence. If, some sixty years after deportation and Auschwitz, a train whistle freezes Wiesel, or the smell of a rotted potato transports Charlotte Delbo's friend and companion back to the Lager, then scholars and teachers of the Holocaust must help students to understand why. Sensory evidence offers students a window into the trauma of history. Through the senses, students bridge time.

In another destabilizing essay, "The Original Yiddish Text and the Context of *Night*" (52–58), Jan Schwarz debunks what early became the truism about Holocaust testimonies, that a fifteen-year silence of survivors was broken by the Eichmann trial in Jerusalem in 1961. Schwarz traces the Yiddish tradition of such narratives, already familiar in its conventions to readers of the Yiddish book series *Dos poylishe yidutum* (Polish Jewry). When, in 1956, Wiesel published *Un di velt hot geshvign/And the World Was Silent*, he wrote in his mother tongue to an audience of Yiddish readers, speakers, and writers, in a tradition that the Nazis had sought to extinguish. Like the editing out of the shattered mirror at the book's close, some of the intimate passion of that address was excised in the French text. While Wiesel confirms that had he not written in Yiddish, he could never have created his memoir, a classroom think/pair/share activity uncovers the world of difference between the Yiddish title and *Night*. Susanne Klingenstein's "*Night*'s Literary Art" further illuminates the Yiddish tradition to which and from which Wiesel wrote. All that her essay lacks is the teacherly context that would help engage students productively in this rich contextual research.

The section "Courses and Classroom Strategies" provides teachers' stories of working with students on this challenging material. Paul Eisenstein's "*Night* and Critical Thinking" (107–114) contrasts Francois Mauriac's preface and its redemptive, progressive view of history with the memoir's irremediable trauma. Through such contrast, Eisenstein invites students to consider a contingency of values, an unsettling of absolute truths. For the students I teach, this is perhaps the most difficult critical thinking opportunity. Similarly, Phyllis Lassner's midrashic method in "Negotiating the Distance: Collaborative Learning and Teaching *Night*" (115–123) invites questions and debate while also pausing for spaces, voids, and silence, in a classroom strategy modeled in the text itself. Jan Darsa's "*Night* and Video Testimony" (140–145) takes the text to high school students, who are upset, puzzled, and even angry. Like Darsa's high school students who ask "Why didn't the Jews leave?" my college students pose questions that derive from American optimism. Students believe themselves to be responding empathetically when they declare, "I would never have . . . " or "If I had been there, I would have. . . . " Their narrative tracks the triumph of individual agency with a naïveté that teachers in all disciplines work to complicate. Yet, paradoxically, Wiesel's narrative insists on the apparently shared ethos of the Jews of Sighet, who cannot credit Moishe the Beadle's warnings. For some students, privilege in the United

States and uncritical adoption of an ideology of free choice and absolute agency seem to grant them superiority of judgment. Darsa's approach, using video testimonies, "allow(s) students to hear a variety of voices speaking about different events and themes, thus reducing the inclination to generalize, find simple answers to complex questions, and doubt the authenticity of the memoir" (145). For students who believe that individuals control their own destiny, often without knowing that alternative beliefs exist, learning about the Holocaust challenges unexamined assumptions. Both through texts and through pedagogy, students learn to pause and reflect before judging the illusory choices Jews faced in the Holocaust.

Philosopher John K. Roth, in "The Real Questions: Using *Night* in Teaching the Holocaust" (146–152), turns to moral and spiritual questions at the anthology's close. Since *Night* is a book of questions, he analyzes the questions that it raises, rather than any answers it may provide. Perhaps we can productively call them problems, like the deep problem Wiesel poses: "In Auschwitz all the Jews were victims, all the killers were Christians . . . as surely as the victims are a problem for the Jews, the killers are a problem for the Christians" (148). Roth finds *Night*'s greatest significance in the "moral and spiritual challenges that it creates for humanity's future" (152).

While I began this essay reflecting upon the communal enterprise of the interdisciplinary team of Holocaust studies scholars at Keene State College, representing history, women's studies, English, psychology, sociology, anthropology, film, and religious studies, I return to my confession that I had not taught Wiesel's *Night* for several years in my Literature of the Holocaust class. One important thread in the course was inspired by Sidra DeKoven Ezrahi's discussion of the controversy over *Life Is Beautiful,* the Roberto Benigni film that some see as reductive, others as a tool to remember and teach about the Holocaust. Ezrahi situates the movie within the distinctive tradition of Jewish humor, from, for example, Sholom Aleichem's "Dreyfus in Kasrilevka" through Becker's *Jacob the Liar,* and to Englander's short story "The Tumblers." Englander imagines the villagers of a fictional Chelm disguising themselves as circus tumblers in order to survive a deportation. When the aging Jews board the train, their strange appearance prompts other riders to exclaim that they must be circus performers. Leaping into surreal fantasy, now costumed in scraps and corks as circus dancers, the Chelmites glance, like Wiesel, in the mirror. They too see a truth difficult to accommodate. Their resistance, continuing to perform, even as the disguise may be penetrated and their deaths assured, becomes a metaphor for Jewish survival, whether in the Holocaust or in an Israel besieged by rocket fire and terrorist attacks. Although they see despair in the mirror, they also see their future. Having learned somersaults and earned new knowledge of themselves and their world, they must tumble. It is a rueful humor, one that has long sustained Jewish life, but not a line of cultural richness to which I had understood Wiesel to be attached. It took students to foreground the gallows humor even in *Night*'s narrative. Wiesel, one student wrote, found a moment of humor when talking about Idek, who "moved one hundred prisoners so that he could copulate with this girl! It struck me as terribly funny and I burst out laughing" (57). While Wiesel pays a terrible price in the beating he receives for that moment of ironic laughter at the human condition, the comedy situates even his dark memoir in the line of the Book of Esther, Sholom Aleichem, and tales of Chelm.

A second thread in my class was nurtured by a faculty study group considering gender as a category in the Holocaust, preparing to teach less-studied women's experiences of the Holocaust through Delbo, Segal, Fink, Charlotte Salomon's "Life or Theatre," and Ravensbruck. To this project, Judith Clark Schaneman's "Teaching *La nuit* in Comparative Contexts" (59–68) contributes a welcome comparison between Wiesel's account of the *univers concentrationnaire* and Delbo's experience as a woman and non-Jew, imprisoned for her participation in the French Resistance. Schaneman adds Anna Langfus's *Le sel et le soufre* (translated as *The Whole Land Brimstone*) to those books to read and consider for the next syllabus.

The future of Holocaust studies depends upon student engagement in the problems the texts pose, as well as in shared responsibility to analyze and act upon genocide since the Holocaust. When I next teach the class, I may situate Wiesel's *Night* in the context of the Armenian genocide, or Rwanda, Darfur, or the genocide of American Indians. At Keene State College, students led the way, forming an activist Holocaust and Genocide Awareness Group, teaching their teachers. Students organize teach-ins, roundtables, marches, petition campaigns, and fundraisers in protest against the genocide in Darfur. A sociology colleague spent her sabbatical in Rwanda preparing to lead this semester's student trip to work with a Rwandan relief agency. Faculty members convened the multidisciplinary Genocide Studies Reading Group to discuss Samantha Power's *A Problem from Hell;* Dave Eggers's *What Is the What,* a fictionalized memoir of Valentino Achak Deng, one of Sudan's Lost Boys; a film scholar's lecture on documentaries of the Holocaust; and Franz Werfel's novel of the Armenian genocide, *The Forty Days of Musa Dagh.* Written by a Jewish refugee from Europe in World War II, *Musa Dagh* fulfills the call to remember, to write it down, and to tell the story, but differently. Soon the shared work of faculty colleagues and students will help prepare the college community to expand the Holocaust studies minor into a Holocaust and genocide studies major.

As students know, Wiesel's summons to responsibility demands remembrance as well as action, resistance in the countless shapes that chroniclers of the Holocaust trace, and some that are yet to be found. When study and problem solving take communal shape inside and outside the classroom and in volumes like Rosen's, the project of remembrance and responsibility gathers students and teachers around analysis of the past and the present in order to look clearly toward a future. Alan Rosen's acknowledgments offer a prayer for his children: "They should be blessed to know and make a world where the scenes *Night* renders are confined solely to the past" (3). Wiesel's exhortation as he closes his Nobel Peace Prize speech in 1986 calls humankind to that shared enterprise: "What all these victims need above all is to know that they are not alone; that we are not forgetting them, that when their voices are stifled we shall lend them ours, that while their freedom depends on ours, the quality of our freedom depends on theirs" (120). In our classrooms, Rosen's text inspires critical, analytical, creative approaches to the study of Wiesel's *Night*. One student responded in a final exam: "I could never draw myself away from the fact that we were discussing someone's life and ultimately their death. And, to deviate slightly, which I must do because I cannot think of the Holocaust and not place it into a current context, I am ashamed at the inaction of the world in regard to modern day genocide. The literature of the Holocaust should leave us all with a resounding message of 'never again' and, unfortunately, I do not think it has." For the class, no metaphor proved more resonant than the metaphor of the mirror, both shattered and hauntingly reflective. That is, Wiesel's *Night*, like his moral and ethical life work, establishes the language through which discussions of responsibility are framed. Students learn to articulate their engagement in the text and the problems it poses, including the open-ended close that reaches out into action. One student who at first craved ready answers ultimately testified, "It feels good to be a part of what the writers worked so hard on." The small-group work provided a model for the class activity of reading as problem solving and learning to understand multiple perspectives. More powerfully still, both text and pedagogy hold the mirror up to nature, moving some to act as our brothers' and sisters' keepers.

WORKS CITED

Ezrahi, Sidra DeKoven. 2001. "After Such Knowledge, What Laughter?" *Yale Journal of Criticism* 14, no. 1: 287–307.

Kertesz, Imre. 2003. "Heureka!" *PMLA* 118: 604–614.

Seidman, Naomi. 1996. "Elie Wiesel and the Scandal of Jewish Rage." *Jewish Social Studies* 3: 1–19.

Weissman, Gary. 2004. "Questioning Key Texts: A Pedagogical Approach to Teaching Elie Wiesel's *Night*." In *Teaching the Representation of the Holocaust*, ed. Marianne Hirsch and Irene Kacandes, 324–336. New York: Modern Language Association.

Wiesel, Elie. 2006. *Night*, trans. Marion Wiesel. New York: Hill & Wang.

Chronology

1928	Elie Wiesel is born on September 30, on the Jewish holiday of Simchat Torah, in Sighet, Rumania. Sighet is located in the region of Transylvania, which is annexed by Hungary in 1940 and reverts back to Rumania in 1945.
1934–1944	While living in Sighet, Wiesel attends *heder* (primary school) and later the yeshiva, where he becomes immersed in the study of the Torah and the Talmud.
1944–1945	Wiesel is imprisoned in various concentration camps (Birkenau, Auschwitz, Buna, Buchenwald) from April 1944 to April 1945.
1945	On April 11, Wiesel is liberated from the Buchenwald concentration camp. He is then sent to France with other children who have survived the concentration camps.
1946	He travels first to Taverny and then Paris, where he rents a room in Porte Saint-Cloud. He earns money as a choir director and Bible teacher.
1948–1951	Wiesel studies philosophy, literature, and psychology at the Sorbonne. Camus, Kierkegaard, and Kafka are among the writers who influence him the most.
1948	While working as a journalist, Wiesel visits Israel to report on the Israeli struggle. During the following years, he continues to live in Paris while working as a newspaper correspondent.

1956	Wiesel settles in New York, where he still lives today. *Un di velt hot gesvign (And the World Has Remained Silent)*, an account of Wiesel's experience in Auschwitz, is published. Wiesel states that this account is the foundation for all of his subsequent books. While working as a correspondent to the United Nations for the Israeli newspaper *Yediot Aharonot*, Wiesel is struck by a taxi in Times Square. Later, unable to get his French travel documents extended, Wiesel applies for American citizenship.
1957	Works for the *Jewish Daily Forward*, a New York Yiddish newspaper, as a writer of feature articles.
1958	*La Nuit* published in Paris. Translated and published as *Night* in 1960 in the United States.
1960	*Dawn (L'Aube)* is published.
1961	*The Accident (Le Jour)* is published.
1962	*The Town Beyond the Wall (La Ville de la chance)* is published. Wiesel wins the Prix Rivarol and the National Jewish Book Council Award.
1963	Elie Wiesel becomes a United States citizen.
1964	*The Gates of the Forest (Les Portes de la forêt)* is published. Wiesel now devotes himself full time to writing and lecturing.
1965	Wiesel visits the Soviet Union during the Jewish High Holy Days and writes a series of articles on his impressions of Soviet Jewry for *Yediot Aharonot*.
1966	The articles on Soviet Jews from the previous year are collected and published as *The Jews of Silence: A Personal Report on Soviet Jewry*.
1968	Wiesel's first drama, *Zalmen, or the Madness of God*, is published in France. It is first staged, as *The Madness of God*, in Washington, D.C., in 1974. *A Beggar in Jerusalem* is published and awarded the Prix Medicis, one of France's most distinguished literary prizes.
1969	Wiesel marries Marion Erster Rose, a Viennese, who is also a survivor of the concentration camps. Marion becomes a translator of most of Wiesel's books.

1970   *One Generation After* is published on the twenty-fifth anniversary of Wiesel's liberation from Buchenwald.

1971   *Souls on Fire (Célébration hassidique: portraits et légendes)* is published, consisting of lectures originally given at the Sorbonne and at the Young Men's Hebrew Association in New York.

1972   Wiesel is appointed Distinguished Professor of Jewish Studies at the City College of the City University of New York. Wiesel's son, Shlomo Elisha, is born.

1973   *The Oath (Le Serment de Kolvillàg)* and *Ani Maamin* are published.

1976   *Messengers of God: Biblical Portraits and Legends (Célébration Biblique)* is published.

1978   Wiesel is appointed Andrew Mellon Professor of Humanities and University Professor at Boston University. *Four Hasidic Masters and Their Struggle Against Melancholy* and *A Jew Today* are published.

1979   *The Trial of God*, Wiesel's second drama, is published; Wiesel also appointed chairman of the President's Commission on the Holocaust. He is awarded an honorary degree by Wesleyan University.

1980   *Le Testament d'un poète juif assassiné* is published; translated as *The Testament* in 1981. Wiesel is awarded an honorary degree by Brandeis University.

1981   Wiesel is awarded an honorary degree by Yale University.

1983   *Le Cinquieème fils* is published in Paris. Translated as *The Fifth Son* by Marion Wiesel, it is published in New York by Summit in 1985.

1985   *Against Silence: The Voice and Vision of Elie Wiesel*, three volumes, edited by Irving Abrahamson, is published in New York by Holocaust Library. *Signes d'Exode* is published in Paris by Grasset et Fasquelle. Wiesel receives the Congressional Gold Medal of Achievement from President Reagan.

1986   On October 14 he wins Nobel Peace Prize for *Night;* Wiesel is active with his wife in the Elie Wiesel Foundation for Humanity, aided by money from his Nobel Prize.

1987   *The Night Trilogy: Night, Dawn, The Accident* is published in
            New York by Farrar, Straus & Grioux. *Le Crépuscule, au loin*
            is published in Paris by Grasset et Fasquelle.

1989   Wiesel's tenth novel, *L'Oublié*, is published; it is translated
            by Stephen Becker as *The Forgotten* (1992).

1992   Wiesel is awarded the Presidential Medal of Freedom for
            Literature Arts by the National Foundation for Jewish
            Culture.

1994   The first volume of Wiesel's memoir is published as *Tous
            les fleuves vont à la mer: Mémoires*; it is translated by Marion
            Wiesel as *All Rivers Run to the Sea: Memoirs* (1995).

1996   The second volume of Wiesel's memoir is published as *Et la
            mer n'est pas remplie: Mémoires, 2* and translated by Marion
            Wiesel as *And the Sea Is Never Full: 1969-* (New York:
            Knopf, 1999).

1999   Wiesel's novel *Les Juges* is published; it is translated as *The
            Judges* (2002).

2003   Wiesel's novel *Le Temps des déracinés* is published.

2006   Wiesel is named an Honorary Knight of the British Empire
            in recognition of his services to Holocaust education. He is
            also named Humanitarian of the Century by the Council
            of Jewish Organizations.

Contributors

HAROLD BLOOM is Sterling Professor of the Humanities at Yale University. He is the author of 30 books, including *Shelley's Mythmaking* (1959), *The Visionary Company* (1961), *Blake's Apocalypse* (1963), *Yeats* (1970), *A Map of Misreading* (1975), *Kabbalah and Criticism* (1975), *Agon: Toward a Theory of Revisionism* (1982), *The American Religion* (1992), *The Western Canon* (1994), and *Omens of Millennium: The Gnosis of Angels, Dreams, and Resurrection* (1996). *The Anxiety of Influence* (1973) sets forth Professor Bloom's provocative theory of the literary relationships between the great writers and their predecessors. His most recent books include *Shakespeare: The Invention of the Human* (1998), a 1998 National Book Award finalist; *How to Read and Why* (2000); *Genius: A Mosaic of One Hundred Exemplary Creative Minds* (2002); *Hamlet: Poem Unlimited* (2003); *Where Shall Wisdom Be Found?* (2004); and *Jesus and Yahweh: The Names Divine* (2005). In 1999, Professor Bloom received the prestigious American Academy of Arts and Letters Gold Medal for Criticism. He has also received the International Prize of Catalonia, the Alfonso Reyes Prize of Mexico, and the Hans Christian Andersen Bicentennial Prize of Denmark.

TED L. ESTESS is Jane Morin Cizik Professor in the Humanities at the University of Houston and dean of the honors college. He wrote *Elie Wiesel* (1980).

BENJ MAHLE is a high-school teacher in Minnesota.

SUKHBIR SINGH is a professor and head of English and American literatures at Osmania University, Hyderabad, India.

CARDINAL JEAN-MARIE LUSTIGER (1926–2007) was a cardinal in the Roman Catholic Church and, as archbishop of Paris, was leader of the church in France. Having converted in his youth from Judaism, he remained devoted throughout his pastorate to championing Jewish-Catholic relations.

EVA FLEISCHNER, professor emerita of religion at Montclair State University, is a program leader at the Franciscan Renewal Center in Scottsdale, Arizona. She wrote *Judaism in German Christian Theology since 1945: Christianity and Israel Considered in Terms of Mission* (1975).

DAVID L. VANDERWERKEN is professor of English at Texas Christian University. He has published many articles on twentieth-century American literature. He wrote *Faulkner's Literary Children: Patterns of Development* (1997).

JOYCE LAZARUS is professor of modern languages at Framingham State College.

JOHN K. ROTH is the Edward J. Sexton Professor Emeritus of philosophy and the founding director of the Center for the Study of the Holocaust, Genocide, and Human Rights at Claremont McKenna College. He has published widely in his field, including *Genocide and Human Rights: A Philosophical Guide* (edited, 2005); *Gray Zones: Ambiguity and Compromise in the Holocaust and Its Aftermath*, edited with Jonathan Pertopoulas (2006) and *Ethics During and After the Holocaust: In the Shadow of Birkenau* (2007).

DANIEL R. SCHWARZ is a professor in the Department of Jewish history at the Hebrew University of Jerusalem. He has published prolifically in Jewish history and the historiography of the Second Temple Period.

SAMUEL TOTTEN is professor of curriculum and instruction in the College of Education and Health Professions at the University of Arkansas. He has published widely on the topic of genocide, including *The Prevention and Intervention of Genocide: An Annotated Bibliography* (2006) and *Genocide at the Millennium* (2005), which he edited.

SARA R. HOROWITZ is director of the Centre for Jewish Studies at York University in Toronto. She is the author of *Voicing the Void: Muteness and Memory in Holocaust Fiction* (1997), coedits the journal *Kerem: Creative Explorations in Judaism*, and edits the Azreili Series of Holocaust Memoirs.

GARY WEISSMAN is assistant professor of English at the University of Cincinnati. He wrote *Fantasies of Witnessing: Postwar Efforts to Experience the Holocaust* (2004).

FREDERICK L. DOWNING is professor and department chair of philosophy and religious studies at Valdosta State University. He wrote *To See the Promised Land* (1986) and *Elie Wiesel: A Religious Biography* (2008).

NONA FIENBERG is dean of the College of Arts and Humanities at Keene State College. She has written articles about women in Renaissance literature.

Bibliography

Abramowitz, Molly. *Elie Wiesel: A Bibliography*. Metuchen, N.J.: Scarecrow Press, 1974.

Alexander, Edward. *The Resonance of Dust: Essays on Holocaust Literature and Jewish Fate*. Middletown, Conn.: Wesleyan University Press, 1979.

Alter, Robert. *After the Tradition*. New York: E. P. Dutton, 1969.

Arendt, Hannah. *Eichmann in Jerusalem*. New York: Viking, 1963.

Bar-On, Dan. *Legacy of Silence: Encounters with Children of the Third Reich*. Cambridge, Mass.: Harvard University Press, 1989.

Berenbaum, Michael G. *The Vision of the Void: Theological Reflections on the Works of Elie Wiesel*. Middletown, Conn.: Wesleyan University Press, 1979.

Berger, Alan L. *Crisis and Covenant: The Holocaust in American Jewish Fiction*. Albany: State University of New York Press, 1985.

Berkovits, Eliezer. *Faith After the Holocaust*. New York: Ktav, 1973.

Bettelheim, Bruno. *The Informed Heart*. New York: Avon, 1971.

Brown, Robert McAfee. "The Holocaust as a Problem in Moral Choice," in *Dimensions of the Holocaust*. Evanston, Ill.: Northwestern University Press, 1977, pp. 47–83.

———. *Elie Wiesel: Messenger to All Humanity*. Notre Dame, Ind.: University of Notre Dame Press, 1983.

Bussie, Jacqueline A. *The Laughter of the Oppressed: Ethical and Theological Resistance in Wiesel, Morrison, and Endo*. New York: Continuum, 2007.

Cargas, Harry James, ed. *Harry James Cargas in Conversation with Elie Wiesel*. New York: Paulist Press, 1976.

————, ed. *Responses to Elie Wiesel: Critical Essays by Major Jewish and Christian Scholars*. New York: Persea, 1978.

Davis, Colin. *Elie Wiesel's Secretive Texts*. Gainesville: University Press of Florida, 1994.

Dawidowicz, Lucy S. *The War Against the Jews 1933–1945*. New York: Bantam, 1976.

Downing, Frederick L. *Elie Wiesel: A Religious Biography*. Macon, Ga.: Mercer University Press, 2008.

Erzahi, Sidra DeKoven. *By Words Alone: The Holocaust in Literature*. Chicago: University of Chicago Press, 1980.

Estess, Ted L. *Elie Wiesel*. New York: Frederick Ungar Publishing, 1980.

Fackenheim, Emil. *God's Presence in History*. New York: Harper Torchbooks, 1972.

Fine, Ellen S. *Legacy of* Night: *The Literary Universe of Elie Wiesel*. Albany: State University of New York Press, 1982.

Friedman, Maurice. *To Deny Our Nothingness: Contemporary Images of Man*. New York: Delacorte Press, 1967.

Frost, Christopher J. *Religious Melancholy or Psychological Depression?: Some Issues Involved in Relating Psychology and Religion as Illustrated in a Study of Elie Wiesel*. Lanham, Md.: University Press of America, 1985.

Glatstein, Jacob, Israel Knox, and Samuel Margoshes, eds. *Anthology of Holocaust Literature*. New York: Atheneum, 1975.

Green, Mary Jean. "Witness to the Absurd: Elie Wiesel and the French Existentialists," *Renascence*, Volume 29 (1977): pp. 170–184.

Greenberg, Irving, and Alvin Rosenfeld, eds. *Confronting the Holocaust: The Impact of Elie Wiesel*. Bloomington: Indiana University Press, 1978.

Halperin, Irving. *Messengers from the Dead*. Philadelphia: Westminster Press, 1970.

Hilberg, Raul. *The Destruction of the European Jews*. New York: Franklin Watts, 1973.

Inchausti, Robert. *The Ignorant Perfection of Ordinary People*. Albany: State University of New York Press, 1991.

Kahn, Lothar. "Elie Wiesel: Neo-Hasidism," in *Mirrors of the Jewish Mind: A Gallery of Portraits of European Jewish Writers of Our Time*. New York: Thomas Yoseloff, 1968, pp. 296–300.

Knopp, Josephine. "Wiesel and the Absurd," *Contemporary Literature*, Volume 15 (April 1974): pp. 212–220.

————. *The Trial of Judaism in Contemporary Jewish Writing*. Urbana: University of Illinois Press, 1975.

Lambert, Carole J. *Is God Man's Friend?: Theodicy and Friendship in Elie Wiesel's Novels*. New York: Peter Lang, 2006.

Lang, Berel, ed. *Writing and the Holocaust.* New York: Holmes & Meier, 1988.

Langer, Lawrence. *The Holocaust and the Literary Imagination.* New Haven: Yale University Press, 1975.

————. *Preempting the Holocaust.* New Haven: Yale University Press, 1998.

Mandel, Naomi. *Against the Unspeakable: Complicity, the Holocaust, and Slavery in America.* Charlottesville: University of Virginia Press, 2006.

Paterson, David. *The Shriek of Silence: A Phenomenology of the Holocaust Novel.* Lexington: University of Kentucky Press, 1992.

Rabinowitz, Dorothy. *New Lives: Survivors of the Holocaust Living in America.* New York: Knopf, 1976.

Rittner, Carol. *Elie Wiesel: Between Memory and Hope.* New York: New York University Press, 1990.

Rosenfeld, Alvin H. *A Double Dying: Reflections on Holocaust Literature.* Bloomington: Indiana University Press, 1978.

————, and Irving Greenberg, eds. *Confronting the Holocaust: The Impact of Elie Wiesel.* Bloomington: Indiana University Press; 1980.

Roth, John K. *A Consuming Fire: Encounters with Elie Wiesel and the Holocaust.* Atlanta: John Knox Press, 1979.

Sherwin, Byron L. "Elie Wiesel and Jewish Theology," *Judaism,* Volume 18 (Winter 1969): pp. 39–62.

————. "Jewish Messianism and Elie Wiesel," in Byron L. Sherwin, ed., *Perspectives in Jewish Learning—Volume Five* (Chicago: Spertus College Press, 1973): pp. 48–60.

Sibelman, Simon P. *Silence in the Novels of Elie Wiesel.* New York: St. Martin's Press, 1995.

Steiner, George. *In Bluebeard's Castle: Some Notes Towards the Redefinition of Culture.* New Haven: Yale University Press, 1971.

Stern, Ellen Norman. *Elie Wiesel: Witness for Life.* New York: Ktav Publishing, 1982.

Walker, Graham B., Jr. *Elie Wiesel: A Challenge to Theology.* Jefferson, N.C.: McFarland, 1988.

Wardi, Dina. *Memorial Candles: Children of the Holocaust,* translated by Naomi Goldblum. London and New York: Tavistock/Routledge, 1992.

Weissman, Gary. *Fantasies of Witnessing: Postwar Efforts to Experience the Holocaust.* Ithaca, N.Y.: Cornell University Press, 2004.

Wiesel, Elie. *All Rivers Run to the Sea: Memoir.* New York: Knopf, 1995.

————. *And the Sea Is Never Full.* New York: Knopf, 1999.

Acknowledgments

Ted L. Estess. "Elie Wiesel and the Drama of Interrogation," *Journal of Religion*, Volume 56, Number 1 (January 1976): pp. 18–35. Copyright © 1976 The University of Chicago Press. Reprinted by permission of the publisher.

Benj Mahle. "The Power of Ambiguity: Elie Wiesel's *Night*," *English Journal*, Volume 74 (October 1985): pp. 83–84. Copyright © 1985 National Council of Teachers of English. This article is in the public domain.

Sukhbir Singh. "The Parable of Survival in Elie Wiesel's *Night*," *Notes on Contemporary Literature*, Volume 16, Number 1 (January 1986): p. 6. Copyright © 1986 *Notes on Contemporary Literature*. Reprinted by permission of the publisher.

Cardinal Jean-Marie Lustiger. "The Absence of God? The Presence of God?: A Meditation in Three Parts on *Night*," *America*, Volume 159, Number 15 (November 1988): pp. 402–406. Copyright © 1988 American Press. All rights reserved. For subscription information, call 1-800-627-9533 or visit www.americamagazine.org. Reprinted by permission of the publisher.

Eva Fleischner. "Mauriac's Preface to *Night:* Thirty Years Later," *America*, Volume 159, Number 15 (November 1988): pp. 411, 419. Copyright © 1988 American Press. All rights reserved. For subscription information, call 1-800-627-9533 or visit www.americamagazine.org. Reprinted by permission of the publisher.

David L. Vanderwerken. "Wiesel's *Night* as Anti-*Bildungsroman*," *Modern Jewish Studies*, Volume 7, Number 4 (1990): pp. 57–63. Copyright © 1990 David L. Vanderwerken. Reprinted by permission of the author.

Joyce Lazarus. "Elie Wiesel's *La Nuit* and *L'Oublié:* In Pursuit of Silence," *Essays in French Literature*, Volume 28 (November 1991): pp. 87–94. Copyright © 1991 The University of Western Australia. Reprinted by permission of the publisher.

John K. Roth. "From *Night* to *Twilight:* A Philosopher's Reading of Elie Wiesel," *Religion and Literature*, Volume 24, Number 1 (Spring 1992): pp. 59–73. Copyright © 1992 John K. Roth. Reprinted by permission of the author.

Daniel R. Schwarz. "The Ethics of Reading Elie Wiesel's *Night*," *Style*, Volume 32, Number 2 (July 1998): pp. 221–242. Copyright © 1998 Daniel R. Schwarz. Reprinted by permission of the author.

Samuel Totten. "Entering the 'Night' of the Holocaust: Studying Elie Wiesel's *Night*," in *Teaching Holocaust Literature*, ed. Samuel Totten (Boston: Allyn and Bacon, 2001): pp. 215–242. Copyright © 2001 Pearson Education. Reprinted by permission of the publisher and the author.

Sara R. Horowitz. "Boyhood Unraveled: Elie Wiesel's *Night* (1960)," in *Women in Literature: Reading through the Lens of Gender*, Jerilyn Fisher and Ellen S. Silber, eds. (Westport, Conn.: Greenwood Press, 2003): pp. 211–214. Copyright © 2003 Greenwood Press. Reprinted by permission of ABC-CLIO, LLC.

Gary Weissman. "Questioning Key Texts: A Pedagogical Approach to Teaching Elie Wiesel's *Night*," in *Teaching the Representation of the Holocaust*, Marianne Hirsch and Irene Kacandes, eds. (New York: Modern Language Association of America, 2004): pp. 324–336. Copyright © 2004 Modern Language Association of America. Reprinted by permission of the publisher.

Frederick L. Downing. "The Poetics of Memory and Justice: Elie Wiesel and Post-Holocaust Theological Reflection," *Perspectives in Religious Studies*, Volume 35, Number 3 (Fall 2008): pp. 283–300. Copyright © 2008 Baylor University. Reprinted by permission of the publisher.

Nona Fienberg. "Gazing into the Mirror of Wiesel's *Night*, Together," *Pedagogy*, Volume 9, Number 1 (Winter 2009): pp. 167–175. Copyright © 2009 Duke University Press. Reprinted by permission of the publisher.

Index